Praise for *The Mindfulness Edge*

"This is an extraordinary book! *The Mindfulness Edge* will help you take advantage of your greatest strategic asset: your mind. This book offers a practical path to mastering your mind—and changing your brain in ways essential for effective leadership—with one simple habit. Develop this habit and you will not only be more successful both professionally and personally, you'll be more fulfilled as well."

—**Skip Prichard**, president and CEO,
Online Computer Library Center, Inc.;
Leadership Insights blogger at www.skipprichard.com

"I thoroughly enjoyed this valuable book. Matt Tenney and Tim Gard show quite clearly how mindfulness can transform everyday activities into opportunities to change our brains in ways that improve essential leadership skills. They also offer a practical, enjoyable path to consistently being the leaders we aspire to be."

—**Bob Hottman**, CEO, EKS&H

"This is a game-changing book. Based on cutting-edge research and illuminated by real-world examples and practical guidance, *The Mindfulness Edge* can take your business acumen, leadership skills, and personal growth to a higher level. I have read roughly 2,000 business books and this one is now in my top 10."

—**John Spence**, named one of the top 500 leadership development experts in the world by www.HR.com

"I found this book very insightful. It serves as a practical training manual for improving self-awareness, and shows how self-awareness impacts nearly every aspect of leadership. This book will not only help you to be a better leader, it will also help you to enjoy the journey."

—**Gregory A. Serrao**, executive chairman,
American Dental Partners, Inc.

"In *The Mindfulness Edge*, Matt Tenney and Tim Gard present—in an engaging and inspiring way—a practical method of 'strength training' for the most important 'muscle' in your body: your brain. This insightful book is a game plan on how to apply mindfulness training to create the self-awareness and mental agility needed for impactful leadership. This is a must-read for any leader looking to raise the bar of excellence, while also becoming happier!"

—**Chris Thoen**, senior vice president,
head of Global Science and Technology,
Givaudan Flavours Corp.

"I truly enjoyed this book! The applications and narrative herein apply not only to leadership but also to life. With readable and to-the-point information on mindfulness backed by rigorous neuroscience, I strongly recommend *The Mindfulness Edge* to people new to the practice and to people with a long-standing interest."

—**Tara Swart**, MD, PhD, CEO, The Unlimited Mind;
senior lecturer, Massachusetts Institute of Technology (MIT)
Sloan School of Management; and coauthor of *Neuroscience
for Leadership: Harnessing the Brain Gain Advantage*

"I recommend *The Mindfulness Edge* to leaders of all types. The book offers a path to self-mastery through mindfulness training and guidance for applying that self-mastery to enhance the effectiveness of your employees and company, thereby more positively impacting your clients. The authors explain the practice in great detail, inviting reflection along the way, and show how mindfulness can be easily integrated into daily routines with a measurable impact on your home, social, and business worlds."

—**Rick Staab**, CEO, InterMed

"If you want one book that dives deeply and eloquently into one of the single best ingredients for a healthy and effective brain, *The Mindfulness Edge* is it. Matt Tenney and Tim Gard pair up to give spot-on insights that will unleash some awesome things already hanging out in your head. Bathe your brain in this book and get ready to find a whole new you."

—**Scott G. Halford**, executive educator,
National Hall of Fame speaker, and
author of *Activate Your Brain: How Understanding
Your Brain Can Improve Your Work—and Your Life*

"The brilliance of *The Mindfulness Edge* is that it deviates so significantly from the status quo. Rather than merely add to the cacophonous volume of information and advice that overcrowds our mental faculties, this book offers practical, achievable guidance on how to skillfully embrace the chaos and complexity of today's business environment so that we can uncover truly innovative solutions on our own."

—**Martin Sirk**, CEO, International Congress and
Convention Association

"As the business and investment worlds tentatively shift their focus away from short-term transactions toward longer-term relationships, we need excellent leaders to strengthen this trend: leaders with the skills to align our corporations and institutions with the needs of society, the economy, and the environment. *The Mindfulness Edge* is a timely and practical guide for those aspiring to this task."

—**Colin Melvin**, CEO, Hermes Equity Ownership Services, Ltd.

"*The Mindfulness Edge* brilliantly and scientifically demonstrates why mindfulness is a key ingredient in leadership. This book offers not only insight into the journey of mindfulness, but the road map, the compass, and the tour guide to get you there."

—**Chad Paris**, CEO, Parisleaf

"I thoroughly enjoyed this very entertaining and highly useful read. This inspiring book brings together the sound and thorough interpretation of up-to-date neuroscience research with fun-to-read stories and suggestions for applying mindfulness practice in daily life."

—**Britta Hölzel**, PhD, neuroscientist, mindfulness trainer, and author

"*The Mindfulness Edge* offers a fresh and highly practical approach to mastering mindfulness and creating inspiring, mindful workplaces."

—**Michael Carroll**, author of *The Mindful Leader: Ten Principles for Bringing Out the Best in Ourselves and Others*

"Matt Tenney and Tim Gard haven written the first really practical, neuroscience-based guide for enhancing leadership performance through mindfulness. You can start rewiring your brain now!"

—**Wibo Koole**, director, Centrum voor Mindfulness, Amsterdam, and best-selling author of *Mindful Leadership: Effective Tools to Help You Focus and Succeed*

the
mindfulness **edge**

How to **Rewire Your Brain**
for Leadership and
Personal Excellence
Without Adding to
Your Schedule

the

mindfulness**edge**

matt **tenney**   tim **gard, phd**

WILEY

For general information on our other products and services or for technical support, please contact our Customer Care Department within the United States at (800) 762-2974, outside the United States at (317) 572-3993 or fax (317) 572-4002.

Wiley publishes in a variety of print and electronic formats and by print-on-demand. Some material included with standard print versions of this book may not be included in e-books or in print-on-demand. If this book refers to media such as a CD or DVD that is not included in the version you purchased, you may download this material at http://booksupport.wiley.com. For more information about Wiley products, visit www.wiley.com.

Library of Congress Cataloging-in-Publication Data:

Names: Tenney, Matt, author.
Title: The mindfulness edge : how to rewire your brain for leadership and
    personal excellence without adding to your schedule / Matt Tenney.
Description: Hoboken : Wiley, 2016. | Includes index.
Identifiers: LCCN 2015041523 (print) | LCCN 2016001068 (ebook) | ISBN
    9781119183181 (hardback) | ISBN 9781119183204 (ePDF) |
    ISBN 9781119183242 (ePub)
Subjects: LCSH: Leadership. | Mindfulness (Psychology) | BISAC: BUSINESS &
    ECONOMICS / Leadership.
Classification: LCC HD57.7 .T4578 2016 (print) | LCC HD57.7 (ebook) | DDC
    658.4/092019–dc23
LC record available at http://lccn.loc.gov/2015041523

Printed in the United States of America

10 9 8 7 6 5 4 3 2 1

To my parents, Molly and Gary, for your unconditional support.
—Matt Tenney

To Marasha, Max, and Lex.
—Tim Gard

CONTENTS

A NOTE ON BEST ENJOYING THIS BOOK

Please don't be intimidated by the subtitle of this book, or by the fact that the coauthor is a super genius neuroscientist who has worked at leading research institutions, including Massachusetts General Hospital, Harvard Medical School. The main text, which is in my voice, will not delve deeply into neuroscience and is a fairly easy and highly practical read.

Although I'll mention quite a bit of research and shed some light on the latest understanding of how we can rewire our brains for leadership excellence, the more in-depth discussions of neuroscience research, and other interesting studies, are set aside from the main text in sections called "Neuro Notes." If you'd like to go a bit deeper with the neuroscience for your own education, or so you can sound cool at dinner parties, or just to add to the enjoyment of the book, I encourage you to read the Neuro Notes. If you don't think the extra scientific depth is necessary, you can skip the Neuro Notes and stick with the main text without fear of losing the main thrust of the book.

The Neuro Notes are written by the aforementioned super genius neuroscientist, Tim Gard, PhD. In addition to writing the Neuro Notes, Dr. Gard has been instrumental in finding the most recent, relevant research for this book. He also worked with me on the main text to help improve it in many ways, including ensuring that I didn't overstate the results of the research we cite in this book.

Dr. Gard has helped improve this book significantly. I believe that, thanks to him, you will enjoy the book significantly more than if I had written it alone and that you'll walk away with a much greater understanding of your brain and your power to change it in ways that can help you achieve both leadership and personal excellence.

INTRODUCTION

Think of all the simple activities that you already engage in every day—activities such as brushing your teeth, getting dressed, commuting to work, walking to your desk, waiting for the coffee to brew, waiting for your computer to boot up, and so on. These activities are often labeled as "downtime" or "wastes of time."

Now, imagine that you could transform those activities into some of the most productive moments of the day, while also increasing your happiness. Cutting-edge research in neuroscience suggests that you can actually do just that.

This book is about a simple tool that can help you:

- Improve your business acumen
- Improve your emotional and social intelligence
- Become more innovative
- Manage change more effectively
- See opportunities that other people don't see
- Improve your leadership presence
- Live a more fulfilling life

I know it may sound too good to be true, but the tool we'll discuss in this book can help you do all of the above. In fact, it gets even better.

This tool is absolutely free, and it doesn't require you to add anything to your schedule, which is likely quite full already. All you need to do is change the way you do things you're already doing every day. It takes about as much effort as taking a pill, but you can apply this tool every waking moment of your life. And, when practiced correctly, the side effects include only positive things, such as increased happiness and improved health.

The tool to which I'm referring is a simple practice known as mindfulness training.[1]

EVERYTHING BEGINS IN THE MIND

Over the last couple of years, during workshops and training programs I've offered, I've asked thousands of people the following question: "Would you agree with me when I say that all success and all failure originate in the mind?"

No one has ever disagreed. The question is essentially rhetorical. We know that everything we do, or fail to do, begins in the mind.

The reason I ask the question above is because it makes the next question much more powerful: "How many people do you know who take time every day to intentionally train the mind to function more effectively?"

Typically, in business audiences, only 1 to 3 percent of the people raise their hands.

I find this quite interesting. Everyone seems to agree that an effectively functioning mind is the root of all personal and professional success, yet very few people take time each day to intentionally train their minds. We might add knowledge through study, but we don't do anything to train how the mind actually functions. In most cases, this is because people are not aware that a systematic process of training the mind exists, a method of training that is being applied at highly successful companies, such as Google, Apple, Aetna, Intel, General Mills, and many others.

For most of us, unfortunately, the result of not training the mind is that it can be our greatest obstacle to success. It is often a source of anxiety, self-doubt, and repetitive thought patterns that limit us, keeping us from reaching our full potential.

This book offers several radical paradigm shifts. The first broad shift is that we all have the ability to train our minds in such a way that reverses the situation described above. We can transform the mind so that it is no longer our greatest obstacle to success but, rather, an incredibly powerful tool that allows us to achieve significantly greater success in both our personal and our professional lives, especially as leaders.

YOU CAN REWIRE YOUR BRAIN FOR LEADERSHIP AND PERSONAL EXCELLENCE

It would have been nearly impossible 20 years ago to find a neuroscientist who believed that the physical structure of the human brain could be changed after adolescence. Today, this view is quite different. In 2004, for instance, a neuroscientist named Bogdan Draganski and his colleagues showed that people who have trained in juggling for three months develop measurably more gray matter[2]—the switchboard substance of the brain, so to speak—in brain regions that are associated with the processing and storage of complex visual motion.[3,4]

There is now a whole new focus of neuroscience growing around the fact that the brain can be changed, which is referred to as *neuroplasticity*. One of the most promising discoveries in the realm of neuroplasticity is that we can change our brains throughout our entire lives. An old dog really can learn new tricks!

Neuro Note 0.1: Neuroplasticity

Several studies, such as the juggling study above by Draganski and colleagues, clearly show that we can change the physical structure of our brains—in essence, gray matter increases—and that brain and behavior are closely related. However, it is difficult to say with precision which of the very tiny structures that make up gray matter are changing. Animal studies suggest that these changes are due to the growth of tiny blood vessels (capillaries) that supply the neurons with oxygen and glucose, to increases in dendritic length and branching, to a growth of the number of synapses, and even to the growth of new neurons.[5]

(continued)

(continued)

In addition to increasing gray matter, training can also increase white matter, the wiring of the brain. This was revealed for the first time by Scholz, Klein, and colleagues, who found increases in white matter after only six weeks of juggling training.[6] As with the gray matter, it is not clear yet what exactly at the micro level causes this increase.

If you'd like a more detailed explanation about what white and gray matter are, how we measure changes in brain function and structure, and an overview of the brain regions involved in mindfulness, please see the Appendix.

The aspect of neuroplasticity that I find most exciting is the more recent discovery that we can actually change the physical structure of the brain simply by using the mind.[7] One of the first studies to shed light on the possibility of changing the brain simply by using the mind involved taxi drivers in London, England. As part of their exams for obtaining a license to drive a cab in London, they must acquire what is known as "the Knowledge." They are required to memorize routes in an area that includes roughly 25,000 streets and 20,000 landmarks and places of interest. Acquiring "the Knowledge" can take two to four years of training.

In 2011, when Woollett and Maguire, neuroscientists at University College London, studied the brains of a group of London cab drivers before and after acquiring "the Knowledge," they discovered a significant increase in gray matter in the area of the brain associated with spatial memory (the posterior hippocampi). No such changes have been found in those trainees who failed to qualify as licensed London taxi drivers and a control group who did not go through the training.[8]

As the practice of mindfulness has become more widespread, the scientific community has become increasingly interested in mindfulness training, and a tremendous amount of research has been compiled on the benefits of the practice.[9] There are now numerous studies that strongly suggest that mindfulness training results in physical changes to the structure of the brain—in some cases as quickly as eight weeks—that can be linked to better leadership skills.[10] In this book we'll explore how, with mindfulness training, we can literally rewire our brains for leadership excellence.[11]

WHAT YOU'LL FIND IN THIS BOOK

This book is based on a combination of previously separate training programs that I have offered to leaders. I understand that oftentimes the most pressing issue in an organization is the financial situation. There can be tremendous pressure to "hit the numbers" every single quarter.

Thus, we start by discussing how mindfulness training can help leaders make decisions that have better impacts on gross margins and expenses. This helps us make quick, direct impacts on the bottom line, which means we're more likely to keep our jobs long enough to make a long-term impact. Better business acumen also allows a leader to have more resources available to serve both the customer and the members of the organization.

However, as I explored in great detail in my first book, *Serve to Be Great*, if leaders place too much emphasis on the numbers and fail to serve and care for the people on their teams effectively, the organization will eventually fail. Without happy, loyal team members, it is nearly impossible to keep happy, loyal customers. Without happy, loyal customers, an organization simply can't exist for long. Therefore, we also need to address the leadership skills that allow us to create and sustain a culture that drives the long-term growth and profitability of our organizations.

Fortunately, there is a bridge between better business acumen and better leadership skills. The bridge is the practice of mindfulness. Mindfulness training helps us develop the self-awareness and mental agility that are the keys to better business acumen and the foundation for developing the emotional and social intelligence that allow us to serve and care for the people on our teams more effectively, and thus create sustainable, high-performance team cultures.

The book is divided into two parts to make it easy to approach the topics we'll discuss:

Part 1—We'll introduce and explain mindfulness training and how it can rewire our brains in ways that help us achieve greater success as leaders. We'll discuss how mindfulness training can help leaders make a quick, direct, positive impact on gross margins and expenses. We'll also explore how mindfulness training helps us develop the leadership skills that are essential for the long-term success of our teams.

Part 2—We'll discuss how to integrate mindfulness training seamlessly into our daily lives without having to add anything new to our already-busy schedules.

We sincerely hope that you enjoy reading this book as much as we enjoyed writing it!

PART 1

HOW MINDFULNESS TRAINING REWIRES THE BRAIN FOR LEADERSHIP EXCELLENCE

1

THE SHIFT THAT CHANGES EVERYTHING

In November of 1887, two scientists named Albert A. Michelson and Edward W. Morley published a paper at a prestigious university known today as Case Western Reserve, in Cleveland, Ohio.[1] The paper caused quite a conundrum for physicists of the day.

Michelson and Morley hadn't intended to turn the world of physics upside down. They were simply trying to prove that the *ether* existed.

For many years, scientists believed that there must be some invisible sea, which they called the ether, through which every physical thing in the universe is moving. It was a very convenient theory. It provided the foundation for the then accepted laws of motion and provided a medium for the propagation of light (at the time, light was viewed by most scientists as only a wave-like phenomenon; it needed something to "wave" through).

The ether was an extremely important element of physical theories in the late 1800s. Most scientists agreed that the ether simply had to exist.

There was one significant problem, though. No one had ever seen the ether, nor had anyone been able to measure it in any other way.

Michelson and Morley devised a rather simple experiment to determine whether the ether actually existed. They theorized that if there was an ether, and the earth was moving through it, there should be a sort of ether breeze, similar to what we feel when we put a hand outside of a car window while we're driving down the highway. For instance, the earth travels around the sun at nearly 67,000 miles per hour (mph), so that breeze alone would be fairly significant.

The ether breeze, they postulated, would create substantial resistance for a beam of light and cause the light to slow down. So Michelson and Morley set up an experiment to measure the speed of light traveling in the direction of the earth's motion, through the ether breeze, versus a beam of light not traveling against the ether breeze. The experiment showed quite conclusively that there was no difference in the speed of the two beams of light and therefore that the ether almost certainly did not exist.

Other scientists soon agreed with the findings, and similar experiments were conducted with similar results. Within a short time, there was quite a bit of consternation. It appeared that the beloved and necessary ether had been proved to be nothing but a figment of human imagination.

But the problems caused by the elimination of the ether as a possible component of the laws of motion and light propagation were quite minor compared with what else Michelson and Morley discovered in their experiment. As a side effect of their effort to disprove the ether, they also noticed that the speed of light was unchanged relative to the motion of the earth.

Soon, several other experiments produced similar results. It appeared that the relative motion of the observer did not affect the speed of light. This, of course, makes no sense. It defies the extremely well established and commonsense law of motion that states that velocity *is* relative to the motion of the observer.

For example, if you're in a parked car and a car going 20 mph passes by you, the relative velocity between the two cars is 20 mph. However, if you're in a car going 10 mph and a car going 20 mph in the same direction passes you, the relative velocity between the two cars is 10 mph. The other car pulls away at a rate of 10 mph relative to your car.

But if the speed of light were constant, it would mean that for some reason light wouldn't obey that law. If you were in a parked car and turned your headlights on, light would move away from you at 186,000 miles per second. If you and your car could somehow travel at a velocity of 100,000 miles per second in the same direction as a light beam, that beam of light would still move away from you at 186,000 miles per second.

Again, this defies common sense. In the example above, why doesn't the light have a relative velocity of 86,000 miles per second? Why would light be different from every other single thing we experience through our senses in this world?

These are likely the same questions the physicists of the day asked. The answer the scientists likely settled on at first was that something must have gone wrong in the Michelson-Morley experiment. Everything the experts of the day knew about the world, and how we operate in it, forced them to conclude that there was no way the speed of light could possibly be constant.

But one young physicist, who had been fascinated by light for years, took a different approach to the problem in the early 1900s. Although he was likely at least vaguely aware of the experiments showing that the speed of light is constant, his approach actually began in a very childlike manner when he imagined what things would be like if he were traveling on a beam of light. The result of his thought experiment was that one could never catch up to a light beam because that would result in seeing a stationary electromagnetic wave, which is not believed to be possible. Therefore, he concluded that the speed of light must be constant.

This young physicist later realized that if the speed of light were constant, there would be some very strange consequences. For instance, as a person approaches the speed of light, her mass increases, she becomes compressed in the direction of motion, and she actually ages more slowly relative to a person moving with less velocity. He realized that the speed of light doesn't change relative to time; time changes relative to the speed of light. All of these weird consequences were later proved through experiments to be true.

While everyone else was saying that the constancy of the speed of light is impossible because it totally defies common sense, our young physicist realized that both his thought experiments and other experiments suggested otherwise. He was open to the unlikely possibility that perhaps our world just might be so drastically different from how the conventional wisdom of the time suggested it was. He had to temporarily let go of much of what his training led him, and other physicists of the day, to believe. As Gary Zukav writes in the excellent book *The Dancing Wu Li Masters*, this pioneering physicist had to approach the issue of the constancy of the speed of light with the mind of a complete beginner.[2]

With this beginner's mind, the young physicist began to base all of his math on the idea that the constancy of the speed of light is not a theory; it is a fact. When he used C in his equations for the speed of light, he thought of it as being a constant. His most well-known equation is $E = mc^2$. The young physicist's name is Albert Einstein. Today, $E = mc^2$ is probably the most well-known equation in the world. His insights completely transformed our understanding of how the universe works and became the basis for some of the most useful physical theories in history, which later helped us build countless things we rely on every day.

BEGINNER'S MIND

One of my favorite quotes is from a famous mindfulness teacher from Japan named Shunryu Suzuki. He said, "In the beginner's mind there are many possibilities, but in the expert's there are few."[3]

Albert Einstein offers us a perfect example of this. When he was asked why he was so successful as a scientist, his humble response was: "The ordinary adult never gives a thought to space-time problems. . . . I, on the contrary, developed so slowly that I did not begin to wonder about space and time until I was an adult. I then delved more deeply into the problem than any other adult or child would have done."[4]

When most scientists are children, and are asking the big questions that could change the world, they don't have the math or physics training that would allow them to translate their inquiries into something the world could use. And, by the time they reach the peak of their training, they have also fully developed into adults and have lost much of their sense of childlike wonder.

But Einstein never lost his childlike personality traits. He continued to ask naïve, childlike questions well into his adult life. When he asked those questions, though, he already had the math and physics training that allowed him to test and prove his ideas, and share them in a way that other people could understand and apply.

Fortunately for us, we can train our minds to be like the mind of Einstein. We may not be able to match his IQ, but we can train to see the world with a beginner's mind. We can train to be *free* from the constraints of what we already know, without having to *discard* what we already know.

The benefits of having such a beginner's mind extend well beyond the worlds of science and innovation. A beginner's mind is the essence of mindfulness training. In fact, some schools of mindfulness actually refer to the practice as the practice of "beginner's mind."

THE ATTITUDE OF A BEGINNER IS ESSENTIAL

Beginner's mind is essentially a shift in attitude. Instead of operating from the position of *I've already experienced this* or *I already know about this*, we operate with an open, inquisitive attitude of *Ooh, let's explore what this experience is actually like.* We have a questioning attitude, such as, *What's happening now within me and around me?*

This attitude alone can be very beneficial in a general sense. As we've already discussed, having a beginner's mind opens up a whole realm of possibilities for learning new things, for creative approaches that can lead to breakthrough discoveries, and for seeing opportunities that no else sees.

However, we discover many more benefits when we train to apply this beginner's mind to our moment-to-moment experience, when we adopt and then sustain the attitude of *What's happening now, within me and around me?*

The moment we adopt that attitude, a shift occurs in our awareness. We shift from perceiving the world through the lens of the thinking mind—essentially being the thinking mind—to being self-aware, which includes awareness of the thinking mind. When we become aware of the thinking mind, we are free from it. We no longer see the world through its limited view.

Figure 1.1—a top-down view of a human head—illustrates how most of us spend most of our time perceiving the world and acting in it.

The outer ring of the mind represents the thinking mind as a whole.[5]

The middle ring represents the ego, which is a creation of the thinking mind and its interactions with the world up to this moment.

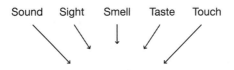

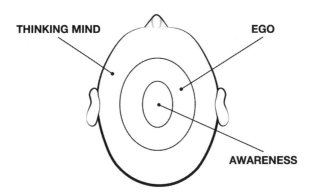

Figure 1.1   The Default Way of Experiencing the World

It is essentially a collection of conditioned habits, thought patterns, emotional patterns, and memories that make up our personal identity—a very strong sense of *me*.

The innermost part of the image represents awareness.

For most of us, most of the time, we operate as though we are the thinking mind and its ego, and we receive all sensory information through those filters, as represented by the arrows in the previous figure. Existing in this way is quite problematic. Following is an overview of three critical ways that our personal and professional success are hindered by operating from the perspective we see in Figure 1.1.

NOT SEEING WHAT'S ACTUALLY HAPPENING

When we operate from the perspective of the thinking mind and its ego—which some neuroscientists refer to as the default mode network (DMN), as Dr. Gard explains in Neuro Note 1.1—everything we perceive is filtered through the thinking mind and the ego. We don't see things as they actually are. We see them with quite a bit of distortion. All of our past experiences, our habitual ways of seeing, and our beliefs and opinions shape what we perceive, as we saw above with the scientists in the late 1800s, whose conditioning caused them to disregard the possibility of the constancy of the speed of light.

As leaders, one of the most critical skills we can possess is the ability to see clearly what is actually happening—to see things not in terms of how we want them to be, or how our conditioning tells us they must be, but how they *actually are*.

Although I'm a huge proponent of being as optimistic as possible about the future, it is absolutely essential that we be extremely realistic about where we, our team members, and our organizations actually are in the present moment. We cannot hope to have any chance of charting a path for future success if we start with an incorrect view of where we currently are. This is akin to trying to get to Paris, France, from Cape Town, South Africa, but thinking that we're actually starting from Rio de Janeiro, Brazil. It would be essentially impossible to get to Paris based on the wrong starting assumption.

Neuro Note 1.1: The Wandering Mind and the Default Mode Network

A large portion of the time (nearly 47 percent), we are not fully engaged in the world around us or in the task that we are conducting.[6] Instead we are lost in self-generated and self-related thoughts, such as remembering our past and planning our future; our mind is wandering.[7]

This mind wandering comes at a cost.[8] It is related to negative emotions and poor performance on demanding tasks, such the scholastic aptitude test (SAT).[9] It also has been hypothesized that this habit or default mode of mind wandering biases the view of ourselves and the world around us, and indeed a recent study suggests that mind wandering is related to decision-making bias.[10]

In the brain, mind wandering is associated with the so-called default mode network (DMN).[11] The DMN is active when we are not engaged in any task or processing of external events. It is involved in remembering the past, envisioning future events, and considering thoughts and perspectives of other people. Roughly speaking, the DMN comprises three midline regions of the brain: the ventromedial prefrontal cortex (vmPFC) that supports emotional processing, the dorsomedial prefrontal cortex (dmPFC) that is related to self-referential processing, and the posterior cingulate cortex (PCC) plus adjacent precuneus that are associated with recollection of prior experiences. Furthermore, the DMN comprises a region in the inferior parietal lobule (IPL), close to the temporoparietal junction (TPJ), which is related to perspective taking.[12]

ACTING IN CONDITIONED, HABITUAL WAYS

Second, when we operate from the position of being the thinking mind and the ego it has created, we act based on our conditioned, habitual ways of reacting. It's as though we are plugged into the proverbial matrix.[13] We are essentially programs that can react to a situation only in the way we've been programmed to react. These programs are constructed from a combination of our genetics and all of the ways the brain has been conditioned by our life experiences up to this moment.

Of course, most of us have programming that can be helpful. There are many cases when reacting based on that programming is likely to yield excellent results. One example is a highly trained doctor reacting—essentially on autopilot—to a medical emergency, allowing her programming to take over and provide the crucial help that could save a person's life.

However, we also have a tremendous amount of programming that does not serve us well. We have numerous conditioned, habitual ways of doing things. Although we might think that we are already free from our programming, as we'll explore in Chapter 2, there are many degrees of being subject to this programming, and much of the programming is completely unconscious for most of us.

In fact, people who think they are completely free from habitual, conditioned ways of thinking, deciding, and acting are often those who are the least free from their programming. They simply don't see their programming because their lack of self-awareness keeps the conditioning completely unconscious.

Often, our conditioned, habitual ways of doing things result in suboptimal outcomes in our personal and professional lives. For example, as we'll see in Chapter 2, this conditioning can affect business acumen and cause very intelligent, experienced leaders to unconsciously make decisions that have significant, negative impacts on gross margins and expenses.

This unconscious conditioning is often quite subtle, and it requires a very high level of self-awareness to recognize the programming and be free from it. Unfortunately, because our minds are untrained, we often lack the momentary self-awareness to notice even very obvious forms of conditioning.

For instance, on several occasions while entering the Jetway at the airport, I've overheard the person in front of me talking with the gate agent. The gate agent said, "Have a nice flight!" The person in front of me replied, "You, too!"

The gate agent smiled politely in each case but was quite likely thinking, "I'm not taking a flight." The reply of the person in front of me was a conditioned, habitual-type response. Each time I've seen this happen, it appeared to me as though the person wasn't even aware that what he just said was nonsensical.

Another example is something I would imagine you've experienced many, many times. You're walking down the street and you're approaching another person walking briskly in the opposite direction. You say, "Hello" to the person. The person replies with "How ya doin'?" as he continues walking by you without even the slightest intention of slowing down to hear the answer to his question.

This is clearly an unintentional, habitual way of responding. The person doesn't actually want to know how you're doing. It's just another way of saying hello. Again, in most cases, I would imagine that most people are unaware of the fact that they are communicating completely out of habit.

If we're unaware of things as obvious as the words that are coming out of our own mouths, imagine how much of our more subtle conditioning we're unaware of. For instance, how do we react when a team member brings us bad news? What types of signals do we send to people in different departments of our organizations as a result of our biases toward sales, quality, or finance? Are we even aware that we have biases toward different areas of our organizations?

Neuro Note 1.2: The Formation of Habits

As we have seen in the main text, our lives are full of habits. In the scientific literature, habits have been described as having the following defining characteristics: "First, habits (mannerisms, customs, rituals) are largely learned; in current terminology, they are acquired via experience-dependent plasticity. Second, habitual behaviors occur repeatedly over the course of days or years, and they can become remarkably fixed. Third, fully acquired habits are performed almost automatically, virtually unconsciously, allowing attention to be focused elsewhere. Fourth, habits tend to involve an ordered, structured action sequence that is prone to being elicited by a particular context or stimulus. And finally, habits can comprise cognitive expressions of routine (habits of thought) as well as motor expressions of routine."[14]

In the brain, habit learning is associated with the basal ganglia and basal-ganglia-thalamocortical loops. The basal ganglia are a group of structures located deep inside the brain (subcortical structures). They are composed of the dorsal striatum (caudate and putamen), ventral striatum, globus pallidus, and sometimes other regions as well. The striatum receives input from a wide range of brain regions all over the cortex and sends its output to the globus pallidus which then via the thalamus sends it back to the cortical regions, thus forming basal ganglia thalamocortical loops. This input from such a variety of regions and output to such a variety of regions enables the learning of a large variety of complex habits, involving motor behavior as well as thoughts.

The actual learning in the basal ganglia takes place under the influence of the neurotransmitter dopamine, which is released in response to reward such as food, sexual activity, money, and praise, but also to more abstract forms of reward. Early in the learning process, behavior is goal directed and flexible and associated with activation in the caudate together with the ventromedial prefrontal cortex, while it later becomes habitual and brain activation shifts from the caudate to the putamen.[15]

SELFISHNESS AND NEGATIVE EMOTIONS

Third, when we operate from the egoic perspective, we operate from and easily get stuck in a place that is the source of all of our negative thought patterns and negative emotions. The ego sees the world from the point of view of self versus others. It has one primary function: self-preservation. Thus, when we operate from ego, we perceive the world and act through varying degrees of anxiety, fear, and selfishness.

In addition to making life a much less enjoyable experience than it can be, operating from the egoic perspective severely undermines our chances for sustained professional success. The negative emotions and mind states the egoic perspective creates result in reduced creativity, burnout, and a tendency to drive negative emotions in our teams instead of positive ones. As we'll explore later in this book, research has verified the intuitive idea that teams with negative emotional climates significantly underperform compared with teams with more positive emotional climates.

THE SHIFT THAT CHANGES EVERYTHING

Fortunately, with the shift that results when we are being mindful with the curious attitude of a beginner, we can operate from a completely different perspective, as shown in Figure 1.2.

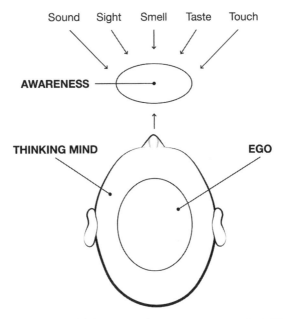

Figure 1.2   The Mindful Way of Experiencing the World

Simply by having the attitude of a beginner and asking in our minds the question "What's happening now within me and around me?" the shift that we see in Figure 1.2 occurs. This image is not meant to imply that we have some sort of out-of-body experience. In fact, when practicing mindfulness correctly, you will likely feel as though you are more in your body than you typically are. This image is meant to demonstrate visually the ability to experience sensations directly, without being filtered through the thinking mind and ego, and to see objectively the body, thinking mind, and ego.

This ability to see ourselves objectively is called *mindful self-awareness*.[16] When we have a beginner's mind and become mindful, we have a balanced, nonjudgmental awareness of both our outer and our inner worlds. The thinking mind and the ego become objects of our awareness. This doesn't mean that we have to shut thinking off. It means we are no longer caught in thinking or distracted by it. Thus, we are no longer controlled by the thinking mind and ego. Rather, the thinking mind is seen as a tool we can use to help us skillfully manage what we experience.

This shift to mindful self-awareness is the shift that changes everything. Self-awareness is the most important leadership skill we can develop. It affects every other aspect of leadership, most notably business acumen and emotional and social intelligence.

Let's start with an explanation of how mindful self-awareness remedies the three problems we discussed above, which result when we operate from the perspective of being the thinking mind and its ego. When we instead operate from the perspective of mindful self-awareness that we see in Figure 1.2, we realize the following benefits.

SEEING THINGS AS THEY ACTUALLY ARE

When we operate from the perspective of mindful self-awareness, we're no longer experiencing the world through the filter of the thinking mind and the ego. We operate from what neuroscience has identified as an entirely different neural network, one that allows us to perceive the world with great clarity, exactly as it is. This allows us to make decisions based on what's actually happening versus some distorted version of what's happening or what we hope is happening or not happening. The journey to Paris, we discussed above is much easier when we know that we're actually starting in Cape Town, instead of Rio de Janeiro.

Neuro Note 1.3: Mindfulness and Shifting from the Default Mode Network to Present Moment Awareness

As we saw earlier, mind wandering is associated with brain activation in the DMN and with biased decision making.[17] In a recent study conducted by University of California, Santa Barbara, scientist Michael Mrazek and his colleagues, it was shown that training mindfulness for two weeks resulted in reduced mind wandering.[18] Even more recently, in 2014, European Institute for Business Administration (INSEAD) scientist Andrew Hafenbrack and colleagues showed that just 15 minutes of practicing mindfulness reduced the so-called sunk-cost bias.[19] The sunk-cost bias refers to the "tendency to continue an endeavor once an investment in money, effort, or time has been made" even if it is not wise to do so.[20]

As one would expect, based on the relationship between mindfulness and mind wandering, and mind wandering and DMN activity, Yale neuroscientist Judson Brewer and colleagues found that during mindfulness practice, practitioners had decreased brain activation in two key regions of the DMN, the PCC and mPFC, as compared with nonpractitioners. Furthermore, the researchers reported greater functional connectivity between the PCC and the dorsal anterior cingulate cortex (dACC), and the dorsolateral prefrontal cortex (dlPFC) during intentional mindfulness practice and rest. These regions are involved in self-monitoring and cognitive control, respectively, and the researchers interpreted the greater connectivity in mindfulness practitioners as greater monitoring and dampening of DMN activity to reduce mind wandering and interference with tasks.[21] Several other studies have reported mindfulness-related changes in DMN functional connectivity as well.[22]

Mindfulness is related not only to decreased mind wandering but also to a shift to increased present moment awareness, in particular awareness of body sensations.[23] For example, in one study the subjectively reported sensitivity of body regions corresponded better to objectively determined body sensitivity in experienced mindfulness practitioners than in nonmindfulness practitioners.[24] Congruent with these findings, several studies have shown increased mindfulness-related brain activity and gray matter in the insula,[25] a brain region that is involved in (body) awareness.[26]

An early study that illustrates the shift from a mind-wandering-like state of being to a more direct-experience way of being is that of University of Toronto neuroscientist Norman Farb and colleagues. The team investigated the brain activity of completers of an eight-week mindfulness training (mindfulness-based stress reduction) and controls during two forms of self-reference: an experiential focus in which participants were asked just to observe thoughts, feelings, and body states as they occur and a narrative focus in which they were asked to judge whatever is experienced, to relate it to oneself, and to get caught up in thoughts.

Completers of the mindfulness training in comparison with nonmindfulness practitioners had decreased brain activation in the midline brain structures mentioned in this Neuro Note and increased activation in lateral brain areas, including the insula and secondary somatosensory cortex, during experiential self-focus as compared with narrative self-focus. Furthermore, a decoupling of the right insula and mPFC was found. The authors interpret this as a clear shift to experiential, sensory grounded self-awareness instead of the habitual integration of narrative and experiential self-reference.[27]

FREEDOM FROM CONDITIONING

Second, when we're ready to take action in response to what we perceive, we experience a small miracle: We can actually choose how we want to respond.

In one situation, it may be true that following our programming is perfectly appropriate (like the doctor above). In another, we may realize that following our programming would not yield the optimal result. The miracle is that when we have the perspective of mindful self-awareness that we see in Figure 1.2, we can see the programming within us that remains completely unconscious for most people. Moreover, we have the space to choose which programming we want to follow.

As neurologist Viktor Frankl famously said, "Between stimulus and response there is a space. In that space lies our freedom and power to choose our response. In our response lies our growth and freedom."[28] A similar phrase was later made popular in the business world by Dr. Stephen R. Covey, who said, "Between the stimulus and the response is your greatest power—you have the freedom to choose your response."[29] As we will see in Chapter 2, we can develop this "greatest power" with a proven practice for systematically training the mind.

EMOTIONAL INTELLIGENCE

Third, self-awareness is the foundation of *emotional intelligence*, which is what allows us to be free from disruptive emotional states, such as anxiety, anger, and lack of motivation, and to spend more time operating from beneficial emotional states, such as inspiration, happiness, and high motivation.

Emotional intelligence also allows us to help the people around us be free from disruptive emotional states and spend more time operating from the beneficial states. The more emotionally intelligent a leader is, the more successful he or she will be at creating a positive emotional climate for his or her team. This is an extremely important leadership skill that some researchers suggest accounts for up to 90 percent of the differences between stellar leaders and average ones.[30]

As we'll explore in Chapter 3, assuming all other things are equal, a team that is emotionally healthy is going to consistently outperform a team where disruptive emotional states are the norm.

CHANGING OUR DEFAULT

Almost everyone is mindfully self-aware quite frequently but unintentionally and for very brief instances. This is a lot like the relationship most people have to running. Most people do run from time to time. However, for people who don't intentionally train for running, the only time they run is when life necessitates it, like when they're trying to catch a subway train or rushing to cross the street before the light changes.

When running is so infrequent like this, and for such short bursts, there are little or no benefits other than arriving a bit more quickly to a destination. However, people who take time to run for periods of 20 minutes or more, three or four times per week, realize a great number of benefits. This type of training results in a stronger immune system, the ability to run faster, better cardiovascular health, better sleep, clearer thinking, and so on.

Most of us unintentionally experience the mindful self-awareness described above many, many times each day (probably more than 100 times each day). We likely bounce back and forth frequently between mindful self-awareness and the default mode of being the thinking mind and its ego. However, these unintentional moments of self-awareness usually last only for a few seconds.

This is especially true during a demanding situation. We become self-aware for an instant, and then we're sucked right back into being our thinking mind and the ego. We spend most of our time being that voice inside our heads that is constantly analyzing, judging, or just blabbering about nonsense, and which is often accompanied by mental images that capture more of our attention than the outside world.

Even in undemanding situations, the default state of being for most of us is being stuck in the thinking mind and its ego. In fact, in the 2010 study mentioned in Neuro Note 1.1, conducted by Dan Gilbert and

Matthew Killingsworth of Harvard University, which involved more than 2,000 people, it was revealed that we spend nearly 47 percent of our time essentially lost in thought, engaged in mind wandering.

As you've likely noticed in your own experience, partial distraction is much more prevalent. When I ask people in the training programs I conduct how much of the time they feel that they are at least partially distracted by thinking, they usually agree that it's at least 90 percent of the time, and many state it's more like 95 percent of the time or more.

Just as with randomly running without intentionally training, we receive few lasting benefits from our random, brief experiences of being mindfully self-aware. However, mindfulness training allows us to go far beyond just randomly being self-aware for brief instances. The practice enables us to *intentionally* become mindfully self-aware and to gradually develop the ability to maintain that mindful self-awareness for as long as we wish, even in demanding situations.

Neuro Note 1.4: Shifting from Mind Wandering to Present-Moment Awareness: It Gets Easier with Practice

Emory University neuroscientist Wendy Hasenkamp and colleagues proposed a model of how fluctuations between mind wandering and attentional states during practicing mindfulness take place. They proposed a cycling between the following states: mind wandering → awareness of mind wandering → shifting attention → sustained attention.[31]

With an innovative study design they then tested what brain activation patterns are associated with each phase in experienced mindfulness practitioners while practicing breath awareness. As expected, during mind wandering the DMN, including the mPFC and PCC, was activated. Awareness of mind wandering activated the salience network, including the dorsal ACC, which plays an important role in conflict monitoring and error detection and here probably was activated because of the mismatch between the intended state of breath awareness and the current state of mind wandering.[32] Switching attention from mind wandering back to the breath was associated with activation in the frontoparietal central executive network, including the lateral PFC, which remained active during sustained attention. This is in agreement with the known role of the lateral PFC in redirecting attention.[33]

Interestingly, in the study by Hasenkamp and colleagues, the more experienced the mindfulness practitioners were, the less brain activation they had while shifting the attention from mind wandering to the breath.[34] This finding suggests that with more practice less effort is required to shift to a state of present-moment awareness. Other authors reported similar findings.[35]

For example, West Virginia University neuroscientist Julie Brefczynski-Lewis and colleagues found an inverted *u*-shape pattern of brain activity in brain regions that support shifting and sustaining attention, including the lateral prefrontal cortex: During focused attention training, mindfulness practitioners with an average of 19,000 hours of experience showed more brain activation than novices, but mindfulness practitioners with an average of 44,000 hours of experience had less activation.[36]

Becoming and remaining mindfully self-aware can eventually become a new habit—a habit we can apply as often we like. Any moment of the day that we remember to try, we can make the effort to shift from being our thinking mind and its ego to becoming and remaining mindfully self-aware. Over time, with practice, we can change our default state from being the thinking mind and its ego to being mindfully self-aware.

We can also train to develop highly refined levels of self-awareness that allow us to routinely see important aspects of ourselves that many people never see in their entire lives and develop the wisdom that is the key to both leadership and personal excellence. This intentional mindfulness training, therefore, is the key to realizing the benefits we'll explore in the coming chapters.

Becoming and remaining mindfully self-aware—and developing highly refined self-awareness—likely sounds incredibly simple, and it is. We don't have to go someplace special like a gym, and we don't have to get sweaty. However, the practice is definitely *not* easy. In fact, training for mindful self-awareness may be the most challenging thing we will ever do in our lives. The mind can be incredibly difficult to tame.

But mindful self-awareness can eventually become a new habit, and the effort we put into developing this habit is certainly worth it. As you'll discover in this book, the payoff is tremendous. When you practice mindfulness, you'll be developing what might be the ultimate habit for leadership and personal excellence.

Review Questions

How would you describe the "shift that changes everything," and why is it so important for leadership and personal excellence?

How can you apply the attitude of *beginner's mind* to realize mindful self-awareness?

What are the three general benefits of being mindfully self-aware that we explored in this chapter?

What is the difference between randomly being mindfully self-aware for brief instances, which almost everyone is many times every day, and intentionally becoming mindfully self-aware and sustaining it for longer periods?

2

MAKING AN
IMMEDIATE AND
DIRECT IMPACT ON
THE BOTTOM LINE

Watching people at Bristol airport in the United Kingdom (UK), everything would have likely appeared normal to you on this day in November 2014. You would have likely seen people rushing to make flights. You would have likely seen people getting impatient as they awaited the arrival of their luggage to the baggage claim conveyor. And you would have likely seen people leaving the baggage claim area to catch a taxi, or perhaps a bus.

It's when you watched the people lining up to catch the bus that you would have discovered your first clues that something very different would be happening that day.

At one of the stops, you would have seen a bench on which to wait. The bench was quite typical. It was made of metal of various shades of gray. However, right next to the bench, you would have seen a white porcelain toilet, which apparently was also meant to serve as a place to rest while you waited. Although newspapers were not provided, you would have been welcome to sit down and read one that you already had. In fact, one man did exactly that.

A few minutes later, that man's bus approached. From the front, the bus looked a little modern but otherwise fairly normal. Upon closer inspection, though, you would have noticed white flowers and the word *Bio-Bus* printed in white letters just below the windshield, both of which stood out from the otherwise green background.

As the bus pulled up to the stop, allowing you to see the side of it, you would have likely smiled, or perhaps even laughed, when you noticed what was painted on the side of the bus. There was a man reading the paper, an old woman knitting, a young man listening to music with headphones, and a young woman reading a book, all sitting one behind the other, appearing almost as though they were real passengers on the bus. However, each one of them was sitting on a toilet with his or her drawers down around their ankles.

After you stopped laughing, you would have likely asked what was going on. You would have then discovered that this was the maiden voyage of a bus now commonly referred to in the UK as the "Poo Bus."

The Poo Bus runs between Bristol Airport and Bath and is powered by nothing other than biomethane gas, which is created from food waste and sewage. The bus is reported to be able to travel 186 miles on a single tank and produces about 30 percent fewer emissions than a comparable diesel-powered bus.

Ironically, the Poo Bus (also referred to as "The Number Two") apparently produces fewer odors than a diesel bus as well. Because all impurities are removed during the treatment process that releases the methane and carbon dioxide from the waste, the emissions from the bus are reported to be virtually odor free.

The Poo Bus is an excellent example of innovation and of creatively avoiding the use of a finite resource—in this case petroleum—to achieve a positive outcome. It serves as a fun reminder of what we should be doing as leaders.

How We Unconsciously Affect
Gross Margins and Expenses

Two key elements of business acumen are making decisions that add more value for the end customer and our organization and achieving goals with the least use of finite resources possible; time and money are important examples. Most, if not all, leaders know that the essence of profitability is the ability to achieve higher gross margins and lower general expenses. However, many leaders are not successful at doing this. The research we'll discuss below from the Perth Leadership Institute suggests that only 12 percent of leaders are naturally hardwired to create and sustain organizations that achieve profitability over the long term.[1]

The problem isn't that we don't know what to do. The problem is that we are subject to *cognitive biases*—ways of deciding and acting that result from a lifetime of conditioning—which cause us to unconsciously make decisions that are less than optimal.

As business psychology expert Dr. Jim Taylor wrote in an article for *Psychology Today*, a cognitive bias "can be characterized by the tendency to make decisions and take action based on limited acquisition and/or processing of information or on self-interest, overconfidence, or attachment to past experience. Cognitive biases can result in perceptual blindness or distortion, illogical interpretation, inaccurate judgments, irrationality, and bad decisions."[2]

The idea of cognitive biases was introduced by Amos Tversky and Daniel Kahneman in the early 1970s. Their work showed quite clearly that humans often make decisions that deviate substantially from what strict rationale would indicate is the correct choice. In other words, we often do things that simply don't make sense.

Tversky and Kahneman also showed that they could predict quite accurately when people would act irrationally, because the irrational behavior was due to measurable cognitive biases. This work on cognitive biases became the foundation for the field of behavioral economics and resulted in Kahneman winning the Nobel Prize in 2002.

There is both good news and bad news that come with this exploration of cognitive biases.

First, the bad news:

1. We all have cognitive biases.

2. Many of them lead to negative impacts on the profit and loss (P&L) statement, both through decisions made directly by the individual leader and the influence the leader has on the decisions of others.

3. Unless we have a very high level of self-awareness, the cognitive biases are usually completely unconscious. We're simply not aware of the conditioned patterns of deciding and acting that negatively affect gross margins and expenses.

There are several pieces of good news:

1. It's possible to measure our cognitive biases quite accurately with a well-designed assessment. Although he didn't win a Nobel Prize, my colleague at the Perth Leadership Institute, Dr. E. Ted Prince, conducted research that was published in highly respected, peer-reviewed journals, which included hundreds of executives over a period of more than 12 years. He discovered 10 cognitive biases that have significant impacts on the P&L: five biases that affect gross margins and five that affect expenses. This research became the foundation for the assessments created by the Perth Leadership Institute designed to measure those 10 cognitive biases.

   With enough self-awareness—which is highly trainable—we can get a relatively good sense of some of the most critical cognitive biases just by applying the guidance we'll discuss below.

2. Once we have a better sense of our cognitive biases, we have a much better chance of being able to recognize when we're about to make habitual, conditioned decisions that would have a negative impact on gross margins or expenses.

3. With continued mindfulness training, we can further enhance our ability to recognize when we're about to make a habitual, conditioned decision.

Mindfulness training also helps us develop the mental agility that allows us to move out of our comfort zone and make decisions that are vastly different than what we would typically do.

Let's explore the good news a bit further.

UNCOVERING OUR COGNITIVE BIASES

In the business acumen training I offer to leaders and leadership teams, the first step in the process is having the participants complete the Perth Leadership Institute assessments. These assessments help leaders discover their business acumen blind spots—how they unconsciously make decisions that have a negative effect on gross margins and expenses.

Bringing these blind spots into conscious awareness is absolutely essential for improving business acumen. By making the cognitive biases conscious, a leader is able to recognize conditioned ways of deciding and acting and make better choices when appropriate. Because this is so important, we will explore how the biases affect gross margin and expenses, as well as how you can get a good estimate of the strength of these biases in yourself.

Although a complete discussion on all 10 of the cognitive biases we focus on with the Perth assessments is beyond the scope of this book, we will briefly discuss four of them here. The effects of the first two are fairly self-evident. However, you may not find the effects of the second two biases we'll explore to be so intuitive.

THE ILLUSION OF CONTROL BIAS

The first bias we'll discuss is the *illusion of control bias*. This bias results in unconsciously believing that the more resources we apply to a given task, the better the outcome will be.

Before reading the description below, how would you guess a strong illusion of control bias in a person affects expenses?

As you likely intuited, a strong illusion of control bias has disastrous effects on resource use. A person with a strong illusion of control bias is very likely to apply considerably more resources to a task than is necessary, which negatively affects expenses.

The higher up in leadership the person is, the more severe the effects. Imagine, for instance, a leader in charge of a $100,000,000 annual budget who, because of his direct decisions and his influence over the decisions of others, unconsciously yet consistently causes spending of only 5 percent more than necessary. This would result in an unnecessary loss of $5,000,000 each year for his organization.

Conversely, a person with little to no illusion of control bias would be much more likely to ask whether it's necessary to apply a finite resource to a solution. She would look for ways to devote the fewest resources possible to achieve a given solution. She would likely be the person to ask, "Why are we spending all this money on diesel fuel for our bus system when we could just use an inexhaustible resource, like our own poo?"

To get a rough idea of the strength of your illusion of control bias, you could ask five people to rate you from 1 to 4 on the question below. You could plot the answers below if you like. This will come in handy as you start to pay more attention to how you make decisions (a 1 on this scale is the best for low resource use).

In her/his personal life, how has ___ tended to spend, or otherwise use up finite resources (such as money) compared with the average person?

1 = ___ has tended to spend/use up a much smaller amount of finite resources than the average person

2 = ___ has tended to spend/use up a slightly smaller amount of finite resources than the average person

3 = ___ has tended to spend/use up a little larger amount of finite resources than the average person

4 = ___ has tended to spend/use up a much larger amount of finite resources than the average person

THE STATUS QUO BIAS

The *status quo bias* results in unconsciously making decisions that conform to the status quo. This bias is quite strong in most people because, as humans, we tend to have a strong, unconscious need to fit in. We generally don't like to do things that could result in being ostracized from the group that we want to belong to.

Before reading the description below, how you would you guess a strong status quo bias in a person affects gross margins?

As you likely intuited, the stronger the status quo bias is in a person, the more likely he is to conform to the status quo and the less likely he is to be an innovator. Conversely, the weaker the status quo bias is in a person, the less affected she is by what others think of her ideas and the more likely she is to move forward on ideas that challenge the status quo and stick with those ideas despite the lack of immediate approval of others.

It is likely quite intuitive for many of us that innovation is strongly correlated with higher margins. The more differentiated a product or service is (or a solution internal to the organization), the more value it potentially adds for the consumer and the easier it is to earn a higher price. Innovation is the most effective driver of gross margins because it allows an organization to earn higher prices without necessarily requiring a lot of overhead. Conversely, noninnovative companies that rely on brand strength to achieve high gross margins are often not very profitable, if at all.[3]

A person with little or no status quo bias is the type of person who is likely to disrupt the status quo and create an innovative solution that results in a significant amount of value for the end consumer and higher gross margins as well.

To get a rough idea of the strength of your status quo bias, you could ask five people to rate you from 1 to 4 on the following question (a 4 on this scale is best for value adding/gross margins):

How often does ____ launch and stick with work on projects that strongly challenge the status quo?

1 = ___ never launches and sticks with work on projects that strongly challenge the status quo

2 = ___ very rarely launches and sticks with work on projects that strongly challenge the status quo

3 = ___ sometimes launches and sticks with work on projects that strongly challenge the status quo

4 = ___ often launches and sticks with work on projects that strongly challenge the status quo

THE LOGIC BIAS

The *logic bias* indicates the type of information a person trusts when he or she makes a decision. Some people are more analytical and place a lot of value on detailed data from sources they believe to be official or scholarly. They don't trust other sources of information.

Other people tend to rely much more on their experiences and their intuition. These people tend to actually distrust data in general. They prefer to listen to what their gut tells them. We refer to these people as being streetwise.

Before reading the description below, who would you guess tends to have a better impact on resource use, the analytical person or the streetwise person?

This one is likely not as intuitive for most of us as the first two biases we discussed. The research shows quite clearly that the streetwise person tends to consume far fewer resources—and thus have a better impact on expenses—than does the analytical person.

An analytical person tends to really trust data. If we can provide him with enough data suggesting that a solution is the correct one, he'll believe in the efficacy of the solution. He will apply the resources—people, time, money, and so on—to act on that solution. Thus, because it's often not very difficult to collect supporting data, it's often not very challenging to persuade a highly analytical person to apply resources.

The streetwise person, however, completely distrusts data. If you bring this type of person a spreadsheet, she'll likely ask you to leave her office. She strongly prefers to listen to what her intuition and experience tell her. Thus, because the streetwise person is so hard to convince, she generally spends much less than does an analytical person.

To get a rough idea of your logic bias, you could ask five people to rate you from 1 to 4 on the following question (a 4 on this scale is best for low resource use):

Compared with the average person, how much does ___ trust data or intuition and experience?

1 = ___, compared with the average person, trusts data much more than intuition or experience

2 = ___, compared with the average person, trusts data a little more than intuition or experience

3 = ___, compared with the average person, trusts intuition or experience a little more than data

4 = ___, compared with the average person, trusts intuition or experience much more than data

❧❧❧

THE REACTION TIME BIAS

The last bias we'll discuss is the *reaction time bias*. This bias affects the speed with which a person takes action.

Before reading the description below, who would you guess tends to have a better impact on gross margins, someone who is a real planner or someone who takes action very quickly?

This one is almost a trick question and is likely not as intuitive for most of us as the first two biases we discussed. The research shows quite clearly that the person who has the best impact on value adding and the resulting gross margins is actually a person who is almost in the middle of the two extremes but slightly favors action over planning.

A person who plans too much simply moves too slowly and often misses opportunities. For example, by the time he constructs and begins executing a plan to take advantage of a market shift, the market has likely shifted again, rendering his plan useless.

A person who acts too quickly often sacrifices quality, which hurts long-term performance. He also tends to change strategies too quickly, which results in confusion and a lack of buy-in from team members, which results in his plans not being executed well, if at all.

The leader who strikes a good balance between the two extremes, but slightly favors action over planning, is the leader who achieves the best results in terms of value adding and higher gross margins. She is able to move quickly enough to take advantage of opportunities but prefers not to act so quickly that the product, service, or other solution being offered fails to create significant value for the end consumer.

To get a rough idea of your reaction time bias, you could ask five people to rate you from 1 to 4 on the following question (a 3 on this scale is the best for value adding/gross margins):

Compared with the average person, does ___ tend to favor planning or taking action?

1 = ___, compared with the average person, tends to strongly favor planning over taking action

2 = ___, compared with the average person, tends to moderately favor planning over taking action

3 = ___, compared with the average person, tends to moderately favor taking action over planning

4 = ___, compared with the average person, tends to strongly favor taking action over planning

MINDFUL SELF-AWARENESS AND BETTER DECISIONS

As Dr. Gard explains below in Neuro Note 2.1, research suggests that mindfulness training significantly increases the likelihood of making rational decisions. Mindfulness training can also help us become free from the cognitive biases described above and make decisions that have better impacts on the P&L.

Neuro Note 2.1: Mindfulness for Better Decisions

Very recently, Sai Sun and colleagues, from South China Normal University, reviewed the growing scientific literature on the effects of mindfulness practice on social and nonsocial economic decision making. They concluded that the 13 studies they reviewed suggest that mindfulness practice "may be effective in promoting good decision making and increasing prosocial behavior."[4]

One particularly interesting study investigated the neural mechanisms of rational decision making in mindfulness practitioners. For this study, Virginia Tech researcher Ulrich Kirk and his colleagues used a tool of behavioral economics: the ultimatum game.[5] In this economic game, two players split a sum of money. One player proposes how the money is split, and the other accepts or rejects the offer. If the offer is accepted, the money will be split as proposed; if the offer is rejected, none of the players will get money. According to the rational choice theory, participants should accept any offer in which they get any money because something is more than nothing. However, in practice, people often decline offers in which they get less than 20 percent of the amount.[6]

The researchers found that mindfulness practitioners accepted twice as many unfair offers as nonpractitioners did, indicating that mindfulness practitioners make more rational decisions.

While deciding about accepting an unfair offer, nonpractitioners showed brain activity in a neural network involving emotion, cognition, and brain areas related to the sense of self, including the medial prefrontal cortex, anterior insula, and anterior cingulate cortex.[7] Mindfulness practitioners had a

(continued)

(continued)

completely different brain activation pattern with increases in the posterior insula and the thalamus, which are associated with body awareness.[8,9]

Years ago, when I was first learning about the research of the Perth Leadership Institute, I asked Dr. Prince what his research indicated was the most important element of good business acumen. He said that it's not the cognitive biases in a person that are most important. It doesn't necessarily matter how a person is naturally hardwired.

The two skills that are most important for good business acumen are self-awareness and mental agility. Self-awareness and mental agility are what allow a person to transcend his or her conditioning and make better decisions. Following is a discussion on how that happens.

Completing an assessment like the informal one described above, or a detailed, more precise assessment like those created by the Perth Leadership Institute, is an essential first step in improving our impacts on gross margins and expenses. An assessment helps increase our awareness of how we tend to decide, act, and influence the decisions of others.

Just as important as knowing what to look for, however, is the ability to actually see, in the moment, our conditioned ways of deciding and acting. In most cases, our conditioning is quite subtle. We need to develop high levels of moment-to-moment self-awareness to be able to catch ourselves leaning toward conditioned, habitual ways of operating and give ourselves the chance to consider a potentially better alternative.

As we discussed in Chapter 1, mindfulness training is essentially self-awareness training and can significantly improve self-awareness. Research conducted by Dr. Sara Lazar and colleagues in 2005 at Massachusetts General Hospital, Harvard Medical School, showed that, compared with controls, longtime practitioners of mindfulness have a thicker insula (an area of the brain associated with self-awareness, particularly awareness of the body).[10] Figure 2.1 is an image from the 2005 Lazar study showing the part of the insula that was significantly thicker for mindfulness practitioners.[11] This study, as well as others like

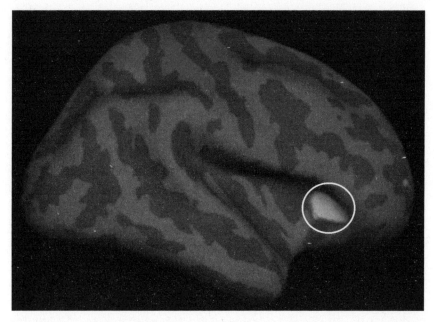

Figure 2.1   Research at Harvard Showing the Thicker Insula of Mindfulness Practitioners
Copyright © Sara Lazar. Used with permission.

it, suggest that mindfulness training can change both the function and the structure of the brain in ways that allow us to have better self-awareness.[12]

Several studies suggest that mindfulness training results in highly refined levels of self-awareness, allowing us to notice aspects of ourselves that untrained people are not able to notice. Jocelyn Sze and colleagues from the University of California, Berkeley, for example, found that experienced mindfulness practitioners had a high correlation between their second-to-second emotional experience and a physiological marker of emotion (the length of time between heartbeats) while watching emotion-inducing film clips. Mindfulness practitioners had greater coherence between subjective and objective markers of emotion than had the control group.[13]

Kieran Fox and colleagues from the University of British Columbia in Canada found that experienced mindfulness practitioners had greater correspondence between subjective and objective measures (average body representation in the brain) of tactile sensitivity of 20 body parts and that the more experience practitioners had, the greater the interoceptive accuracy was.[14]

A very recent and large study by Boris Bornemann and Tania Singer (2015) from the Max Planck Institute in Leipzig, Germany, revealed that after 39 weeks of mindfulness training, participants had significantly improved heartbeat accuracy. That is, they had a greater correspondence between subjectively reported and objectively measured heartbeats.[15,16]

The more refined our self-awareness, the more easily we can see even the most subtle conditioning. We are able to know things about ourselves that very few people will ever know. The greater our ability to clearly see more subtle elements of our conditioning, the more likely we are to catch ourselves getting ready to act or decide in a conditioned, habitual way that may not have optimal results for value adding or resource use and thereby negatively affect gross margins and expenses.

For instance, perhaps you absolutely love data. You scored a 1 on the logic bias assessment above. With the greater self-awareness of your bias for data, and the greater moment-to-moment self-awareness resulting from mindfulness training, you might catch yourself wanting to see data as you consider a purchase and decide to refrain from looking it at right away.

Instead, you might pay more attention to your body and notice how you *feel* about the purchase based on intuition and your past experiences with similar purchases. Just this pause, this space around your habitual way of deciding on a purchase, may be enough to prevent you from making or approving a purchase that isn't necessary. You might still look at the data, but it will no longer be out of habit.

MENTAL AGILITY

FREEDOM FROM AUTOPILOT MODE

In addition to changing the brain in ways that allow us to have stronger self-awareness, mindfulness training also helps us be less likely to follow our conditioning. As discussed in Chapter 1, mindfulness training helps us systematically develop the space between stimulus and response so that we aren't forced to react to situations out of habit. Dr. Gard elaborates on this below in Neuro Note 2.2.

Neuro Note 2.2: Mindfulness and Mental Agility

In 2005, Heidi Wenk-Sormaz demonstrated that practicing mindfulness can reduce habitual responding.[17] One of the tasks that was used in this study was the Stroop task.[18] In this task, participants are asked to name the font color of words that are presented on a screen as fast and accurately as possible. Reading is so habitual that when the meaning of the word conflicts with its font color (e.g., the word *red* printed in blue), it is much more difficult to name the font color correctly. Performance on these incongruent trials is thought to be related to attention control and flexible, nonhabitual behavior. Since this first study, several other studies have shown that mindfulness practitioners perform better than nonpractitioners on the trials with word–color interference.[19]

Neuroscientist Elisa Kozasa and colleagues investigated the brain mechanisms of the Stroop task in mindfulness practitioners. Mindfulness practitioners did not have reduced performance in the interference condition, but they also did not do better than the nonpractitioners.[20] In the brain, word–color interference is associated with increased activation in the anterior cingulate cortex (ACC), which plays a role in the performance monitoring of attention.[21] Mindfulness practitioners, while performing equally well as nonpractitioners, had less activation in several brain regions, including the medial frontal gyrus, close to the ACC. These findings suggest that practicing mindfulness is related to greater brain efficiency in controlling habitual behavior. Very recently researchers have suggested that the emotionally accepting attitude of mindfulness might be even more important than enhanced performance monitoring in the brain for overcoming habitual behavior.[22]

(continued)

(*continued*)

As described in Neuro Note 1.2, an area of the brain called the caudate is involved in goal-directed and flexible behavior, while an area called the putamen is involved in habitual behavior.[23] Together with a growing number of studies that have reported mindfulness-related activation of the caudate as well as connectivity between the caudate and a wide range of brain areas, it could be possible that behavioral flexibility through mindfulness is supported by a shift to caudate-mediated basal ganglia-thalamocortical loops, which are explained in Neuro Note 1.2.[24] However, this interpretation is still very speculative.

Mindfulness training can also help us be free from our conditioning by decreasing the prevalence and the severity of the stress response in the body. There tends to be a strong correlation between the experience of the stress response in the body and doing things in habitual, conditioned ways. The stress response essentially forces us into autopilot mode.

Because many of us have not been trained to effectively deal with the stress response in the body, we spend a lot of time in mild to severe states of that response. As a result, we are significantly more likely to be on autopilot and unconsciously act and decide in conditioned, habitual ways.

Neuro Note 2.3: Stress and Habits

When a situation is perceived as stressful, two systems are activated. In addition to activating the fight-or-flight response, which involves the release of the hormone adrenaline, stress also results in the activation of a slower but longer-lasting system, the hypothalamus-pituitary-adrenal (HPA) axis. This system involves a cascade of activations of the hypothalamus, the pituitary gland, and the adrenal cortex, which releases the stress hormone cortisol. These activations result in increased heart rate and the release of sugar from the liver.[25]

Stress, whether acute or chronic, results in a shift from goal-directed, flexible behavior to habitual behavior. As discussed in Neuro Note 1.2, goal-directed, flexible behavior is associated with the involvement of the ventromedial prefrontal cortex and the caudate, while habitual behavior is associated with activation in the putamen.

Because stress and the stress hormone cortisol are associated with decreased activation and gray matter in the medial prefrontal cortex and caudate, and increased activation and gray matter in the putamen, it is thought that the stress-related shift from flexible behavior to habitual behavior is associated with a shift from caudate to putamen involvement.[26]

Mindfulness training has been shown to be extremely effective at increasing our resilience to stressful situations. In fact, the earliest rigorous research of the practice of mindfulness training occurred at the University of Massachusetts Medical School. For decades, researchers studied the effects of the practice on stress and pain as it was taught through a program called mindfulness-based stress reduction (MBSR), cofounded by the well-known author and teacher Jon Kabat-Zinn.

We will discuss in great detail in later chapters how mindfulness training helps us be more resilient in stressful situations, allowing us to experience increasingly demanding situations without becoming a victim of the stress response. For now, let's consider the benefits inherent in increased stress resilience as they relate to business acumen.

By spending less time experiencing the stress response, we spend less time on autopilot. We are much more likely to consider and take courses of action that deviate from our conditioned, habitual ways of deciding and acting. This is one way that mindfulness training can help us be more mentally agile.

A Persistent Beginner's Mind

One of the counterintuitive findings of Dr. Prince's research is that there is an inverse correlation between education and business acumen. Assuming a person has no real-world experience, his business acumen would actually be worse if he had a master of business administration (MBA) than if he had only a college degree. His impacts on gross margins and expenses would be significantly worse if he then went on to get a doctor of philosophy (PhD). Why do you suppose this is?

Dr. Prince, whose PhD is in economics, has offered an explanation for why his research shows that people with high-level degrees who lack real-world experience tend to have poor business acumen. It is because they tend to be less flexible in their thinking. They tend to believe very strongly in what they've learned in school, so much so that they are often not as open to new approaches. They find it difficult to let go of what they already know—as we saw in Chapter 1 with the scientists in Einstein's day—and be open to what real-world, real-time experience is demanding.

Neuro Note 2.4: Mental Habits

In Neuro Note 1.2, you can see how habits are created in the basal ganglia-thalamocortical loops in the brain. These mechanisms apply both to simple behaviors and to complex thought processes.[27]

This understanding of why people with high-level degrees and little or no real-world experience lack mental agility points to a clear path that all of us can take to improve our agility. As you've likely intuited already, mindfulness training is extremely helpful for increasing mental agility. It is, by definition, the practice of letting go of what we already know and opening to present-moment experience. Research suggests that, over time, mindfulness helps us be more flexible in our thinking and can help us be free from even the strongest conditioning, including a powerful reflex, such as the startle reflex.[28]

When we're more flexible in our thinking, we're able to maintain and apply our existing knowledge when necessary, but we are no longer a prisoner of our existing knowledge. We are much more likely to let go of our conditioned ways of acting and deciding and act or decide in a way that's most appropriate based on the real-time, real-world information we are receiving.

Neuro Note 2.5: Self-Regulation, the Anterior Cingulate Cortex, and Mental Agility

We saw above with the example of the Stroop task that mindfulness leads to more flexibility and responding in nonhabitual ways. We also saw that the Stroop task involves the anterior cingulate cortex (ACC). The ACC is a hub in the salience network and well known to play a role in conflict monitoring.[29] As such, it is thought to play a role in cognitive flexibility, the ability to adjust behavior to changing demands of the environment.[30] It also has been implicated in self-regulation, which enables us to resist temptations, choose from alternatives, control impulses, and inhibit unwanted thoughts.[31] Considering that we fail to resist temptations 20 percent of the time, self-regulation is a valuable skill.[32]

Mindfulness is often conceptualized as enhancing self-regulation. Several functional magnetic resonance imaging (fMRI) studies have found the involvement of the ACC during mindfulness practice, and structural MRI studies have even shown that mindfulness practitioners have increased gray matter in this region.[33]

DOING WHAT'S UNCOMFORTABLE

As you have likely experienced in your own life, it can be very uncomfortable to act and decide in ways that deviate substantially from our conditioned, habitual ways of acting and deciding. When we do, it's very likely that we feel like the proverbial fish out of water. This discomfort can range from a mild sense of dislike all the way to an experience of moderate to severe stress response in the body. The unpleasantness can cause us to quickly abandon ways of acting and deciding that deviate from our conditioning.

As we've discussed above, mindfulness training can help us be more resilient to stressful situations. As we'll explore further in Chapter 12, the practice also helps us develop the ability to experience unpleasant and uncomfortable situations that we don't like with an increasing sense of equanimity. Thus, in addition to helping us consider a decision and initiate a course of action that deviates from our conditioning, mindfulness training also helps us stick with that course. Mindfulness training helps us improve execution.

QUICK IMPACT AND GREAT POTENTIAL

Many leaders have found that by taking the time to go through the assessment process to become more aware of the cognitive biases that affect gross margins and expenses, they can quickly make adjustments in their decisions and behaviors that have significant impacts on the bottom line. In some cases, leaders have reported significant impacts on expense reduction in just a week or two after being assessed and discussing ideas for improvement.

However, there is tremendous room for growth here. We can continue to refine our business acumen for years and years, yielding increasingly better impacts on the P&L, by improving and refining our self-awareness and mental agility. Mindfulness training helps us do precisely that.

REVIEW QUESTIONS

What causes intelligent leaders, who know what to do, to make decisions that have negative impacts on gross margins and expenses?

What are the four cognitive biases discussed in this chapter and their impacts on gross margins and expenses?

What two skills are even more important for good business acumen than our hardwired cognitive biases?

What are the four key ways that mindfulness training help improve our business acumen?

What are the three ways that mindfulness training can change the brain in ways that support the effects above?

3

ORGANIZATIONAL CLIMATE CHANGE

In 1869, Joseph Campbell and Abraham Anderson started a canned goods company in Camden, New Jersey. Anderson left the company in 1876, and after a couple of name changes, the company gradually settled on Campbell Soup Company, commonly referred to as Campbell's.

In 1897, Campbell's introduced five varieties of condensed soup, including the tomato soup that is still one of its best-selling products. In 1911, the company started distributing its soup throughout the United States. By the early 1970s, Campbell Soup Company had become an international firm and one of the largest food companies in the world.

The company had invested heavily in advertising—which significantly strengthened the brand—as early as the 1930s when the famous "M'm m'm good" jingle first started to hit the airwaves over radio. Ronald Reagan was an early spokesperson for the company, promoting the V8 brand. The Campbell's brand grew to become extremely strong, perhaps even iconic, and it gradually acquired a variety of other strong brands as well. In 1990, Campbell's produced their 20 billionth can of condensed tomato soup.

Despite Campbell's brand strength and its apparent success, by the end of the 1990s the company was in serious trouble. Sales were falling because of a decision from senior management to raise prices. Campbell's share price was falling quickly, and the firm was gradually becoming one of the worst-performing major food companies in the world. By 2001, the company's share price was about half of its previous high.

Senior management attempted to remedy the error that was made when prices were raised by cutting costs. The decision was made to reduce spending on advertising and to lay off large numbers of employees. The reduction in advertising further reduced sales, and the layoffs exacerbated the root cause of the problems Campbell's was facing: The emotional climate at the company was horrible.

The headquarters office in Camden was surrounded by a fence with barbed wire. It looked a bit like a prison, and many people felt as though their workplace wasn't much different from a prison. They were only there because they had to be.

When the Gallup organization measured the engagement levels of managers at Campbell's in 2002, more than 60 percent of them reported that they were not engaged in their work (which means that they were producing little or nothing while at work), and more than 10 percent reported that they were actively disengaged (which means they were so unhappy that they were likely undermining the efforts of the few people who were actually performing). These were among the worst results ever recorded within a Fortune 500 company.

THE POWER OF A POSITIVE EMOTIONAL CLIMATE

There is no doubt that factors such as business acumen and intelligence play a critical role in leadership. But they are not enough to succeed as a leader. As I wrote about in *Serve to Be Great*, to succeed over the long term, a leader must also be able to serve and care for team members consistently and effectively. He or she must be able to create and sustain a workplace culture that people enjoy being a part of. In other words, the emotional climate of the workplace must be positive.

It doesn't really matter how smart a leader is or how strong his or her business acumen is. If the leader is unable to drive positive emotions in team members, he or she will eventually fail. In general terms, this failure would come about because disengaged team members would eventually fail to serve the customer. The quality of the product or service would decline, as would customer service. No organization that fails to serve its customers can survive for very long. As we saw above, Campbell Soup Company was a good example of this downward spiral toward collapse.

Conversely, when the emotional climate is strong, the customer is better served. Happy, loyal team members lead to happy, loyal customers. Happy, loyal customers drive positive business outcomes.

Intuitively, most people see this quite clearly. There is also research that supports our intuition and quantifies the effect of a positive emotional climate. One study suggests that for every one percent increase in service climate, there is a corresponding two percent increase in revenues.[1] In another study involving 19 insurance companies, researchers found that in 75 percent of cases emotional climate alone served as an accurate prediction of both profitability and growth.[2]

THE LEADER DRIVES THE EMOTIONS OF THE TEAM

It is now commonly accepted that emotions are contagious, so to speak. Likely because of the way humans evolved in groups—which meant it was important for people to be able to affect the emotions of others—the emotional areas of our nervous systems operate in what is often referred to as an "open loop." Our emotional state affects the emotional state of the people around us, which can actually alter hormone levels, sleep, heart function, and the immune system in others.[3]

When strangers share the same space, the most emotionally expressive person tends to affect the mood of the others without even speaking.[4] But this effect is much stronger when people know each other. People who work together are more likely to affect each other's moods, and the effect is stronger when the group is more cohesive.[5]

Neuro Note 3.1: Mirror Neurons and the Emotionally Contagious Brain

Emotional contagion has been proposed to play an important role in leadership through different organizational levels.[6] A brain system that is often implicated in emotional contagion in the mirror neuron system. In the 1990s, it was discovered that, in the brains of monkeys, neurons fire when the monkey performs a specific action but also when it just observes the execution of the action by the experimenter.[7] Research suggests that humans also have a mirror neuron system that comprises similar regions as in monkeys, namely the posterior inferior frontal gyrus (IFG) and the rostral inferior parietal lobule (IPL).[8] There is research indicating that this mirror neuron system plays an important role in emotional contagion or emotional empathy by making it possible to simulate, for example, the situation or facial expression of the other person.[9,10]

As we would likely guess, the person who has the greatest impact on the emotions of others tends to be the leader. Whether we like it or not, as leaders, people are watching us, and our emotional state affects them emotionally. This is even true for leaders who tend to hide in their office a lot. A chief executive officer (CEO) who doesn't interact a whole lot with anyone but senior management can significantly affect the emotional climate of the organization through a sort of "ripple effect" that starts with direct reports who in turn influence others.[11]

THE EMOTIONALLY INTELLIGENT LEADER

Understanding how the leader affects the emotional climate of the organization makes it clear that our people skills, our emotional and social intelligence, are essential for being effective as a leader over the long term. Emotional and social intelligence are what close the gap between *wanting* to serve and care for team members—and thereby creating a positive emotional climate and a sustainable, high-performance culture—and *actually doing it.*

This is why I strongly encourage clients to begin any training for emotional intelligence with an anonymous, 360-degree assessment of each participant's emotional and social intelligence called the Emotional and Social Competency Inventory (ESCI), which was developed by Daniel Goleman, Richard Boyatzis, and the Hay Group and is based on years of research that links emotional and social intelligence competencies to business outcomes.[12]

Although we cannot administer the full ESCI in this book (it is an anonymous, 360-degree assessment done online with much more precisely calibrated questions that measure much more specific aspects of the core competencies listed below), I'd like to give you an idea of the core competencies that the ESCI measures so that you can get at least a rough idea of your strengths and weaknesses in these areas by asking people you work with to rate you informally. For each competency, you could ask a few people who know you well to rate you on the following scale:

1 = Never displays (emotional self-awareness) __
2 = Rarely displays __
3 = Sometimes displays __
4 = Often displays __
5 = Almost always displays __

If you'd like to learn more about these critical competencies and how to apply them, I highly recommend the excellent, internationally bestselling book by Daniel Goleman, Richard Boyatszis, and Annie McKee, *Primal Leadership.* In that book, the authors list four areas of emotional and social intelligence, which are then divided into specific leadership competencies. The ESCI follows the same general outline. The first area is *self-awareness*, which is the foundation of all emotional and social intelligence.

SELF-AWARENESS

Under the domain of self-awareness is the leadership competency of emotional self-awareness.

Emotional Self-Awareness

Emotionally self-aware leaders are able to recognize even their own very subtle emotions, understand why they occur and how they are affecting performance, know their strengths and limits, and be open to feedback on how to improve.

SELF-MANAGEMENT

Under the second domain, self-management, are the following leadership competencies:

Achievement Orientation

Leaders with high achievement drive are self-motivated and tend to anticipate obstacles, take calculated risks, and take action rather than wait.

Adaptability

Leaders who are adaptable tend to juggle multiple demands well, handle rapid change easily, and adapt their ideas based on new information.

Emotional Self-Control

A leader with high levels of emotional self-control doesn't become a victim of his or her emotions and is able to remain calm and collected under very demanding situations.

Positive Outlook

A leader with a positive outlook tends to see opportunities rather than threats, have positive expectations about the future and about other people, and see the positive side of difficult situations.

SOCIAL AWARENESS

Under the third domain, social awareness, are the following leadership competencies:

Empathy

This crucial skill is what allows leaders to listen well and understand the perspectives and emotional states of others.

Organizational Awareness

A leader with organizational awareness is able to understand office politics, the social networks and norms of an organization.

RELATIONSHIP MANAGEMENT

Under the fourth domain, relationship management, are the following leadership competencies:

Inspirational Leadership

Effective leaders are able to inspire team members by connecting their work to a larger purpose and being a living example of the team's values.

Influence

The ability to influence the behaviors of others is the essence of leadership. Emotionally intelligent leaders are able to build influence with others by understanding others and appealing to what's important to them.

Coach and Mentor

Leaders who coach and mentor offer feedback that improves others' performance, recognize strengths, and truly care about the development of team members.

Conflict Management

Leaders who skillfully manage conflict are able to draw out and recognize the needs of all sides and help the parties involved find a shared solution.

Teamwork

Leaders who are most effective at fostering good teamwork are living examples of good team players. They seek to collaborate often and they value and invest in personal relationships.

A More Emotionally Intelligent Brain

It should be quite clear that, assuming relatively equal levels of cognitive ability and business acumen, a leader who excels in most of the emotional and social competencies above (very few people excel at all of them) is going to significantly outperform a leader who is poor in most of the competencies above. More important than knowing about these competencies, though, is knowing how to develop them. Let's explore that now.

I wish I could tell you that after reading this chapter, you will have greater emotional and social intelligence. But that is not the case. If you want to be a highly effective leader, you will need to practice. There are two widely accepted methods for improving emotional and social intelligence that have been shown to result in positive changes to the function and structure of the brain.

The first method is simply to make the effort to practice the competencies in real-world situations. You might like to begin in relatively easy situations, perhaps even away from work. Emotional intelligence is something that's acquired through what is known as *implicit learning*, which happens in areas of the brain other than the neocortex, where thinking occurs.

Fortunately, this means that practicing behaviors in one setting, such as leading a group of volunteers on the weekend, will make it more likely that we exhibit the same behavior in other leadership contexts, such as at our workplace. The more often we practice a given behavior, the stronger the neural network associated with that behavior becomes and the easier it is to behave that way in the future.

The second method for rewiring the brain to be more emotionally intelligent is to practice mindfulness training. Mindfulness training affects, either directly or indirectly, every emotional and social intelligence leadership competency. We'll explore the competencies most affected by mindfulness training—emotional self-awareness, emotional self-control, achievement drive, adaptability, positive outlook, empathy, inspirational leadership, and conflict management—in various ways throughout this book.

Perhaps most important, though, is that mindfulness training is essentially the very foundation of emotional intelligence development. Every emotional and social intelligence competency can be improved by improving self-awareness. Thus, as Daniel Goleman often stresses, self-awareness is the core competency of emotional and social intelligence.

As we've discussed in earlier chapters, mindfulness training is at its essence self-awareness training and has been shown to change both the functioning and physical structure of the brain in the areas associated with self-awareness. Because self-awareness is the foundation, or core competency, of emotional intelligence, it follows that mindfulness training is perhaps the most powerful tool there is for developing emotional intelligence.

Neuro Note 3.2: Mindfulness and the Emotionally Intelligent Brain

Several studies have shown that greater mindfulness is related to greater emotional intelligence (EI).[13] Researchers have found that EI mediates the relationship between mindfulness and lower negative emotions, stress, and mental distress and greater positive emotions and life satisfaction.[14] Emotion regulation is an important aspect of EI,[15] and one study found that in particular the emotion regulation aspect (e.g., "I am quite capable of controlling my own emotions") of emotional intelligence mediated the relationship between mindfulness and perceived stress.[16]

Emotion regulation, alongside attention control and self-awareness, has been proposed as one component of enhanced self-regulation through mindfulness.[17] Several types of studies have shown that mindfulness enhances emotion regulation.[18] For example, Amishi Jha and colleagues found that the more mindfulness soldiers practiced, the more positive and the fewer negative emotions they experienced.[19]

Véronique Taylor and colleagues found that emotional pictures resulted in less intense emotions in a state of mindfulness,[20] and Fadel Zeidan and colleagues found that after a short mindfulness intervention, heat stimuli were experienced as less painful.[21] With regard to patients, many studies have found improvement in conditions in which emotions play an important role, including chronic pain,[22] depression, and anxiety disorders.[23] Liz Hoge and colleagues, for example, found that in patients with generalized anxiety disorder, participating in an MBSR class resulted in decreased anxiety.[24]

In the brain, three networks can be identified with regard to emotion experience and regulation. The ventral affective network, which includes the amygdala, serves to indicate how dangerous or rewarding a stimulus is. The dorsal affect processing system includes medial prefrontal regions and is responsible for how we evaluate our emotional state.[25] Emotion regulation, in particular through positive reappraisal, which means giving the emotional stimulus or situation a new, more positive meaning, involves prefrontal regions, such as the lateral prefrontal cortex.[26] Overall, the research literature shows that mindfulness affects all three systems, but there is still a debate about how exactly.[27]

So far, two distinct brain activation patterns have been observed with regard to emotion regulation through mindfulness. One pattern that looks like reappraisal involves increased brain activation in emotion regulative brain areas, such as the lateral prefrontal cortex, and at the same time decreased brain activation in emotional brain regions, such as the amygdala. This form of emotion regulation is called "top-down" because the "higher" regulatory brain regions down regulate the "lower" emotion-related brain regions. The other pattern involves no activation or decreases in activation in regulatory brain areas and no activation or even greater activation in "lower" emotion-related regions and is called "bottom-up." In beginning mindfulness practitioners, the top-down pattern is typically observed, while in experienced mindfulness practitioners, the bottom-up pattern is often seen. However, it is not clear yet whether the

(continued)

(*continued*)

different patterns observed in beginning and advanced practitioners are mostly because of different strategies or decreased effort that comes with practice.[28]

One of the most successful EI training programs in the business world was created as a result of the cofounder, Chade-Meng Tan ("Meng"), making a connection, similar to the one described above, between mindfulness, self-awareness, and EI. The program, which was started at Google in cooperation with Daniel Goleman, is called Search Inside Yourself (SIY). The SIY program offers an excellent approach to developing emotional intelligence, which is a combination of mindfulness training and practical application of emotional and social intelligence leadership competencies.

Since the early days of the program, SIY has been one of the most popular and highest-rated programs at Google. People often comment that the program helped them improve performance, get promoted, be a better leader, or discover their best work. Even more important, participants have reported that the program changed their lives.

Based on the success of the SIY program at Google, Meng wrote a book by the same name, which became a *New York Times* bestseller. Demand for the program outside of Google also began to increase rapidly, so Meng cofounded the Search Inside Yourself Leadership Institute (SIYLI—pronounced "silly." Yes, on purpose), along with the current CEO of the organization, Marc Lesser. The institute is growing and experiencing increasing demand for the SIY program.

A TRAINING REGIMEN FOR EMOTIONAL INTELLIGENCE

I hope that you are as excited as I am about the fact that the emotional and social competencies so essential for leadership excellence are skills we can develop with practice. With mindfulness training, every one of us can systematically train to change our brains in ways that increase our EI.

Because mindfulness training and the self-mastery and people skills that fall under the umbrella of EI are so interwoven, we will be touching on emotional and social competencies—and how they are cultivated with mindfulness training—throughout much of the rest of this book. Thus, you will be able to create a sound EI training regimen by practicing the competencies listed in this chapter and engaging in the mindfulness training methods outlined in Part 2 of this book.

For now, let's return to the story that opened this chapter and consider a real-world example of the power of emotional intelligence.

A Human Approach

When Douglas Conant took charge of Campbell's in 2001, he was given what appeared to be mission impossible: turn around a company that seemed destined to either fail or be bought out. But he believed that a turnaround was possible.

His plan included two major elements. Of course, strategy and business acumen played a role. Conant realized that sales had to be restored, so his approach included strategies for changing the consumer perception of Campbell's products, making in-store displays more appealing and redesigning products that hadn't been changed in decades. However, he also realized that none of these strategies could be executed without the help of thousands of employees. Without a huge change in culture, Conant knew that the help he needed wouldn't come and that his plan would never be executed.

The main focus of Conant's plan was based on his insight that "you can't win in the marketplace if you aren't winning in the workplace." He needed to help leaders better serve and care for the team members at Campbell's and transform the culture from a veritable toxic prison where engagement levels were extremely low to a winning culture with a positive emotional climate where people are highly engaged in their work. This required him to apply many of the emotional and social competencies discussed in this chapter.

One of Conant's first moves was to change the most obvious elements that would contribute to a more positive emotional climate, such as taking down the fence so that the headquarters building no longer looked like an actual prison. He also created an inspiring vision of future success and communicated it often, in person, which required him to go out of his comfort zone (Conant is a self-proclaimed introvert).

Next, Conant worked on transforming the leadership team into one focused on building trust with team members and being, in his words, "tough-minded on standards and tender-hearted with people." Conant designed and personally ran a two-year leadership development program to help leaders grow, which included homework assignments that he would personally grade, often within 24 hours.

In his efforts to boost engagement, Conant led by example. He made it a goal to take 10,000 steps per day and have meaningful interactions with as many employees as possible. As he points out in his book *TouchPoints: Creating Powerful Leadership Connections in the Smallest of Moments*, instead of seeing conversations in the hallway as something that got in the way of his work, Conant approached them as opportunities to listen deeply to team members, build trust with them, and learn about their ideas for making the company better.

When Conant was in his office, he spent a good deal of his time there appreciating team members who were performing well. On most days, he would handwrite 20 notes of appreciation. It is estimated that during his 10 years at Campbell's, Conant sent roughly 30,000 handwritten notes thanking the 20,000 employees for jobs well done.

Little by little, Conant's efforts to improve the emotional climate at Campbell's bore fruit. At first, there was a lot of change. Many people weren't a good fit for the leadership team, so turnover of senior leaders was high. But, eventually, the leadership team became highly engaged and built high levels of trust with team members. When Gallup polled the workforce at Campbell's in 2010, it learned that for every 17 engaged employees, only one was disengaged. To put this in perspective, Gallup considers an engagement ratio of 12 to one world-class. Even more incredible, the engagement ratio for the top 350 leaders was 77 to one!

Because of the improved emotional climate and the increased engagement, innovation and performance soared at Campbell's, and

Conant's marketplace plans were successfully executed. Over a period of eight years, Campbell's averaged 4 percent growth in earnings per year, which was among the best in the industry. Over a six-year period, Campbell's had a cumulative shareholder return of roughly 60 percent, which was more than four times the 13 percent return of the Standard & Poor's 500 during the same period.

One afternoon, though, in July of 2009, Conant's streak of successes seemed as though it might abruptly end. He was being driven from Campbell's headquarters in Camden to his home in Morris County. As Conant and the driver approached Exit 6 of the New Jersey Turnpike, the Lincoln Navigator they were in struck the rear end of a tractor trailer. Although the drivers of both Conant's vehicle and the semi were not seriously hurt, Conant was taken to the hospital with broken ribs and later required surgery.

But what seemed like a great misfortune actually highlighted what may be Conant's greatest success. During his recovery, Conant was soon flooded with get well notes from people from many areas of Campbell's and even people from outside the company. Conant said of the notes, "As my wife and I sat and read them in the hospital room, I could feel them helping to speed my recovery. The blessings of their notes reminded me that the more supportive feedback you give to others, the more you may very well receive in return."

Conant's efforts to create superior engagement and to serve and care for team members by listening to them, building real human relationships with them, and appreciating them did more than help turn Campbell's around. His efforts afforded him a wonderful taste of those priceless, intangible riches that are realized only when we prioritize people over the numbers.[29]

REVIEW QUESTIONS

In a general sense, why is the emotional climate of a team culture so essential for sustainable bottom-line results?

Who tends to have the greatest influence on the emotional climate of a team?

What are the 12 emotional and social leadership competencies that research suggests have the greatest impact on business results?

What is the foundational emotional competency that influences all other emotional and social competencies?

How does mindfulness training change the brain in ways that improve emotional and social intelligence?

4

FUELING THE FIRE
OF INNOVATION

I n 2001, Debbie Sterling was finishing up high school in Rhode
Island and starting to apply to colleges. She asked her math teacher
to write a recommendation letter for her. Her teacher asked what
Debbie planned to study so that she could make the letter more specific.
Debbie replied simply, "I don't know."

Her math teacher suggested, "Why don't you major in engineering?
I think you would really excel in that field."

Debbie wasn't quite sure what it meant to be an engineer. The first
thought that came to mind was the person who drives a train. She
thought there was no way that an "artistic and creative girl" like her
could ever be interested in that. But the confidence that Debbie's math
teacher had in her inspired her to look further into the matter.

Debbie was accepted into Stanford University. She decided to enroll
in a survey level mechanical-engineering course but with a little bit of
fear. She thought that for the first time in her academic career she might
fail a course.

It was in that class, ME 101, which consisted of inventing and
designing a wide variety of items, that Debbie discovered that engineers

build the amazing tools, gadgets, and machines that make people's lives better. That was something she could see herself doing.

But Debbie also learned in her early engineering classes that she didn't fit in. There were only a few girls in each of her classes. Engineering appeared to be a field for men.

In fact, although (as of this writing) 50.8 percent of people in the United States are women, only 11 percent of engineers are women. Debbie realized that half of the population could benefit a great deal from having more things built by people who more closely share their perspective. This realization fueled her desire to become an engineer. She wanted to disrupt the status quo.

Although there would be a lot of subtle opposition to her becoming an engineer from the men who dominated the field, she also faced some internal challenges. Debbie discovered one of those challenges in an engineering drawing class.

She quickly realized that while engineering drawing appeared to be very easy for the men in her class, it was extremely difficult for her. She seemed to have a mental block that kept her from being able to draw in a three-dimensional perspective. Debbie was worried once again that she might actually fail. But she worked extremely hard, spending many nights in the library until the early morning hours. She eventually learned to draw in perspective.

She later learned that the cards had been stacked against her at an early age. Like many other young women, she had underdeveloped spatial skills. She also learned that people who score the highest on spatial skills tests played more with construction toys when they were kids than those who don't score well in spatial skills.

Debbie realized that construction-type toys had been marketed exclusively toward boys for generations. Girls are conditioned to believe that those are boys' toys, and encouraged to play with dolls and other girly things by both their parents and the marketing that has resulted in the girls' toy aisle in stores being dominated by pink, pretty things.

By this point, Debbie had an engineering degree. She decided that she would challenge the notion that girls wouldn't want to play with construction-type toys. If she was right, she could help young girls realize that they could be builders, too, and she could help them develop the skills they needed to be successful engineers.

She decided to quit her job and devote herself 100 percent to creating an engineering toy for girls. She worked late hours for months to create her first prototype. She spent a lot of time observing girls playing with construction toys so that she could learn how to improve the toys in ways that would make them better for girls. Debbie noticed that with almost every toy, the girls would quickly get bored.

Instead of giving up on the idea, though, she started asking the girls to go get their favorite toys. In case after case, the girls would return with a book. The girls would say that they loved reading and ask Debbie to read with them.

This led to her aha moment. She realized that if she could combine books with construction-type toys, she could weave acts of building things into a story that would get girls excited about playing with toys that develop spatial skills.

Debbie created a prototype that included a book about a girl named Goldie Blox, who went around solving problems by building things, as well as a construction toy that would allow the girls to live out the story they were reading. With much anticipation, she tested the toy with more than a hundred girls in the San Francisco Bay area.

It worked. As Debbie said in her Technology, Entertainment, Design (TEDx) Talk, little girls in tutus were getting excited about building belt drives!

Knowing that she had a found a winner, Debbie started looking for ways to take the next step and bring an actual product to market. After she asked around a bit regarding how to do that, a friend introduced her to one of the most elite tech accelerators in Silicon Valley. She got an interview.

On interview day, Debbie walked into the accelerator and noticed that she was surrounded by men with laptops and tablets. She, on the other hand, was carrying a physical prototype covered in a napkin. One of the guys said, "Oh, that's nice. Did you bake us all cookies?"

She felt her confidence seep out of her. She did not get accepted into the accelerator. The staff members there didn't agree with the idea of adding a book with the toy.

Despite this initial opposition, Debbie persisted. She decided to take her prototype to the New York Toy Fair, a large international toy show. She assumed that a toy fair would surely be full of creative people and kids playing with toys. When she arrived with her prototype, she discovered that the buyers were nearly all old men in suits.

Each of the buyers, upon seeing Debbie's prototype, looked at her with what appeared to be a sense of pity and told her that construction toys for girls simply don't sell. They took her to the so-called "pink aisle" to show her what does sell.

Although the toy show left her feeling temporarily dejected, Debbie was not about to give up. If anything, the toy show further fueled her aspiration to challenge the status quo. She wasn't going to stop until she could disrupt the pink aisle with her engineering toy for girls.

THE ARCHETYPE OF AN INNOVATOR

An important first step for fueling innovation in our organizations is to determine the characteristics of successful innovators. Understanding the basic archetype of an innovator helps us understand the traits we need to develop to become more innovative ourselves. As we discussed in Chapter 2, being more innovative helps us make a greater impact on gross margins. Being more innovative also helps us be better able to identify, attract, and retain highly innovative people to our teams and thereby further fuel innovation in our organizations.

One important element of understanding the archetype of an innovator is realizing that an innovator may not necessarily be the creative type. Although many people use the words *creative* and *innovative* as synonyms, the two are actually quite distinct. Creativity simply refers to the generation of new ideas. An innovation is something that actually disrupts the status quo. It is an idea that has been turned into a reality that is somehow disrupting other current realities.

With this understanding, we see that a person doesn't need to be creative to be an innovator. An innovator could take an idea that someone else had, but decided not to act on, and make the effort to transform that idea into a reality that disrupts the status quo. A well-known example of this is Bill Gates. Gates didn't create disk operating system (DOS). He bought it from the people who created it and then applied their idea to bring Microsoft software to market.

Thus, a good working definition of an innovator is "a person who is able to bring to reality an idea that actually disrupts the status quo." This definition makes it much easier to define the characteristics of a successful innovator. We simply need to ask, "What type of person is most likely to bring to reality an idea that actually disrupts the status quo?"

RESILIENCE IN THE FACE OF OPPOSITION

Debbie Sterling displays one of the most defining characteristics of an innovator—an apparent obsession with disrupting the status quo. As we discussed in Chapter 2, the research of Dr. Prince of the Perth Leadership Institute suggests that people with the greatest propensity to innovate are those least affected by a cognitive bias called the status quo bias.

People who are naturally innovative tend to be influenced very little by what others think of their ideas. They are perfectly comfortable being alone and tend to be introverts. If they do something that others don't accept, they are not affected at all. Peter Thiel cited anecdotal evidence for this common trait of innovators in his book *Zero to One*. Thiel notes that many of the great founders in Silicon Valley have Asperger's syndrome and that they are essentially wired to have no need to fit in.

Many people who score very high on the Perth Leadership Institute assessments for their propensity to innovate seem to have some innate compulsion to do so. It's almost like an addiction. They thrive on doing things no else is doing. In fact, if other people oppose something an innovator is doing, this tends to make him or her want to do it even more, as seemed to be the case with Debbie Sterling.

Conversely, a person with a strong status quo bias tends to be extroverted and doesn't like to be alone. Whether consciously or unconsciously, he or she wants to avoid being rejected and excluded by others. He or she would be extremely uncomfortable doing something that rocks the proverbial boat.

Thus, we can see that if we want to be more innovative, we need to develop the aspiration to challenge the status quo and learn to be more resilient to the opposition others have to unique ideas we want to advance. There are several ways that mindfulness training helps us develop those skills.

Thriving with Change

As we've discussed, a person with a strong status quo bias strongly prefers to keep things the way they've always been. Such a person sees change as something that brings discomfort and so must be avoided as much as possible. Conversely, an innovator thrives on change.

As we'll discuss further in Chapter 12, one of the core elements of mindfulness training is becoming more familiar and comfortable with change. Although we all understand intellectually that change is the only constant in this world, very few of us have had any sort of actual insight into the truth of impermanence. We haven't seen it clearly with the powerful, highly stable awareness that comes with consistent mindfulness training.

Those of us who do practice mindfulness regularly make an effort to pay attention quite often to how the things we experience change. When we see the truth of impermanence with the incredible clarity that results from consistently training our awareness, we discover that insight into impermanence is one of the most liberating and joyful experiences we can possibly have. We learn not only to become comfortable with change but also to thrive in it.

Neuro Note 4.1 How Mindfulness Helps to Effectively Manage Change

As we have previously seen, the current body of research supports the notion that mindfulness enhances emotion regulation, attentional control, self-awareness, and self-regulation, which allows for behavioral flexibility and goal-directed behavior in changing environments.[1]

This is an important first step toward being a person who aspires to challenge the status quo. By developing increased levels of comfort with change, and even a deep appreciation for it, we are much more likely to be open to, or even aspire to, disrupting the status quo. This will help us to be more innovative personally and to help our organizations be more innovative as we become more open to the potential innovations of our team members.

LESS NEED TO FIT IN

Mindfulness training helps us learn to be much more comfortable with being alone. Continued training allows us to become intimately familiar with the deep inner workings of our minds. We recognize and fully accept all of our strengths and our shortcomings. We learn to be at peace with our own minds. This results in a profound feeling of being completely comfortable in our own skin.

Along with this deep sense of comfort with who we are comes a reduced need to have the approval of others. Although we still respect the views of others, our peace of mind is no longer tied to whether others approve or reject our ideas. Thus, we gradually become free from another one of the most significant obstacles to advancing ideas that disrupt the status quo.

EMOTIONAL RESILIENCE

As previously mentioned, mindfulness training also helps us be more resilient to the emotions that arise when others oppose an idea we're trying to advance. This emotional resilience keeps us from being stopped in our tracks by an unpleasant emotion that is likely to arise because of rejection or conflict. As we'll explore further in Chapter 9, mindfulness training reduces the strength, duration, and frequency of unpleasant emotions.

Emotional resilience is quite important because it can take some time to become free from the strong yet often unconscious human need to have the approval of others and fit in. Fortunately, the ability to become very resilient in the face of unpleasant emotions is something that arises much more quickly. While we are developing our ability to be free from the need for approval, emotional resilience can help us innovate despite the unpleasant emotions that arise when our ideas aren't met with approval.

Neuro Note 4.2: Mindfulness for Emotional Resilience

As discussed in Neuro Note 3.2, mindfulness can effectively regulate emotions. The earlier mentioned study by Elizabeth Hoge and colleagues not only revealed that participating in a mindfulness-based stress reduction (MBSR), as compared with a stress-management intervention, intervention reduces anxiety during rest, but it also showed reduction in anxiety during a highly stressful task: the Trier Social Stress Test. In this test, participants have to give a public talk with very little preparation, and they have to publicly do an arithmetic task, all in front of a conspicuous camera and three unfriendly evaluators in lab coats. This study suggests that mindfulness helps regulate emotions even in highly stressful situations.[2]

EMPATHY

In addition to having an aspiration to challenge the status quo and the ability to stick with an idea despite opposition from others, successful innovation also requires empathy. The greater our ability to empathize with others, the easier it is for us to understand the needs and values of our peers and leaders. When we understand the needs and values of these team members, we are better able to point out how our innovation helps them achieve what's important to them.

In an article published in the *Harvard Business Review*, authors Jeffrey Cohn, Jon R. Katzenbach, and Gus Vlak describe how their research suggests that the single most important characteristic of a person who is successful at advancing an idea in an organization is empathy. They write: "Innovators must be able to walk into a conference room full of diverse constituents, including colleagues, customers, subordinates, bosses, vendors, and partners, and quickly discern the underlying motivation of each one. They leverage that information to craft and communicate a message that resonates with every constituent. This is the art of bringing a diverse group onto the same page—and it is absolutely essential to transforming an interesting idea into a company-wide innovation."[3]

Fortunately, empathy is a highly trainable skill, and a growing body of research suggests that mindfulness can help us develop it. For example, in a study conducted by Paul Condon and Dave DeSteno of Northeastern University, Willa Miller of Harvard University, and Gaëlle Desbordes of Massachusetts General Hospital, Harvard Medical School, the research team sent a group of people to an eight-week mindfulness-training course. Afterward, they tested the people who received the mindfulness training and people who had no such training. Each subject was tested to see how he or she responded when a woman on crutches wearing a medical boot, who gave visible and audible signals of being in pain, entered a waiting room with only three chairs in it. The test subject sat in one of the chairs, and the other two chairs were occupied by two members of the research team who were not going to give up their seat.

Only 16 percent of the members of the control group gave up their seats for the woman on crutches. However, 50 percent of the members of the test group gave up their seats. The study suggests that only eight weeks of mindfulness training is enough to significantly increase our ability to empathize with another person and to take compassionate action.[4]

Further supporting the study above, neuroscientists Helen Weng, Richard Davidson, and colleagues at the University of Wisconsin confirm that even relatively brief training in elements of mindfulness practice aimed specifically at developing compassion can alter neural functioning in brain areas associated with empathic understanding of others' distress.[5] Additionally, the earlier cited research by Sara Lazar at Massachusetts General Hospital, Harvard Medical School, and colleagues shows that practitioners of mindfulness tend to have a thicker insula, an area of the brain associated with empathy.[6]

Neuro Note 4.3: Mindfulness and Empathy

The study by Paul Condon and colleagues and other studies have shown that mindfulness-based interventions can enhance empathy and compassion.[7,8] Half of the participants in the Condon et al. study received mindfulness training, and half were given compassion training. Interestingly, the participants who were trained in mindfulness were just as likely to have empathy for the woman and act with compassion as those who received the compassion training.

EMPATHETIC DESIGN

Perhaps even more important than advancing an idea is ensuring that the idea we're advancing is worth the effort. If the innovation doesn't provide value for the end consumer, it doesn't matter how differentiated it is from the competition; it would be worthless. The greater our ability to empathize with the end consumer of our potential innovation, the more likely it is to provide value for that consumer.

The story of Debbie Sterling and GoldieBlox illustrates the importance of truly understanding the needs and values of the end consumer. Debbie could easily put herself in the shoes of the potential users of GoldieBlox. In essence, she was creating a toy for the younger version of herself. She also discovered the key insight for potential success, an essential element that even expert entrepreneurs at a prestigious tech accelerator couldn't see: *Girls like stories.* For GoldieBlox to be a success, the toy would have to be accompanied by a book.

This ability to understand what girls would truly enjoy gave her confidence in her idea and her ability to disrupt the status quo. Despite significant initial opposition to GoldieBlox, Debbie kept plowing along until she eventually found a factory that could produce a prototype, and she soon had a real toy in her hands.

The factory required a minimum run of 5,000 units to produce the toy at an affordable price, which she couldn't afford on her own. Because of all the initial opposition, Debbie was a little concerned about attracting investors to help with the production of the toy. She decided instead to use the Kickstarter platform to confirm that people would actually buy GoldieBlox and potentially raise the funds to pay for the initial production run.[9]

She set a goal of $150,000, which she would have to raise in 30 days. She did all the work necessary to set up her Kickstarter campaign, she launched it, and she hoped for the best.

Debbie hit her goal in four days and then far surpassed it, raising more than $285,000. The initial production run wasn't 5,000 units. It was more than 20,000 units.

The press got word of GoldieBlox, and articles started appearing about the toy everywhere. Phone calls came in with moms pronouncing that "Yes! My daughter is more than just a princess!" Letters and e-mails started pouring in.

In one of those e-mails a mother wrote about how her four-year-old daughter stopped in the middle of playing with GoldieBlox to ask, "Mommy, am I an engineer?" To which the mother replied, "You certainly can be. You can be anything you want."

Orders from stores poured in, too. GoldieBlox can now be found in even the largest toy retailers. Apparently, the world was waiting for a disruption in the pink aisle.[10]

REVIEW QUESTIONS

What is the cognitive bias that tends to keep people from innovating?

What are the three ways that mindfulness training can help you be less constrained by the effects of the cognitive bias above and thus help you be more innovative?

What is the role of empathy in successful innovation?

5

DEVELOPING
EXTRAORDINARY
LEADERSHIP
PRESENCE

S everal days earlier, the U.S. Army's eighty-third Infantry Division closed in on the last strategic stronghold of the Nazi forces, the industrial area in and around Ruhr, Germany. They had surrounded the roughly 300,000 soldiers of Nazi Army Group B, led by Field Marshal Walter Model. The outcome was inevitable. The Nazi soldiers began surrendering in large numbers.

It seemed, at this point, that the outcome of the entire European front was inevitable, and U.S. troops could sense it. They knew that they would be going home soon. The larger Nazi units also knew the end was near and that resistance was futile. In case after case, they began to surrender with increasing haste. But some of the smaller Nazi units fought viciously to the end of the war in Europe, which would arrive only two months later.

On April 6, 1945, the soldiers of the second Platoon of Company F of the U.S. Army's 109th Regiment, thirtieth Infantry Division, were nearing the small town of Hamelin, Germany, about 100 miles east of the Ruhr pocket. Although Hamelin is the gateway to the Weserbergland Mountains, the soldiers were walking across relatively flat, open ground, which made them quite vulnerable. Suddenly, they encountered one of the smaller units, mentioned above, that would fight viciously to the end.

A group of Nazi soldiers armed with machine guns and other automatic weapons opened fire on the platoon with devastating effect. The soldiers hit the ground but with little cover to protect them. They were pinned down in a terrible position.

The platoon was led by First Lieutenant Raymond O. Beaudoin, who assessed the situation and began taking decisive action. He ordered his men to rotate into and out of firing positions in a way that allowed them to suppress the enemy long enough to allow each of them to dig a deeper fighting position that would protect them from the enemy fire. While his men were digging in and returning fire when they could, Beaudoin alternated between returning fire himself and darting around, exposed to enemy fire, to distribute ammunition and encourage his men.

Once all of his men were dug in and effectively firing at the Nazi soldiers, Beaudoin moved to the front of the platoon's position, dug his own fighting position, and led his men in suppressing the enemy by returning fire. Despite being severely outnumbered and outgunned, because of the defensive positions they dug, Beaudoin and his men were able to gain the advantage and inflicted heavy casualties on the Nazi unit.

But that advantage would end quickly when Nazi reinforcements arrived. Again, Beaudoin had to think quickly and take decisive action. He ordered one of his men to run back to the rest of Company F for ammunition and reinforcements. The soldier was shot by a Nazi sniper.

Beaudoin knew that they would be overrun if they didn't get more ammunition and reinforcements, so he ordered a second soldier to make the run to Company F. That soldier was shot by a sniper as well, as was the third soldier Beaudoin ordered to make the run.

He could not stand to lose another man, but he had to act quickly. He couldn't abandon his men to make the long run himself, but he knew that getting a runner to Company F was the only way his platoon would survive. He decided to make a one-man attack on the sniper nest that had been taking his men down. It was about a football field away from the platoon's right flank.

Beaudoin ordered another soldier to attempt the run to Company F once the enemy appeared to be distracted by his own advance toward the sniper nest. He started to crawl toward the snipers over completely exposed ground, which apparently caught the enemy's attention. As Beaudoin crawled, he began receiving an onslaught of enemy fire.

During his assault, the Nazi soldiers fired eight explosive rounds from a bazooka at him. None of the rounds struck close enough to cause injury, but the explosions threw mud and stones over him. Rounds from rifle fire, however, actually ripped his uniform. None of this was enough to deter him, though.

Beaudoin stood up 10 yards from the enemy position and charged the four Nazi soldiers in the nest. He was able to take down three of them on his own. The fourth adversary was cut down by the platoon's rifle fire as he attempted to flee.

Beaudoin never had a chance to determine whether the runner had started his journey back to Company F. He continued his attack to further distract the enemy. He ran toward a Nazi fighting hole but was taken down by a burst of fire from a machine gun before he reached the target.

Although he didn't live to see it, the last runner Beaudoin ordered to attempt the trek actually made it back to Company F. Reinforcements arrived in time to save the rest of the platoon from what appeared to be certain death. For his actions, First Lieutenant Beaudoin would post-humously receive the United States' highest military award, the Medal of Honor.

STAYING COOL UNDER PRESSURE

Stories like that of Lieutenant Beaudoin offer us glimpses of our potential for leadership presence. Leading others in the middle of a horrific situation in which our team members are being shot at—and human lives, including our own, are in grave danger of being lost—is perhaps the greatest test there is of leadership presence. We give leaders like First Lieutenant Beaudoin awards because in situations like this the ability to remain confident and clearheaded, and quickly make good decisions, is absolutely extraordinary.

Many of us see leaders every day who falter under even the slightest amount of pressure. This may cause us to presume that only a special type of person could have the leadership presence Beaudoin displayed. We may think that leaders like Beaudoin are born with great presence.

Fortunately for us, however, this is simply not true. Although, because of our genetics and life experiences, some of us may have a greater natural propensity to remain cool under pressure, this ability is actually highly trainable. As we touched on in Chapter 3, stress resilience is the benefit of mindfulness with the greatest amount of research supporting it.

Because of the abundance of research suggesting the effectiveness of mindfulness training for developing resilience to stressful situations, the U.S. military has begun to offer mindfulness training as a way to help leaders develop battlefield presence. A training program Dr. Elizabeth Stanley founded, called Mindfulness-based Mind Fitness Training (MMFT, pronounced "M-fit"), has been offered to a large number of U.S. Marines and soldiers.

A recent study conducted by University of California, San Diego, researcher Douglas Johnson and colleagues demonstrated the effectiveness of an eight-week MMFT program with U.S. Marines stationed at Marine Corps Base Camp Pendleton in California. The team studied four infantry platoons who received mindfulness training matched against a control group of four platoons that received the standard training regimen to prepare for combat. The Marines were assessed before they started the MMFT program and after they completed a highly stressful training exercise designed to replicate the combat conditions experienced when responding to an enemy ambush like the one First Lieutenant Beaudoin experienced in 1945.[1]

The Marines who received the eight weeks of mindfulness training showed a significantly greater capacity for stress resilience. Using several methods, including brain scans, the researchers found that the Marines who were trained in mindfulness experienced less of the fight-or-flight response compared with the controls. This ability to experience a demanding situation with a diminished fight-or-flight response is the key to being able to think clearly under pressure.

The Marines who received MMFT also recovered faster from the stressful situation. This quicker recovery can help reduce symptoms of posttraumatic stress syndrome, which is another reason the military is interested in mindfulness training. It makes me smile to know that the young men and women who are put in harm's way by the U.S. government are receiving training to help them remain psychologically healthy during and after their service to our country.

Of course, this also has positive implications for everyday civilian leaders. The more quickly we can recover from stressful situations, the sooner we can return to maximum effectiveness and the healthier we remain both physically and psychologically.

Neuro Note 5.1: Mindfulness and Resilience to Stressful Situations

The above-mentioned study by Douglas Johnson and colleagues also found that after the stressful combat training, participants who got mindfulness training had decreased brain activation in the anterior insula and the dorsal anterior cingulate cortex, as compared with soldiers who didn't get mindfulness training. This can be interpreted as more efficient processing in two main regions of the so-called salience network to detect cues that signal perturbation of homeostasis to improve adequate responses to stress.[2]

Another region that is part of the salience network is the amygdala, which plays a role in detecting and evaluating emotional stimuli.[3] In stressful, fear-inducing situations, we typically see increased amygdala activation, and chronic stress and anxiety disorders are associated with increased activity and gray matter in the amygdala.[4] As we have seen in Neuro Note 3.2, mindfulness down regulates activation in the amygdala, especially in novice practitioners.[5]

For example, in the study earlier mentioned by Véronique Taylor and colleagues of the University of Montreal, after just one week of training, novice mindfulness practitioners showed decreased amygdala activation during a state of mindfulness as compared with a normal state when viewing emotional pictures.[6] Neuroscientist Britta Hölzel from Massachusetts General Hospital, Harvard Medical School, and colleagues found a relation between changes in amygdala gray matter and perceived stress after an eight-week mindfulness-based stress reduction course: Participants with greater decreases in perceived stress had greater decreases in amygdala gray matter.[7] These and several other studies indicate that through mindfulness training, we can regulate stress pathways involving the amygdala.[8]

FEARLESSNESS

Another key trait of a person with extraordinary leadership presence is fearlessness or, more accurately stated, freedom from fear. First Lieutenant Beaudoin, of course, displayed a great degree of freedom from fear. Fear was very likely present when he left his dug-in fighting position to crawl across open ground toward snipers who had already killed three of his men. The fear was probably amplified when explosions threw mud and stones on him and he could feel the heat of a rifle round as it ripped his uniform. But the fear that Beaudoin surely experienced did not prevent him from taking action. He was free from his fear.

One aspect of being free from fear is essentially identical to staying cool under pressure. This is the ability to experience less emotional reactivity when we are in situations highly likely to produce fear. As we discussed above, mindfulness training allows us to develop this ability.

With enough training, we can eventually reach a point where fight-or-flight emotions, such as fear, rarely arise and, when they do, are so subtle that they have no effect on us other than to alert us that there may be an issue we need to deal with.

Even after years of mindfulness training, however, there will still likely be situations where fear arises to some degree. It may not be as strong as it would have been before training in mindfulness, but it's still there. Another aspect of being free from fear is to have enough space around the emotion to be able to think clearly and take appropriate action, despite the fact that fear is present. This ability to see fear objectively and take action despite its presence helps us appear fearless in the moment, as Lieutenant Beaudoin appeared.

Neuro Note 5.2: Mindfulness and Reduced Emotional Interference

As we saw in Neuro Note 5.1, mindfulness training can regulate stress pathways and reduce emotional reactivity. Studies also have shown that mindfulness training results in less interference of emotional or stressful situations with cognitive tasks.

Do you remember the word–color interference Stroop task from Neuro Note 2.2? It is the task where the font color of a word had to be pronounced, which is particularly difficult when the color of the word and the spelled color are conflicting (e.g., the word *red* written in green font). Neuroscientist Micah Allen and colleagues from Aarhus University in Denmark and from the University College London used a version of the Stroop task but made it more difficult by inserting emotion-inducing pictures, such as snakes, in between the images of words. Because of the emotional processing, when participants see the emotion-inducing images, performance on conflicting trials tends to be even worse than without the emotional pictures. The researchers found that after completing a six-week mindfulness course, performance on this emotional Stroop task improved. This was not the case in the control group. While performing the emotional Stroop task, participants of the mindfulness training had increased brain activation in the lateral prefrontal cortex, which suggests increased top-down control, as we already have seen in Neuro Note 3.2.[9]

In a similar study (this one without brain imaging), Catherine Ortner and colleauges from the University of Toronto found that a seven-week mindfulness training resulted in better performance on an emotional interference task, and that a relaxation training did not improve performance.[10] In this task participants had to judge whether a tone is high or low while watching emotion-inducing pictures. The better performance on this task by participants after the mindfulness training suggests that through mindfulness training one can better focus on the task at hand and be less distracted by emotions.

Also, the more often we take action despite our fears, the more often we see that our fears are often worse than the actual experiences themselves and the more often we realize that we can do things we didn't think we could do. Together, these two elements combine to increase our self-confidence gradually and create a sense of general courage that permeates more and more areas of our lives.

THE MOST IMPORTANT ASPECT
OF LEADERSHIP PRESENCE

Although First Lieutenant Beaudoin was certainly free from his fear and able to remain cool under the extreme pressure of the horrific situation he faced during World War II, that's not why he was awarded the Medal of Honor. He was awarded the United States' highest military honor because he was *selfless*. He put the lives of his team members ahead of his own.

As an officer, Beaudoin was very likely aware that the end of the war was near. He had likely already thought about what he would do when he returned to a normal life in his hometown of Holyoke, Massachusetts. Nevertheless, he sacrificed his life so that others might enjoy their homecoming.

Although we may never be required to sacrifice our lives for the people on our teams, we can certainly demonstrate that we are willing to put their needs above our own. We can selflessly sacrifice in subtle ways that demonstrate to team members that we love them in the same way First Lieutenant Beaudoin loved the men in his platoon. The ability to help another person feel loved by us is the most important aspect of leadership presence.

Loving the people around us like this is incredibly rewarding personally. It is also quite helpful for achieving better business results. The most effective team is one in which people consistently do much more than their job requires of them and go the extra mile to make an impact. Beaudoin's men knew that he was willing to die for them. It would be almost impossible to imagine that those men wouldn't go the extra mile for him. In fact, as we saw above, four of Beaudoin's men were willing to risk their lives for him and the rest of the platoon by attempting the run back to Company F.

Mindfulness training can help us become less egotistic and self-centered and therefore more likely to selflessly serve and care for the members of our teams. There is an abundance of research suggesting that mindfulness training, especially when it includes intentional compassion training, changes both the structure and function of our brains in ways that result in a greater propensity for selfless mind states and behaviors.

Neuro Note 5.3: Mindfulness and Other-Centered Mind States

A growing body of research suggests that mindfulness training enhances other-centered mind states, such as empathy, compassion, and altruism.[11] Compassion and mindfulness are closely related; mindfulness-based interventions often include compassion practices, and compassion-based interventions often incorporate mindfulness practices.[12] It is not only the case that mindfulness-based interventions increase compassion; compassion-based interventions also enhance mindfulness.[13]

In the study mentioned in Chapter 4, Helen Weng and colleagues from the University of Wisconsin studied the effects of compassion training on altruistic behavior and the brain. They used an economic game (such as the ultimatum game that we saw in Neuro Note 2.1) in which the participant observes how a so-called dictator shares money in an unfair way (e.g., keeping $9 and giving $1) with another person. The participants can choose to use their own money to transfer double the amount the dictator pays to the victim of unfairness.

After two weeks of compassion training, participants spent more of their own money to help the victim. In the brain, this increase in altruistic behavior was associated with increased brain activation in the inferior parietal cortex and the dorsolateral prefrontal cortex (DLPFC). In addition, an increased connectivity between the DLPFC and the ventral striatum was found.[14] As we have seen in Neuro Notes 1.2, 3.1, and 3.2, these regions play important roles in feeling the emotions of others, emotion regulation, and reward processing, respectively.

Another study that assessed altruistic behavior with a similar dictator game found that the more altruistic people were, the greater gray matter volume in the temporoparietal junction they had.[15] Neuroscientist Britta Hölzel and colleagues at Massachusetts General Hospital, Harvard Medical School, found that gray matter concentration increased in this region after an eight-week mindfulness training.[16,17]

Fortunately, though, we don't have to give our lives for another person for him or her to feel loved by us. In fact, we don't have to give much at all. One of the most powerful things we can do to help someone feel loved is simply to be mindful when we're with him or her. We just need to be fully present, giving him or her our complete, undivided attention.

Can you remember the last time you were talking with someone, and he or she was barely with you? (Unfortunately, I would imagine you don't have to think back very far to remember a situation like this.) Physically the person was there, but his or her attention was all over the place and rarely with you. How did that feel?

Can you remember a time when someone you admired was with you; gave you his or her full, undivided attention; and made you feel that during your time together, you were the most important person in the world? How did *that* feel?

Although this is one of the most subtle benefits of mindfulness training, it is also one of the most powerful. The practice is, at its essence, making the effort to be fully present with what we're doing or whom we're with right now. Just as with any other skill, the more we practice at this, the better we get at it. The more consistently present we are with the people on our teams, the more loved they feel in our presence.

Some people don't think the word *love* should be used in a business context. They say it's an irrelevant, soft skill. But love is highly relevant in a business context, and it may be the hardest skill there is to develop. It's easy to learn technical skills and management techniques. If we can read and have a functional level of intelligence, we can learn those things.

However, cultivating the ability to consistently be fully present with people, and help them to feel cared for in our presence, takes a lot of training. It's by no means easy. It's also not easy to extend ourselves to help a person meet the legitimate needs he or she has when we have tremendous demands placed on us. But the return on our investment in developing these abilities is tremendous.

Feeling loved is one of the deepest human needs there is. Sadly, many people rarely feel loved, even at home. If you can create a workplace culture where people feel loved by you, their other leaders, and their peers, you will be offering people something incredibly valuable and often quite rare.

This tremendous competitive advantage is extremely difficult to copy. It's an advantage that can allow you to attract and retain the most talented people in your industry and help ensure that those people consistently go the extra mile, doing much more than you ask them to do. What would happen in your organization if you had more talented people who gave more discretionary effort and who stayed with you significantly longer, which reduced your costs significantly? What would that do for the bottom line?

You can create that type of impact. You can create that type of team culture by developing your ability to offer people one of the most valuable things in the world—a place where they are consistently loved.

Review Questions

How does mindfulness training increase your ability to stay cool under even the most intense pressure, such as leading others in a life-or-death situation like combat?

How does mindfulness training help you cultivate freedom from fear?

What is the most important aspect of leadership presence, which may be the most important competitive advantage there is?

How does mindfulness training help you cultivate the most important aspect of leadership presence described above?

6

WHY MINDFULNESS IS THE ULTIMATE SUCCESS HABIT

After putting on the blue jumpsuit, the guards also put a leather belt—which looked quite similar to the type of belt weight lifters wear—around my waist. But this belt was clearly not for weight lifting. Attached to the front of the belt was as a set of stainless steel handcuffs.

One of the guards locked my wrists in the handcuffs. A moment later he locked leg irons around my ankles. Apparently, these precautions were part of the standard operating procedure for admitting a detainee to special quarters, which was the maximum-security area of the base brig at Marine Corps Base Camp Pendleton.

During my time in the U.S. Marine Corps, as many Marines have, I once hiked more than 20 miles at a pace of 4 miles per hour, after spending a week patrolling in the forest, with burning blisters on my feet, carrying a heavy pack and a 25-pound M240 G machine gun, which combined to create an incredibly sharp pain in my trapezius muscles that flared with every step. The walk to special quarters was likely less than 100 yards in total, my feet were free of blisters, shoulders free of pain, and I wasn't carrying anything. But it was the longest walk of my life. The humiliation, the fear, the regret, and the confusion grew within me with each step.

With each turn around a corner, I prayed that it would be the last. I wondered, "How many corners could there possibly be in this place?" Where on earth is special quarters?"

After one left turn, I had my answer. We approached an entryway that looked like the entrance to a castle. Two walls of steel bars stood in front of us. On the other side of this gate were two guards standing by a desk situated in front of a cinderblock wall.

The door to the first set of steel bars clanked and rattled as it slid open. We stepped inside the area between the bars. Once the door behind us had closed, the second door opened, and we walked into what I felt had to be special quarters.

We turned to the right down a hallway, which curved to the left. We stopped in front of the first cell in the hallway. The door was a solid piece of steel with a 3-by-3-inch window at eye level and a 2-inch-by-12-inch slot at waist level, which was used to pass food into the cell. One of the guards spoke into his radio and asked for the cell door to be opened. A second later, the door clanked and rattled as it moved.

We walked into the 6-foot-by-9-foot cell, which had a steel toilet at the far end and a steel bed with a thin green mat on it to the right. The guard told me to walk over and kneel on the bed. He removed the leg irons. He told me to turn around and face him. He removed the handcuffs and the belt.

The guard walked out of the cell and called on his radio for the cell door to be closed. The door rattled and clanked as it slid to the right, culminating in a loud clank as it slammed shut. That abrasive noise spoke to me. It said, "You will never leave."

⤜✠⤏

TWO LIFE-CHANGING DISCOVERIES

I had no one to blame for the situation I was in but myself. In January of 2001, while serving as an officer in the U.S. Marine Corps, I had partially attempted a shortcut to success. I arranged the unauthorized delivery of a large sum of U.S. government money.

My conscience wouldn't allow me to go any further than arranging the delivery, and I made no attempt to actually take anything that wasn't mine. But the steps I had taken to arrange the delivery made me guilty of fraud. As a result of being both dishonest and stupid, I would end up spending five and one-half years confined to military prison.

I spent roughly the first year of that time in special quarters, in what was essentially solitary confinement. The first few months were the worst months of my life. At one point, I had frequent thoughts of suicide.

But this time in confinement eventually became the most important experience of my life. About one year into my sentence, I started learning about the practice of mindfulness through books that I had asked my mother to send to me. The practice seemed so logical and practical to me, so I began to practice immediately. Within a few months, I was making the effort to practice mindfulness during nearly every moment of the day.

The books I was reading were either written by monks or composed of talks monks gave that were recorded and later transcribed. I was so inspired by the ideals of the monastic life—as I understood them through the books I was reading—that I eventually decided to transform the prison into a monastery. I spent the last three years of my time in confinement living and training exactly as monks live and train. I followed all the strict rules that monks follow regarding behavior, and I spent most of every day training my mind.

This monastic training resulted in two very important discoveries for me. The first discovery was the power of living a life devoted to serving others.

THE POWER OF SERVING OTHERS

The core ideals for monastic training are to let go of the tendency to chase after desires for things that we don't need, to become the most kind and compassionate person we can become, and to devote ourselves 100 percent to serving others, with a focus on helping others be free from their suffering. I found these ideals both inspiring and liberating.

I realized that I could be of help to people, even while I was confined, by doing whatever I could to bring happiness to the inmates and guards around me. This newfound purpose of helping others be free from suffering made my time in confinement deeply meaningful. It has been my purpose ever since.

After leaving confinement, I spent some time living and training in a real monastery. Although I was almost ordained, I decided to continue living and training much like a monastic and to find ways to serve others as a layperson. I went on to cofound and lead two small nonprofit organizations.

I noticed that the more focused I became on serving others, the more success I had. This gradually led me to the intuition that the most effective way to lead an organization is by focusing more on serving and caring for team members than we do on numbers. As I wrote about in *Serve to Be Great*, this intuition was validated by many highly successful companies.

This realization that the most effective leaders over the long term are those who can consistently and effectively serve and take care of the members of their teams led to an epiphany for me. I had significant experience with highly effective tools for helping people more consistently and effectively serve and care for team members. If I worked to help leaders develop in this area, it would not only help them achieve better long-term business outcomes but also make our world a better place. With that basic idea in mind, I started my work in leadership development in 2012.

UNCONDITIONAL HAPPINESS

About six months after beginning mindfulness training, I noticed something that took me by surprise. I was standing and waiting in a yard at the consolidated brig in Miramar, California. I was looking at a drop of dew on a blade of grass. The sun was reflected through the dew drop in such a way that was absolutely brilliant. I was filled with joy.

A few moments later it dawned on me that I was experiencing happiness like that almost all the time. I realized that I was more generally happy right there in a military prison, with nothing, than I had ever been in my life.

Many people can't imagine that it would be possible to be happy without good food, a comfy bed, entertainment, romance, or any of the myriad experiences and things that we enjoy daily. Some people do believe that it would be possible to be happy with nothing, but they've never had the opportunity to realize it for themselves.

This is one reason why I consider my time in confinement the most valuable gift of my life. I now know, through years of experience, that the only thing I require to be happy in this life is to be alive and free of biologically created mental illness. No other conditions need to be met. My happiness is essentially unconditional.

Fortunately, you do not need to spend time in confinement (and I hope you never do) to discover unconditional happiness for yourself. My experience is by no means unique. Unconditional happiness is something that you can train to develop.

THE STUDY OF HAPPINESS

For nearly two decades, a large body of research has been developed, conducted by psychologists such as Martin Seligman who operate from a different initial assumption than the one traditional psychologists have started with. Generally speaking, psychologists have traditionally worked to research and/or treat mental illness. If a person was experiencing difficulty functioning in daily life, he or she would see a psychologist or psychiatrist, who would attempt to help him or her function normally again.

The new assumption was that life for an average or normal person isn't really that great. The average person tends to lead a life that is, well, average.

Some of these psychologists noticed that oftentimes, when conducting research on people's levels of emotional well-being, there would be an outlier: a person who seemed to be experiencing significantly higher levels of happiness and fulfillment in life than the average person experiences. As former Harvard professor Shawn Achor describes (only half-jokingly) in his excellent book *The Happiness Advantage*, many researchers tend to ignore outliers in their studies or find ways to eliminate them by writing them off as resulting from a measurement error, because those outliers can throw a monkey wrench in the researchers' efforts to support their hypotheses.

The psychologists like Seligman and his colleagues, who were approaching psychology from a new angle, decided to look at the outliers they found in a different way. Instead of trying to eliminate them on the assumption that a measurement error had occurred, they decided to investigate them a bit. They started to look at different studies on similar topics and look at the outliers from each of them to see whether there were any commonalities among them.

It turns out that there were commonalities. These innovative psychologists realized that if they focused on what was similar among these people who were apparently experiencing extraordinary levels of well-being in their lives, they could identify ways to help the average person live a much more fulfilling life as well. Instead of being a field that only helps people get to average, it appeared that psychology could become a field that helps people get to *awesome*. Thus was born the field of *positive psychology*.

There is now an abundance of scientific research from the field of positive psychology that can be applied to help people lead lives that are significantly more fulfilling. Below, we'll explore two elements of the field that are most relevant to the discussion of leadership excellence.

Happiness Is Good for Business

As we discussed in Chapter 3, emotional intelligence is essential for stellar performance as a leader. One component of emotional intelligence is the ability to spend much more time in a positive emotional state than in a negative one. A happy person tends to do this quite easily.

Independent from the studies done specifically on emotional intelligence, researchers in the field of positive psychology have conducted studies on the effects of happiness on success in general and as leaders. One of the interesting findings in general is that it appears the widely held notion that achieving success causes happiness is incorrect. Apparently, the causal relationship is actually the inverse. It's not success that leads to happiness; it's happiness that leads to success.

As Achor explains in *The Happiness Advantage*, achieving success results in only a brief feeling of happiness and leaves a void that soon requires another achievement to feel the same happiness again. Conversely, a more pervasive happiness results in numerous effects that increase the likelihood of achieving worldly success, including more optimal levels of performance.

Some examples of research findings Achor cites are doctors making accurate diagnoses 19 percent faster after being primed to feel happy, optimistic salespeople outperforming their peers by 56 percent, students far outperforming their peers when primed to feel happy before taking an achievement test, and leaders in more positive moods better able to think creatively, problem solve, negotiate, and influence higher performance from employees.

As we discussed in Chapter 3, we likely don't need research to convince us that all other things being relatively equal, a generally happy leader is going to significantly outperform a generally unhappy one. A happy leader is going to be able to more easily attract and retain talented people because people much prefer to be around a happy person than someone who is miserable. A happy leader is also going to be able to more easily drive positive emotions in the people around her, which boosts the performance of everyone on the team.

HAPPINESS IS PREDETERMINED, KIND OF (BUT YOU CAN CHANGE THAT)

The second key finding of positive psychology that relates to our discussion on happiness and leadership is the idea that we have what is known as a baseline level of happiness. This baseline level of happiness is determined partly by our genetics and partly by our early life experiences. For the most part, it is determined when we are still children.

This idea of a baseline level of happiness explains why what happens to us has only a short-term effect on our happiness. Achieving success of some type makes us feel great for a time. But, after a while, we return to normal.

For instance, research conducted in 1978 at Northwestern and the University of Massachusetts (UMass) suggests that people who win the lottery report high levels of happiness for a while. Within a year, however, most lottery winners report being no happier than they were before they won the lottery. Their happiness levels return to baseline.[1]

At first glance, this idea of a baseline level of happiness may seem like a negative thing. We might think that our happiness is essentially predetermined for us. Fortunately, though, we can change our baseline level of happiness.

Positive psychology offers us an important lesson on changing our baseline level of happiness: Having pleasant experiences, such as success or winning the lottery, won't do it. We can change our baseline levels of happiness only by engaging in certain behaviors.

A large body of research suggests that mindfulness training is one of the most beneficial behaviors in which we can engage for improving happiness. One study conducted by Richard Davidson's team at the University of Wisconsin involved measuring subjects' abilities to change the ratio of brain activity in the left prefrontal cortex (associated with positive emotion) to activity in the right prefrontal cortex (associated with unpleasant emotions).[2] Changing that ratio, shifting activity from the right prefrontal cortex to the left, is often called *left tilt*. Davidson and his team measured the left tilt a longtime practitioner of mindfulness, named Matthieu Ricard.

Ricard's ability to create such left tilt was like nothing the researchers had ever seen before and resulted in the team stating that he is the happiest man, by far, ever measured by science, which was reported in a variety of media.[3] Ricard's apparent ability to generate happiness on demand, and his baseline brain activity, suggest that both the function and structure of his brain are radically different from people who have not trained their minds.

Other longtime practitioners of mindfulness (most with more than 50,000 hours of training) have demonstrated similar differences in their brain function both on demand and at baseline. Fortunately for us,

50,000 hours of training is not required to see changes in the function and structure of our brains.

In fact, some research suggests that such changes can be observed in a matter of weeks. One study that included researchers from UMass and the University of Wisconsin demonstrated that after completing an eight-week mindfulness-based stress reduction (MBSR) course, practitioners had significant increases in activation of the left prefrontal cortex.[4] Another study researchers at Massachusetts General Hospital, Harvard Medical School, conducted found that subjects who had participated in an eight-week MBSR course had increased gray matter in areas of the brain associated with well-being.[5]

Neuro Note 6.1: Mindfulness and Well-Being

What does well-being mean for you? In the fourth century BC, the Greek philosopher Aristotle distinguished between hedonic and eudemonic well-being, a distinction that is still made in modern psychology.[6] Hedonic well-being refers to pleasure and happiness and is often measured by the presence of positive emotions, the absence of negative emotions, and life satisfaction. Eudemonic well-being refers to flourishing and self-realization and is typically measured with a psychological well-being questionnaire, which taps into six domains, including autonomy, personal growth, self-acceptance, life purpose, mastery, and positive relatedness.[7] We have already mentioned the first study that investigated the effects of mindfulness training on gray matter in the brain over time, conducted by neuroscientist Britta Hölzel and colleagues from Massachusetts General Hospital, Harvard Medical School. A subset of the participants in that study also completed questionnaires to measure psychological (eudemonic) well-being. It turned out that the participants with the largest increase in psychological well-being after the mindfulness course also had the greatest increase in gray matter concentration in several regions of the brain stem that affect mood and alertness.[8]

A study by Olga Klimecki and colleagues from the Max Planck Institute in Leipzig, Germany sheds some light on our ability to increase hedonic well-being.[9] They found that after a compassion training, negative emotions were decreased and positive emotions were increased together with increased brain activation in the compassion network, which includes regions that are related to reward and positive emotions, such as the orbitofrontal cortex (OFC) and the ventral striatum.

In a very recent study, Feng Kong and colleagues from Beijing Normal University in China investigated how functional connectivity within a brain region is related to mindfulness as well as hedonic and eudemonic well-being. Congruent with the finding of Klimecki and colleagues, the researchers found that greater local connectivity in the OFC was associated with greater mindfulness and greater positive emotions and that mindfulness mediated the relation between the OFC and positive affect.

The researchers also found that lower local connectivity in the inferior frontal gyrus (IFG) related to greater mindfulness and greater eudemonic well-being and that mindfulness mediated the relation between the IFG and eudemonic well-being.[10] The IFG, or lateral prefrontal cortex, is part of the central executive network and implicated in inhibitory control. The negative relation between IFG connectivity and mindfulness and eudemonic well-being might be the result of greater efficiency or different mechanisms involved in persons with greater mindfulness.

THE ULTIMATE SUCCESS HABIT

As we have discussed, mindfulness training affects every area of leadership in some way because it improves self-awareness, attentional control, and other aspects of mind function, and everything we do or fail to do is a result of how effectively the mind functions. Based just on the improvements to self-awareness—which is arguably the most important leadership skill we can develop—we might conclude that mindfulness training is the ultimate success habit and that devoting time to mindfulness training is the best investment we can make because it positively influences so many areas of leadership excellence.

However, often I refer to mindfulness training as the ultimate success habit for reasons other than its effects on professional success. One of those reasons is that mindfulness training helps us develop unconditional happiness. Yes, being happier helps us be more effective professionally, especially as leaders. But happiness is ultimately much more important than professional success. Reflecting on this for a moment, we could conclude that happiness is one of the primary goals of our lives. Actually, isn't everything we do essentially motivated by the aspiration to be happy?

Ultimately, why do we pursue professional success? Because we believe success will help us be happy.

Why do we seek out relationships? Because we believe relationships will help us be happy.

Why do we look for meaning in our personal and professional lives? Because we believe that meaning in our lives will help us be happy.

Why do we want to make more money? Because we believe more money will help us be happy.

Why do we work to become a better person? Because we believe that becoming a better person will bring happiness to both others and ourselves.

Unfortunately, it seems that the message we hear all too often is that happiness is an if-then proposition. If we do something or get something, then we'll be happy. This message is severely flawed.

The truth is that happiness is available right here, right now. Happiness requires no condition outside ourselves to be met. Mindfulness allows us to realize this through our own experience.

When we are able to tap into the happiness that is always available to us, we realize that the treasure we have been searching for all our lives is something we've always had. We just didn't realize it. Discovering this truth is incredibly liberating.

Have you ever been looking all over your house for your keys or phone, and after 10 minutes or so you realize that the object is in your purse, your pocket, or perhaps even your hand? It is such a relief, isn't it? Realizing that happiness has always been in our hands is a lot like that but significantly more powerful.

With the continued practice of mindfulness, we gradually realize with increasing frequency the happiness that is always available. We realize one of the primary goals of life, which makes the practice very enjoyable. At the same time, the practice is rewiring our brains in ways that make us better leaders and better human beings.

It doesn't really matter what our motivation is for beginning the practice. We may want to be better leaders, and we're okay with discovering unconditional happiness as a side effect. Or, we may want to realize unconditional happiness, and we're okay with becoming better leaders as a side effect.

Either way, if we practice correctly, as outlined in Part 2 of this book, the results will be the same. We will gradually realize unconditional happiness with increasing frequency, and we will become better leaders.

❧

Review Questions

What are three ways that increasing your own happiness improves your effectiveness as a leader?

Why is it that what happens to you has little or no lasting effect on your level of happiness?

How would you describe some of the research suggesting that mindfulness training is a highly effective tool for changing your baseline level of happiness?

What is one reason, other than effects on leadership excellence, why I call mindfulness training the ultimate success habit?

PART 2

DEVELOPING THE ULTIMATE SUCCESS HABIT

7

THE PERFECTION
OF THE PRESENT
MOMENT

S tarting the practice of mindfulness training is very simple. You could try it right now if you like. Just be a beginner.

Ask yourself in your mind, "What is it like to sit here right now?" Don't try to answer the question. Just be intensely curious about and open to what's happening within you and around you right now, then now, then now, and so on. Keep that curious attitude alive.

You might notice what it feels like to sit. You might notice what you hear or see or smell. If you're really curious and open, you might notice that you're breathing. You might notice what it feels like as the body breathes in and breathes out. Please take 10–15 seconds to explore what it is like to sit there right now.

How was it? Were you able simply to be open to what was happening without being distracted by your thinking? With the guidance above, my guess is that you were successful for about 10 or 15 seconds. However, I would also guess that 10 to 15 seconds is about as long as most people can be mindfully self-aware before they revert back to being that voice in their heads that wants to analyze or judge experience or before they are completely distracted by their thinking.

As a species, we are not very good at sustaining our attention without being distracted. We are likely quite aware of this through our own experience, and research confirms that experience. By one measure of attention span, researchers recently concluded that the average attention span for human beings is about 8 seconds. By contrast, it is rumored that the average attention span for goldfish is 9 seconds.[1] (I'm not sure how that is measured, but if it's at all accurate, it's certainly a little embarrassing.)

An essential element of mindfulness practice is training to stabilize awareness. We are training to be able to sustain present-moment awareness for a given time without being distracted by our thinking. Most precisely, we are training to be aware of our thinking, instead of being pulled into becoming our thinking. When we are able to remain aware of the thinking mind, we are no longer distracted by it and thus able to remain aware of what else is coming in through our senses in the present moment.

Neuro Note 7.1: Mindfulness Enhances Cognitive Functioning

Upon first learning about mindfulness training, many people raise the concern that they may somehow lose their amazing intellect if they spend less time being their thinking and more time being aware of their thinking. Actually research suggests that the opposite is true.

Several studies have shown that mindfulness can enhance cognitive function.[2] For example, remember (this will be easier after some mindfulness practice ☺), the Stroop task that I have mentioned several times? Several studies have shown that mindfulness practitioners perform better than nonpractitioners on the trials with word–color interference,[3] and Elisa Kozasa and colleagues from the Federal University of São Paulo, Brazil, have shown that mindfulness practitioners have less brain activation in a region close to the anterior cingulate cortex during conflicting trials, suggesting more efficient executive control.[4] Do you also remember the emotional Stroop task that Micah Allen and colleagues from Aarhus University in Denmark used? They found better performance on this task after a mindfulness training and found increased brain activation in lateral prefrontal cortex, suggesting increased executive control.[5]

More and more research suggests that even in older adults mindfulness can increase cognitive functions and prevent their decline.[6] For example, my colleagues from Massachusetts General Hospital, Harvard Medical School, and I found that among the aging participants we studied, the decline in fluid intelligence, which is the ability to reason and solve novel problems and is assessed with standard intelligence tests, was slower in mindfulness practitioners than in controls. The functional brain networks of the mindfulness practitioners had greater global efficiency and were more resilient to simulated damage. The higher the level of mindfulness, the more globally efficient and resilient the functional brain networks were. These findings suggest that mindfulness can possibly reduce normal age-related decline in fluid intelligence and integration of functional brain networks.[7,8]

Imagine how much more effective you could be both personally and professionally if you were able to sustain present-moment awareness for longer periods, perhaps even indefinitely, without being distracted by your thinking. I'm sure that a list of potential benefits would be nearly endless.

As William James, the father of American psychology, said more than 100 years ago, "The longer one does attend to a topic the more mastery of it one has. And the faculty of voluntarily bringing back a wandering attention, over and over again, is the very root of judgment, character, and will. No one is *compos sui* (a master of one's self) if he have it not. An education which should improve this faculty would be the education *par excellence* (superior to all others)."[9]

The ability to remain free from distraction improves our safety, improves performance during whatever task we're working on, improves our ability to learn new things, improves our ability to notice important details that we might otherwise miss, and so on. The possibility of mastering our ability to sustain present-moment awareness should be a sufficient reason alone to undertake some form of mindfulness training.

BEGINNING TO PRACTICE IN DAILY LIFE

A simple and enjoyable way to begin mindfulness training in our daily lives is training to sustain present-moment awareness during daily activities. We don't have to add anything to our already-busy schedules. We can just subtly change the way we do things that we already do every day so that they become part of our mindfulness training.

To begin practicing mindfulness in your daily life, I recommend that as your first step you make a list of all the simple, mundane things that you do every day in relative solitude.

The list should include things such as:

- Waking up
- Using the bathroom (at home and work)
- Washing the hands (at home and work)
- Taking a shower (including during working hours should you be so lucky as to be able to work out onsite or over a lunch break)
- Getting dressed (including during working hours should you be so lucky as to be able to work out onsite or over a lunch break)
- Brushing the teeth (including at work if you're really into great dental hygiene)
- Flossing or water picking (your dentist would agree that this should be done every day)

- Drinking water (at home and work)
- Preparing food (at home and work)
- Eating food (at home and work)
- Preparing coffee (at home and work)
- Washing the dishes (at home and at work should you wash a dish at work)
- Taking short walks, like the walk to the car or public transportation or walks to take bathroom breaks at work (These should be individual activities at first—you can eventually commit to being mindful at any time you are walking.)
- Driving
- Standing and waiting in lines
- Sitting and waiting (for the computer to boot up, for a meeting to start, etc.)
- Listening to the phone ring

There are, of course, many more activities that we engage in daily. Eventually, we may reach a point in our practice where we're making the effort to be mindfully self-aware during every moment that doesn't require us to actively plan, analyze information, or otherwise be actively engaged with the thinking mind. We'll gradually replace our current habit of becoming the thinking mind as our default mode of being with the new habit of becoming and remaining mindfully self-aware as our default mode of being. However, to start the practice, I recommend you start your list with the simple, mundane activities that don't require you to engage with others or your own thinking, such as the activities listed above.

The second step is to pick one of the activities from your list and commit to making the effort to train awareness by being mindful during that activity each time you perform it, for one week. For instance, let's imagine that you start with brushing the teeth.

What is brushing the teeth typically like for you? If you're like most people, brushing the teeth is something that you rush through to get on to what's next, and you're likely thinking about all sorts of things while you're brushing the teeth. Have you ever paused in the middle of brushing the teeth and started over because you forgot which parts of the mouth you had brushed due to being lost in thought?

Let's look at what brushing the teeth is like as a mindfulness practice and how that's different from how we normally brush the teeth. When you get ready to start brushing the teeth, you could pause for one in breath and one out breath, opening your awareness to whatever you notice right now within you or around you. This simple pause is a very important part of mindfulness training during daily activities. The pause helps reestablish mindfulness in the event you were caught in your thinking, and it also helps you mentally commit to making the effort to be mindful throughout the activity of brushing the teeth.

Your only goal when brushing the teeth should be to know that you are brushing the teeth, almost as though you are observing yourself brush the teeth, aware of what each moment of brushing the teeth is like. Thoughts will likely arise quite often during the 2 minutes recommended for brushing the teeth. That's perfectly fine and quite natural.

There's no need to push thoughts away or try to get rid of them. Your job is simply to notice when there is thinking or when there isn't, which allows you to keep from being distracted by your thinking. In any moment that you're aware of your thinking, you are not caught in that thinking, which means you can be aware of what else is happening while you brush the teeth.

You may notice what the muscles in the body feel like, what the brush feels like in the hand, what the bristles feel like on the teeth and gums, what sounds are present, or perhaps even what breathing in and out is like. You don't need to try too hard to notice these things. If you just have the curious attitude of "What's happening now? What's this moment like?" you will have achieved mindful self-awareness, and you'll be open to whatever is happening in the present moment.

You may occasionally become lost in thought. Again, this is quite natural and very likely to happen. Whenever you notice that you're lost in thought, though, you have just become mindful and self-aware again. You might like to smile to appreciate your accomplishment! This process of noticing that you've become distracted and reestablishing mindfulness is a key part of training the mind. Once reestablished, you can sustain that mindful self-awareness by once again applying the curious attitude of "What's happening now? What's this moment like?"

If you find it difficult to remember to practice, you could try leaving a little sticky note somewhere you can easily see, which can serve as a reminder to practice being mindful while brushing the teeth. Assuming you remember, after practicing in the way described above for one week, it is quite likely that you'll be able to stick with brushing the teeth as a mindfulness practice, and you should. Brushing the teeth will have become one of your anchors for mindfulness. Even if you never intentionally practice mindfulness the rest of a day, you'll at least have a few moments of training each morning and evening (or perhaps even over lunch if you're a little obsessive about oral health).

For the second week, you should continue with the practice of brushing the teeth and add another activity. Each week from that point on, you should continue with the activities you're already using for training and add another activity to your training regimen. With this approach, you will find that after just a few months you are making the effort to practice mindfulness during many moments of the day.

At this point, you may be asking, "What in tarnation does brushing the teeth have to do with leadership excellence?" That's a great question. I'm glad you asked.

The Brain Is a Habitual Machine

The brain is a very malleable machine (remember neuroplasticity), but it tends toward what is habitual. This can become a sort of vicious cycle. We favor what is comfortable, which means we're more likely to behave in that particular way. The more often we behave in a certain way, the stronger the neural pathways in the brain that are associated with that behavior become. Over time, the neural pathways become strong enough that the particular behavior becomes our default. The behavior becomes habitual.[10]

As we discussed in Chapter 1, the essence of mindfulness training is simply learning to be mindfully self-aware more often and eventually having the ability to be mindfully self-aware at will, whenever we like, even in the most challenging situations. By gradually transforming how we approach the activities we engage in every day, we can also gradually change our neural pathways and thereby rewire our brains so that being mindfully self-aware becomes our default during those activities. This helps lay the neural foundation for being able to remain mindfully self-aware in increasingly demanding situations.

It is our ability to sustain mindful self-awareness—and to develop increasingly refined self-awareness—that allows us to realize all the benefits described in Part 1 of this book. As we discussed in Chapter 1, making the effort to be mindfully self-aware from the beginning of an activity to the end of it, versus just being randomly mindful for a few seconds at a time, is much like intentionally running for 20 minutes at a time, versus only randomly running for a few seconds to cross the street. In the case of both mindfulness and running, only when we train to intentionally sustain the effort for longer periods do we realize the many benefits of intentional training.

Also, by developing our ability to sustain present-moment awareness without being distracted during daily activities, we develop a highly refined awareness that allows us to see both our inner and our outer worlds with much greater clarity. As we'll explore in the following chapters, this greater clarity is crucial for cultivating the wisdom that is essential for leadership excellence. Thus, there is a clear and direct connection between practicing mindfulness during simple activities, such as brushing the teeth, and rewiring the brain for leadership excellence.

The First Step to Unconditional Happiness

In addition to being an essential part of rewiring the brain for aspects of leadership excellence, such as improved business acumen, emotional intelligence, innovation, and leadership presence, practicing mindfulness during the simple moments of each day also helps us realize an aspect of leadership excellence that is often overlooked: happiness.

As we discussed in Chapter 6, happiness is also one of the primary goals of our lives. In that chapter, we introduced the idea that things external to us create only temporary happiness. What happens to us has little or no effect on our baseline level of happiness.

Pleasant things and experiences cannot bring lasting happiness because they are impermanent. Thus, the happiness that they bring is also impermanent. A new car, good food, and even personal relationships are wonderful while they last, but eventually we will lose them. This leaves us only wanting more. Seeking happiness outside ourselves is like drinking saltwater to quench our thirst—it only makes us thirstier.

Because pleasant things and experiences are not necessary to be happy, and in fact cannot provide lasting happiness, we can see that lasting happiness cannot be found in anything outside ourselves. It has to come from within. This is why I call this type of happiness unconditional. It does not depend on any external condition being met.

Have you ever thought about why we don't experience such unconditional happiness in every moment? I believe that it is very important for us to understand exactly what keeps us from realizing happiness. Increased awareness of the cause of the problem helps us better understand and apply the remedy for our dilemma.

When we look closely enough, we discover that the reason we do not experience satisfaction from moment to moment lies within ourselves. We find that our dissatisfaction is a result of a lack of space around thinking.

We habitually cling to and become the thoughts that arise in the mind, which leaves no space around them. When there is no space around these thoughts, they have a huge effect on our happiness. If our thoughts are good, we feel satisfied. If they are bad, we feel unsatisfied, stressed out, or downright miserable.

At the simplest level, we can see that our dissatisfaction is the result of a lack of space around the comparisons the mind makes between our experience here and now and our memories of all the pleasant things that we have had or done or our hopes for a better future. Of course, because our present-moment experience could almost always be more pleasant, it often pales in comparison to our pleasant thoughts of the past or future. As a result, we are not satisfied in the present moment.

However, if instead of identifying with these comparative thoughts, we see them objectively and have some space around them, they don't have the power to obscure the truth that the present moment is actually perfect just the way it is. My first deep realization of this was during my time in confinement and actually occurred while I was brushing the teeth. While brushing the teeth with sustained mindfulness for a minute or so, I found myself smiling. I was no longer in prison. I was just brushing the teeth, and there was simply nothing wrong with that moment. It was perfect.

I have since had countless experiences of realizing the perfection of the present moment in mundane situations that you likely experience daily, such as sitting in traffic. The problem with sitting in traffic is created by the thinking in the mind that keeps reminding us that we're going to be late and that we'd like to move faster, both of which are completely out of our control. But, if we're not caught in the thinking that compares the experience of sitting in traffic to thoughts of arriving on time or moving faster, what's wrong with it? There's nothing wrong with it. It's just sitting in a car.

In fact, let's take it a step further. Let's imagine that we just came into existence right in that moment. We would probably find the experience of sitting in the car quite miraculous. We would think, "Wow! I can see things. I can hear things. I can feel my feet on the floor. I can feel my hands on the steering wheel. I'm in this human body that is breathing. There's a heartbeat. There are thoughts coming and going. This is incredible!"

Why isn't every moment like that?

It's simple, right? Our minds ruin such moments. The mind automatically starts comparing the present experience to thoughts of the past or future. "Well, sitting here in this car is okay, but we're just crawling and I'm going to be late! If I could only go faster, things would be so much better and I would be happy." All of our dissatisfaction is created by the mind.

In Chapter 1 we discussed the research of Harvard PhD Matt Killingsworth, which showed that the 2,250 people in the study reported that their minds wandered nearly 47 percent of the time.

The research also suggests that such mind wandering is a significant cause of unhappiness. This was true even when people were experiencing something unpleasant, such as sitting in traffic during a commute. We might think that we would be happier in a traffic jam if we allowed the mind to wander off to some tropical island. However, the people in the study who were fully present with the activity of commuting reported being significantly happier than people who allowed their minds to wander, even when those thoughts were pleasant.

This habit of mind wandering and looking elsewhere for happiness is likely a very old one for most of us. The neural pathways associated with that habit are likely very, very strong.

When we were in middle school, we likely said, "Once I get to high school, then I'll be living. Then I'll be happy." Once there we said, "When I graduate and go to college or start my dream job, then I'll be living." Once there, we need a better career. Then, many of us struggle through every workweek, hoping that the weekend will bring us happiness. Next, we need a spouse, then kids. Once we have the spouse and kids, we might long for the freedom we felt during the college days. Right now we might feel as though if we could just get or do the next thing, then we'd finally be happy.

However, this is only an illusion if the mind still habitually looks to the past or the future for happiness. If we don't change our minds, we are destined to continue the lifelong habit. Even when we don't wish we were elsewhere, the good times will always end, and if we still rely on external conditions for our happiness, we'll be unhappy when they do.

Conversely, if we can develop the ability to be satisfied with the present moment, even during mundane moments, then when we're with loved ones, we will be fully there with them and be more able to accept them as they are. When we're at work, we'll be fully at work instead of wishing we were elsewhere. We'll enjoy whatever we do much more completely, and our lives will be much more fulfilling.

Fortunately, our habitual tendency to cling to and become our comparative thinking is not how we started off in this world. This tendency is something that has come about through conditioning. When we observe infants during their first few months, we see that as long as their basic needs are met, they are perfectly happy just to be alive and breathing. They appear to live in a veritable heaven on Earth. Before developing object permanence, infants' moment-to-moment experience is not likely corrupted by thoughts of the past and future.[11] Thus, for the infant, each mundane moment is perfect.

This infant mind is essentially our original mind. We experienced this heaven on Earth for many months before our minds began filling up with memories and comparative thinking, which began pulling us around with increasing frequency. As this pull became stronger, we in turn became less contented. We required more complicated, pleasant experiences to realize the happiness that we used to realize during nearly every moment.

Now, for many of us, true happiness is realized only for brief instances, flashes of complete satisfaction and wholeness that we cannot describe. The rest of our time consists of a never-ending search through the outside world for something that we've always had within ourselves.

However, if we can train ourselves to see comparative thinking objectively, which creates some space around it, whatever we are doing in the present moment will be much more satisfying and potentially even perfect. Each moment has the potential to reveal its perfection. We only need to train ourselves to realize this. The practice of mindfulness allows us to do just that!

A WIN-WIN-WIN PARADIGM SHIFT

Those of us who tend to be skeptical may be thinking, "I agree that we could realize happiness during any normal moment, but what about during the extreme moments when life is really frightening, depressing, or painful?" This is an excellent question, which will be addressed thoroughly in the coming chapters. For now, let's consider the fact that for most people reading this book only about five percent of our entire lives are extremely pleasurable and exciting, and only five percent of the moments are extremely painful or difficult. The vast majority of life, probably more than 90 percent of it, consists of simple, neutral moments, such as walking, standing, sitting, using the toilet, and so on. Most of us become easily bored during such moments, and we rush to get them over with—adding to the anxiety that we experience each day—so we can get back to the seemingly exciting moments of life. This means that we are anxiously skipping over the vast majority of our lives in our rush toward the future—a future that is not guaranteed for any of us. This increase in anxiety also inhibits our ability to effectively accomplish whatever we do next.

Are you beginning to realize what an incredible paradigm shift can occur simply by practicing mindfulness during your daily activities?

When we are mindful during the mundane activities in our lives, we transform those moments into useful opportunities to rewire our brains for leadership excellence. They also become opportunities to let go of at least a little bit of the anxiety that can build up during a workday, which improves performance on both the current and upcoming tasks. Perhaps most important, these mundane moments become opportunities to realize unconditional happiness right now, in the present moment, and they become joyful reminders that complete satisfaction is always available during the simple moments of our lives.

With mindfulness, each act can become an opportunity to touch the perfection of the present moment. Those of us who regularly practice mindfulness often realize complete satisfaction, and even joy, during simple, neutral moments, such as standing in lines, eating rather bland food, waiting for a meeting to start, and changing the paper in the printer. And moments that are inherently pleasant—being in the company of loved ones, accomplishing something great at work, eating good food, watching a sunset—seem amplified by the practice of mindfulness.

Have you ever noticed how rich and vivid an experience seems to be during a slow-motion scene in a movie? In slow motion, even in a simple scene, such as walking into a room, everything seems more vivid. We notice little details that we don't normally notice. With sustained mindfulness, we often experience moments with this type of surreal vividness, almost as though we're in a slow-motion scene in a movie. With mindfulness, a glimpse of a leaf blowing in the wind can be a magical experience that evokes joy.

Although our daily practice may start with just one or two simple, mundane activities, over time mindfulness begins to permeate more and more moments of each day. Whenever it's not necessary for us to be actively engaged in planning, analyzing, or otherwise intentionally thinking, we find that we incline toward being mindfully self-aware. Mindfulness becomes a new habit—the ultimate habit for personal and professional success.

One of my clients is a large dental practice management company. The president of the company discovered a major turning point in his practice as a result of focusing more on practicing mindfulness during daily activities. He noticed that as mindfulness started to permeate activities such as hiking on the weekends and doing the dishes after dinner, he started to enjoy the practice more. It became less of something he had to do to improve as a leader, and more of something he did just to enjoy doing it.

He also realized that the time he spends practicing mindfulness in his personal life makes it easier to practice while at work during activities such as attending meetings, planning, sending e-mails, and listening to team members. He saw a clear connection between doing the dishes and improving his leadership skills. He also realized that while he was doing the dishes, the most important thing he could do to realize happiness, become a better leader, and be more present for his family was to let go of any desire to achieve anything—even the desire to have clean dishes—and just be fully engaged with the activity of washing the dishes.

Ironically, this is also the best way to have clean dishes. We do a much better job of cleaning the dishes when we really pay attention to what we're doing. Of course, this is true for any activity. By temporarily letting go of our desire to achieve a certain outcome and instead being fully engaged with the task we're currently working on, the outcome is much better than when we're wasting mental energy thinking about what we hope to achieve.

If we want to achieve an optimal result in any endeavor, a good general formula to follow is to set goals that excite us and encourage us to begin and stick with activities that help us achieve those goals. But, in the moments when we're engaged in the activities that help us reach our goals, we should be 100 percent engaged in the activity at hand. This formula is absolutely essential for success with mindfulness training.

I cannot stress enough how important this point is. The most important thing we can do to realize the benefits of mindfulness training discussed in this book is let go of the desire to achieve those benefits in any moment we're engaged in the practice. Our lives are filled with moments of striving. We must learn to balance those moments with more moments of mindfulness, of *nonstriving*, of being completely open to what is actually happening. The more often we do that, the more often we realize the perfection of the present moment and the sooner we'll see impacts on our leadership skills.

REVIEW QUESTIONS

What are the three areas of your life that would be affected the most if you were no longer distracted by your thinking against your will?

How can you begin practicing mindfulness without adding anything to your schedule?

How is practicing mindfulness during daily activities linked to developing leadership excellence?

How does practicing mindfulness during daily activities allow you to significantly increase your happiness?

How would you describe the incredible paradigm shift that occurs when you practice mindfulness during the mundane moments of your life?

What is a good general formula for achieving optimal results in your efforts to achieve a goal?

8

THE POWER OF
SITTING STILL

I f you took a break between this chapter and the last and practiced a bit of mindfulness, began practicing after reading Chapter 1, or began practicing some time ago, you have surely discovered something that may be a bit troublesome. The practice can be incredibly difficult!

It sounds so simple, right? Just be objectively aware of thoughts, emotions, and other sensations as they are happening in the present moment, and try to sustain that awareness for a while. And, it is that simple. But it's certainly not easy.

The mind is crazy, isn't it? If you've made any effort to sustain mindful self-awareness without being distracted, you've likely noticed that you're frequently switching back and forth between being mindfully self-aware and being the thinking mind, often completely distracted by thinking.

Many people report that they actually feel more distracted when they first start practicing than before they began. Although this is likely not the case, it can certainly seem that way because we're likely more aware of where our attention is directed than we ever have been before. An analogy often used to describe this phenomenon is that of a really old, oily shop rag that's completely stained.

When we first start to clean the rag up a bit, we start to notice that there isn't just one big stain. There are lots of individual stains. With a bit of cleaning, we start to see some space between the stains, and we become aware of just how many there are. In the same way, when we start to intentionally become and remain mindfully self-aware, we also start to notice how little time we actually spend resting in that awareness and how often we operate from the perspective of being the thinking mind, either partially or completely distracted by our thinking.

The practice is also often described as similar to training a puppy. At first, it's almost impossible to get the puppy to sit. When we're finally able to get the puppy to sit, he doesn't sit for more than a second or two before he's prancing around in play again.

Just as with the puppy that seems never to stay on task, we try to remain mindfully self-aware, but we are constantly pulled into and distracted by the thinking mind. We have to keep starting over, over and over. This is part of the training.

There is good news on this front. It gets easier with practice. By practicing mindfulness during simple, mundane, daily activities, as we discussed in the last chapter, we are already beginning to train the mind in a way that allows us to change our default mode from being the thinking mind to being mindfully self-aware. By constantly recognizing when the mind has wandered and gently reestablishing the mindful self-awareness that allows us to be open to what else is coming in through our senses, we are breaking old habits and developing new, more beneficial ones.

A helpful shortcut that can make the practice significantly easier is to take some time each day to practice mindfulness while sitting still. There is a highly mutually beneficial relationship between practicing mindfulness during daily activities and practicing while sitting still. Practicing during daily activities helps develop our ability to intentionally become and remain mindfully self-aware, both during activity and while sitting still. However, daily activities can also be seen as the actual main event we're training for, and taking time to sit still each day is a key part of training for that event.

There are two main reasons why taking time to practice while sitting still is so helpful for improving our ability to intentionally become and remain mindfully self-aware during our daily lives. First, because we can reduce the number of incoming stimuli, or potential incoming stimuli, while sitting still, we can decrease the likelihood that we'll be required to intentionally engage in thinking. This provides us a much better chance of spending more time sustaining mindful self-awareness, which strengthens the neural networks involved, making it easier to sustain mindful self-awareness during daily activities.

The second reason taking time to engage in mindfulness training while sitting still is so beneficial is that it allows us to dramatically improve our self-awareness and thereby learn significantly more about ourselves and how we operate in this world. Sitting still allows us to let go of the concerns we rightly have while we're in motion regarding what might happen to us. When we're sitting still in a safe place, we can turn our attention inward toward the body and mind. This allows the awareness of the inner world to become much more stable and powerful than it is during activity, which in turn allows us to learn so much more about the mind and body and how they function. This self-knowledge is the key to self-mastery.

The ability to see the mind and body, and how they function, is essential for developing a very special type of wisdom that is one of the keys to realizing all of the benefits we've explored in this book. It is the wisdom that breaks the habit of continually becoming our thinking rather than remaining aware of our thinking. The training exercises in this chapter will help you begin cultivating that wisdom. We'll also explore that wisdom in depth, as well as additional exercises for developing it, in Chapters 10, 11, and 12.

SEAMLESSLY INTEGRATING THE TRAINING INTO DAILY LIFE

Just as with practicing mindfulness during daily activities, to incorporate some sitting-still practice into our daily lives we shouldn't have to add anything to our already-busy schedules, assuming that we take at least one break in the morning and one in the afternoon. If you are not taking at least one 10-minute break in the morning and afternoon, you almost certainly should be. Taking breaks can dramatically improve the accuracy of our work, creative problem solving, safety, and productivity.

Many productivity experts encourage taking a 5-minute break every 25 minutes (the Pomodoro Technique) or a 10-minute break every 50 minutes (my preference). The idea is to be hyperfocused on whatever task we're working on for a specified period and then intentionally relax the mind for a period. Over the long term, this allows us to actually spend more time focused and less time partially or mostly distracted from what's important.

Neuro Note 8.1: Breaks Improve Performance

Several recent scientific publications with titles such as "Mental Breaks Keep You Focused" and "Rest Is Best" report studies that show that performance on sustained-attention tasks improves when one takes breaks in which one completely disengages from the main task.[1] One study even suggests that the longer one performs a task, the longer breaks need to be to prevent decline in performance.[2] The general idea here is that resources for sustained attention deplete over time. In the brain, longer time on task is associated with decreased activation in regions of the salience and central executive networks, including the anterior insula and lateral prefrontal cortex.[3]

Assuming that we are taking at least two 10-minute breaks per day, all we need to do to incorporate some sitting-still practice into our daily lives is change the way we take a portion of each of those breaks by taking what I call a *minivacation*. This is a very special type of short but incredibly rewarding vacation. This vacation is likely to leave us feeling more relaxed than we often feel on our full vacations, and we're likely to return to work significantly recharged, with greater clarity and peace of mind, and with the enhanced self-awareness that is so crucial for leadership excellence. At the same time, this minivacation is a crucial part of rewiring the brain in ways that help us realize all the other benefits described in this book.

Although our motivation for exploring this training is to develop leadership and personal excellence, the moment we begin practicing mindfulness while sitting still, it is very helpful to think of it as a minivacation. We shouldn't see it as work or as something we *have* to do. We should think of it as something we *get* to do.

If you have a type A personality, like me, at first you'll have to take it on faith that sitting still and doing nothing can be seen as something we look forward to, as something we *get* to do. You may see it more as something that gets in the way of getting stuff done. Whether or not you're a type A personality, you will quite likely find it difficult at first to be alone with your thoughts. Many of us seem programmed quite strongly to seek external stimulation and avoid being alone to face our minds.

In a study conducted at the University of Virginia in 2014, psychologist Timothy Wilson and colleagues discovered that many people so dislike being alone with their thoughts that they would actually rather give themselves an electric shock than continue doing nothing but facing their minds. When asked to sit alone in a room for 15 minutes, participants were given the choice to do nothing or, if they preferred it, to give themselves a mild electric shock delivered from a 9-volt battery. Six of the 24 women who participated elected to shock themselves, and 12 of the 18 men who participated preferred electric shocks to being alone with their minds. One of the men shocked himself 190 times.[4]

Many of us face some variation of this discomfort with being alone with our thoughts. This is the mind many of us bring to work every day. Fortunately, it doesn't have to be that way. If you practice correctly, you will gradually become extremely comfortable in your own skin and facing your thoughts. You will bring a much healthier mind to your interactions with the outside world.

In fact, if you practice correctly, you will soon see the time you spend sitting still as one of the most enjoyable parts of your life. Many people who practice regularly come to find the practice as so enjoyable that it can almost become addictive. We have to restrain ourselves to take only

30 minutes or so each morning and evening to sit still, knowing that we have other things that need to be done. The practice is truly like a minivacation.

Ironically, approaching the practice as something we get to do is one of the secrets to realizing the benefits we have discussed in this book. During our practice of sitting still in mindfulness, there is no need to try to go anywhere, change anything, or achieve anything. The practice becomes very easy if we can just sit back, relax, and objectively observe the incredible show that is our moment-to-moment experience.

A BEGINNER'S GUIDE TO SITTING STILL IN MINDFULNESS

An easy way to begin your practice of sitting still in mindfulness during your breaks is to find some ways to make it clear that you are on break, which might mean going to a room or some other place where no one will demand your attention. If you're staying close to or in your office, you might take some extra steps to let people know you are on break by putting earbuds in your ears and creating a sign that reads, "Taking a 10-minute break. Please do not disturb." (If you're working to make the practice available to other team members, you might even like to eventually designate a room for silent breaks or even specifically for mindfulness training.)

Step One—Set a timer on your watch or phone for the length of time you intend to practice while sitting still. A great time with which to start is 5 minutes. If you can commit to only 1 minute, though, that's much better than nothing.

Read these instructions before starting the timer. If you'd like to be guided through this practice, you can download a recorded version of a 5-minute practice at www.TheMindfulnessEdge.com.

Step Two—Sit with good posture. You don't have to be rigid. Just sit upright without leaning on anything.

Although you may find yourself more relaxed after practicing, that is not the main goal. Being alert is more important for the practice so that we can have greater clarity of awareness. Good posture helps facilitate that.

Once you have good posture, you can find a general area to look at and hold your gaze steady in that area with your eyes open, or you can just close your eyes. Once you've read the following instructions and become comfortable with the idea of this practice, you would start the timer at this point, just before settling your gaze or closing your eyes.

Step 3—Open your awareness, with a curious beginner's mind, to what's happening now.

What do you notice while sitting still? Perhaps you notice what the body feels like as it sits in the chair. Perhaps you notice some subtle sounds. Perhaps you notice what the muscles feel like in various areas of your body. Perhaps you notice that there are thoughts passing through the mind and that you can see them without losing awareness of what else is happening. You might also notice that the body is breathing in and out. What is that like?

Allow yourself to watch the body breathe, with curiosity, without trying to control the breathing in any way. The attitude is one of "What's it like when the body breathes out?" then "What's it like when the body breathes in?"

This curious awareness of the body breathing can become the foundation that helps you sustain your open, curious awareness of what's happening in the present moment. You don't need to focus on the breath. Just be aware that it's happening, noticing whatever aspect or aspects of the breath are most prominent for you.

The only goal of this exercise is to have—and then sustain—mindful self-awareness with the curious, open awareness described above. You don't need to sustain that awareness for the entire length of time you've committed to sitting still. It's much better to have a smaller, more manageable goal. Just try to sustain mindfulness for one in breath. Then, try it again for one out breath. If you just take it one breath at a time, you will likely find the practice much easier.

You might find it helpful to use the inner voice to mentally note what is happening as a way to skillfully guide awareness. You could mentally note "In" as the body breathes in and "Out" as the body breathes out. As you hear the words in *and* out *in the mind, they should serve as gentle reminders to be curious about what the in breath or out breath is like and remain open to whatever is happening in the present moment. So the attitude is something like "In—what's happening now? Out—what's this moment like?"*

When the timer goes off, see whether you can continue to be mindfully self-aware during the next activities you engage in. During activity, the breath is no longer the foundation for sustaining mindfulness. Rather, the activity itself becomes the foundation. For instance, if you walk someplace, try to maintain mindful self-awareness while walking, occasionally mentally noting, "Walking" to keep awareness alive to that activity, and try to remain open to the physical sensations associated with walking. You could then make the same effort with drinking water, sitting down and writing an e-mail, and so on.

You might notice a couple of minor differences between the experiences of practicing while sitting and practicing during activity. You will likely not be as aware of the breath during activity, and you will not likely see your inner world as clearly during activity. However, the effort should be essentially identical: maintaining curious awareness of what's happening now both within you and around you. You can achieve this by simply keeping the question alive: "What's happening now?"

Please take a moment just to reflect on the experience of sitting still in mindfulness. What was that like? Were you able to maintain mindfulness for one full breath, for several breaths, or perhaps for the entire time? Was there a lot of thinking or not as much? Did you notice anything internally or externally that you weren't aware of before you sat still in mindfulness?

For most of us, there will likely be a lot of thinking passing through the mind while we practice sitting still in mindfulness. This is perfectly fine and quite normal. In a general sense, thinking results from the stimuli to which we are exposed. As leaders, most of us are exposed to a tremendous amount of information and other stimuli. The brain's job is to process all that information, analyze it, make sense of it, and determine what's best to do with it. Much of this processing occurs consciously. Because of this, for most of us, it would be very unrealistic to expect our minds to be empty of thinking.

There is no need to worry about how much thinking is present, to try to get rid of thinking, or to struggle with it in any way. All we need to do is recognize it. In fact, as we'll see in the more advanced practices, thinking is actually a wonderful gift that will help us develop the wisdom that is essential for developing both personal and leadership excellence.

It doesn't really matter how many thoughts arise during our sitting-still practice. We should not consider the presence of thinking, or lack thereof, a metric for whether we are practicing well. The effort is simply to remain mindfully self-aware and not to get pulled into thinking. To help with this, you might find it skillful just to mentally note when thoughts arise and then use mental noting to keep awareness open to what else is happening.

For instance, if a thought about performance evaluations arises, you might just mentally note with the inner voice, "Thinking about performance evals." Then with the next in breath or out breath, return to "In" or "Out" as a reminder to be curious about what's happening right now. Maybe the thought is still there, or maybe it has passed. Either way, just keep yourself open to what you notice *right now*, then *right now*, then *right now*, and so on.

If the mind is very busy, and you find yourself distracted by thinking often, you might just mentally note that, with "In, there's a lot of thinking right now," or "Out, the mind is very busy," and then keep a curious attitude about what the experience is like with each succeeding in breath or out breath.

Remember, the only goal with this beginner-level exercise is to be aware of what's happening in the present moment without being pulled into being the thinking mind. If you'd like to have a metric for your progress with this practice, you might like to try counting each mindful breath.

For instance, if you're able to maintain mindful self-awareness for one full breath (an in breath and out breath), without being distracted by thinking, then you would count that as "One." If you can do it again, you would count the second full breath as "Two." If you ever get distracted and lose count, then you start over. After each time you practice sitting still for 5 minutes, you could write down how high you were able to count before becoming distracted. Over time, you should notice that you can spend more time being mindfully self-aware, often coexisting with thoughts passing through the mind, without being pulled into and distracted by thinking.

Although this counting is a much more skillful metric than trying to empty your mind of thinking, or achieve some other feat that has little or no benefit for improving your ability to become and remain mindfully self-aware at will, even this metric should be applied with caution. If you try too hard, and really focus on counting, it actually won't be very helpful.

To apply this metric skillfully, we should focus more on the quality of our awareness with each breath. If awareness is open and curious for a full breath, without being pulled into our thinking, then we should certainly count that breath. However, if we're so focused on counting that we aren't really aware of the body breathing or open to what else is happening now, then we're missing the point. The key here is to apply just enough effort not to lose count but not so much that counting becomes the primary goal or activity.

AN INTERMEDIATE-LEVEL GUIDE TO SITTING STILL IN MINDFULNESS

You are free to move on to this intermediate-level exercise whenever you like. Although the breath-counting exercise is not necessary, if you can practice sitting still in mindfulness for 5 minutes without losing count of your breaths (and without being overfocused on counting), you are more than ready to begin enjoying this intermediate-level training exercise.

There are only two things different about this intermediate-level practice. First, it should be a little bit longer than 5 minutes. I recommend setting a timer for about 10 minutes for this practice.

Second, because we spend so much time caught in our thinking, we're going to practice refining awareness of the body. This is very important for developing emotional intelligence and for developing a foundation for the more advanced exercises.

Neuro Note 8.2: Body Awareness and Emotional Intelligence

The insula is one of the brain regions that is most consistently affected by mindfulness, in terms of function as well as

(*continued*)

(*continued*)

structure.[5] As we have seen in Neuro Notes 1.3, 3.2, and the discussion on the differences between empathy and compassion in the first endnote for Neuro Note 5.3, this region is involved in body awareness,[6] empathy,[7] and emotional intelligence.[8]

We'll begin the instructions for the intermediate-level exercise right at the point from the beginner-level exercise where you've assumed good posture and started your timer.

With the curious mind of a beginner, what do you notice while sitting still? Perhaps you notice what the body feels like as it sits in the chair. Perhaps you notice some subtle sounds. Perhaps you notice what the muscles feel like in various areas of your body. Perhaps you notice that there are thoughts passing through the mind and that you can see them without losing awareness of what else is happening. You might also notice that the body is breathing in and out. What is that like?

Allow yourself to watch the body breathe, with curiosity, without trying to control the breathing in any way. The attitude is one of "What's it like when the body breathes out?" then "What's it like when the body breathes in?"

This curious awareness of the body breathing can become the foundation that helps you sustain your open, curious awareness of what's happening in the present moment. You don't need to focus on the breath. Just know that it's happening, noticing whatever aspect or aspects of the breath are most prominent for you.

The only goal of this exercise is to have—and then sustain—mindful self-awareness with the curious, open awareness described above. However, you don't need to sustain that awareness for the entire length of time you've committed to sitting still. It's much better to have a smaller, more manageable goal. Just try to sustain mindfulness for one in breath. Then, try it again for one out breath. If you just take it one breath at a time, you will likely find the practice much easier.

You might find it helpful to use the inner voice to mentally note what is happening as a way to skillfully guide awareness. You could mentally note, "In" as the body breathes in and "Out" as the body breathes out. As you hear the words in *and* out *in the mind, they should serve as gentle reminders to be curious about what the in breath or out breath is like and remain open to whatever is coming through the senses in the present moment. So the attitude is something like "In. What's happing now? Out. What's this moment like?"*

To help you become more aware of the body, you can sweep through the body with awareness, starting with the feet.

Each time the body breathes in, mentally note, "In," and notice whatever there is to notice with the feet. If you feel nothing, just note that. If there's any tension in the feet, just note it without judgment and without trying to fix it.

Each time the body breathes out, mentally note, "Out," and notice whether there are any little muscles contracted in the feet. If there are any muscles contracted, however small, let them relax.

Continue in this way for three to five breaths.

Follow this same guidance for each part of your body, moving from the feet to the lower legs, to the upper legs, to the lower back, to the upper back and chest, to the arms, to the neck and shoulders, ending with the face.

Thoughts are sure to arise during this time, which is fine. You can just note them and keep your awareness open to the portion of the body you're at. If at any time you find yourself distracted by thinking, you could just mentally note with the inner voice, "Thinking about performance evals" (or whatever thought is there). Then with the next in breath or out breath, return to "In" and "Out," as reminders to be aware of the part of the body you're at.

After three to five breaths of awareness of the face, allow your awareness to open up to include the entire body. Each time the body breathes in, mentally note, "In," and notice whatever there is to notice with the body. If you feel nothing, just note that. If there's any tension in the body, just note it without judgment and without trying to fix it.

Each time the body breathes out, mentally note, "Out," and notice whether there are any muscles contracted anywhere in the body. If there are any muscles contracted, however small, let them relax (except, of course, for the muscles needed to hold the spine upright).

Allow yourself to watch the body breathe, with curiosity, without trying to control the breathing in any way. The attitude is one of "What's it like when the body breathes out?" At the end of the out breath, you might wonder, "Is it

THE MINDFULNESS EDGE

going to breathe in?" and wait with anticipation for the body to breathe in. Then, "What's it like when the body breathes in?"

Gradually allow the mental noting of "In" and "Out" to become quieter and quieter in your mind until your inner voice is silent and you're simply watching the body breathe and open to whatever passes through your awareness. For instance, you might notice how you can be aware of a sound and your body breathing at the same time.

You will likely notice that as you maintain this refined awareness of the body breathing, you are also aware of the mind. You may notice that thoughts are among the sensations that pass through your awareness. You may notice that you can observe the mind, without losing awareness of the body breathing, almost as though you are watching a television screen. You're simply watching the body breathe, aware of the mind and body, and open to whatever passes through your awareness now, then now, then now, and so on.

Continue in this way until the timer sounds.

SPILLING OVER INTO ACTIVITY

The fruits of this intermediate-level exercise include developing more refined levels of self-awareness, especially awareness of the body. With practice, you will likely find that the skills you develop during your sitting-still practice become easier to apply during your daily activities. Feel free to explore your body awareness, and even awareness of the mind, during the daily activities you're practicing with, as outlined in Chapter 7.

REVIEW QUESTIONS

How does practicing mindfulness while sitting still improve your ability to be mindfully self-aware during daily activities?

How can you integrate the practice of mindfulness while sitting still into your daily life without adding anything to your schedule?

When practicing sitting still in mindfulness, what is a good goal to have regarding how long you sustain mindful self-awareness?

9

FROM 4 HOURS TO 4 MINUTES

MASTERING EMOTIONS FOR OPTIMAL PERFORMANCE

I n the last two chapters, you were encouraged to begin your mindfulness training during activities that are conducted in relative solitude and that don't require you to be actively engaged in thinking. It is during those types of activities that it is likely easiest to begin your training and to realize some of the fruits of the practice. However, the life of a leader is certainly not lived in isolation.

As you add more and more activities to your training regimen, mindfulness will begin to spill over into many areas of your life. You will gradually notice yourself making the effort to practice being mindfully self-aware during more complex activities, such as interacting with others, which we'll explore in great detail in Chapter 13.

Although it is certainly possible, and quite likely, that we experience unpleasant emotions during time in relative solitude because of negative thought patterns, unpleasant emotions tend to arise equally as easily, and oftentimes much more easily, when we interact with other people. This is likely because we tend to take our interactions with people quite personally and are more likely to assign blame based on assumed intent when we're dealing with people.

The causes of those unpleasant emotions are probably somewhat different for each of us, but the experience of emotion is something we have in common as human beings. We know that there are certain situations or people that can easily provoke an unpleasant emotion in us, such as anxiety, sadness, fear, annoyance, frustration, or even anger.

When a strong, unpleasant emotion arises, there is usually a period of continuously experiencing that strong emotion combined with lots of negative thinking that fuels it. After some time, the emotion may be much more subtle, and we stop thinking about the perceived cause of the emotion. Then, often when we're no longer fully engaged in an activity the mind wanders back to thoughts of the perceived cause of the emotion, which reignites the emotion, taking it from subtle to strong again.

Once again, after some time, the emotion may be much more subtle, and we stop thinking about the perceived cause of the emotion. This cycle often continues until the thoughts about the perceived cause of the emotion eventually cease to arise, and we return to a pleasant emotional state for some time. This time often ends when we experience another event that provokes an unpleasant emotional state.

Have you ever contemplated the cost of being caught in one of the unpleasant emotions listed above? How does being caught in an unpleasant emotion affect your performance? How does it affect the performance of team members?

Of course, we know that being caught in an unpleasant emotion—most of which are variations of the fight-or-flight response—can have devastating effects on our own performance. We're not as creative; we don't think as clearly, so there's a greater risk of making a costly, poor decision; and it's harder to concentrate. And, as we discussed in

Chapter 3, leaders set the emotional tone for teams. The more time we spend caught in an unpleasant emotion, the greater negative impact we have on relationships with team members and on their performance.

When conducting training programs, I often ask how long it takes people to fully recover from the experience of a strong, unpleasant emotion. How long does it take for you? Imagine the last time you were a bit worked up emotionally. How long did it take before the process described above was completely finished—all the thoughts about the perceived cause of the emotion had ceased, the emotion was completely gone, and you returned to a pleasant emotional state?

I get a wide variety of answers, ranging from 2 hours to several days, depending on the gravity of the situation and the person's skill in dealing with emotions. For the sake of this discussion, let's assume a conservative average of 4 hours, roughly half of a workday. This allows us to get an approximation of how much unpleasant emotions cost us.

How often do you experience an unpleasant emotion, such as anxiety, for a minimum of 4 hours? For a conservative estimate (many people experience unpleasant emotions daily and are almost always mildly to moderately anxious), let's assume that we are caught in an unpleasant emotion only once per week on average. If that's the case, then we experience roughly two full days each month where we probably should not be at work because our performance is lackluster at best, and if we interact with others while we're caught up in the unpleasant emotion, we're having a negative effect on the performance of team members. Furthermore, there's a good chance that decisions we make during those times will be very poor and potentially be very costly. Considering all of these things, what might unpleasant emotions be costing you?

Clearly, being caught in unpleasant emotions can be costly from a business perspective. The cost can be even greater from a personal perspective. When we're caught in an unpleasant emotion, it can seem as though we are trapped in a sort of hell on Earth where happiness appears to be an impossible dream and where we can easily cause serious harm to the relationships we have with others. Many relationships have been ruined when one or both parties said or did something they normally wouldn't say or do because they were caught in an unpleasant emotion.

RETURNING TO COOL: FROM 4 HOURS TO 4 MINUTES

In Chapter 3, we discussed how absolutely essential emotional intelligence is for helping us create the type of winning workplace culture that drives long-term success and that mindfulness training is perhaps the most powerful tool there is for developing emotional intelligence. In addition to being the very foundation of emotional intelligence—self-awareness—mindfulness also provides us some very powerful tools for mastering our emotions. This emotional mastery allows us to be free from the grip of unpleasant emotions.

Mindfulness training helps us gradually reduce the amount of time we're losing as a result of being caught in an unpleasant emotion. Right now it may be about 4 hours before an unpleasant emotion completely passes and we are once again performing at the optimal level. With training, this can gradually be reduced to 3 hours, then to 2 hours, and then to 1 hour. In time, it is quite possible to reduce the time we lose from being caught in an unpleasant emotion to a matter of minutes or even seconds. This doesn't happen overnight, but it certainly can happen.

Neuro Note 9.1: Mechanisms of Mindful Emotion Regulation

As we discussed in Neuro Note 3.2, the study conducted by Véronique Taylor and colleagues illustrates the difference between how beginning and experienced practitioners regulate emotion. They found that both beginning mindfulness practitioners (after only seven days of training) and experienced practitioners (with on average more than 1,000 hours of practice) had less intense emotions in response to emotionally arousing pictures, so both groups were successful in regulating their emotions. However, the brain mechanisms employed to achieve this differed. Beginners had decreased brain activation in the amygdala, suggesting top-down control. Experienced mindfulness practitioners did not have decreases in affective regions but instead decreased brain activation in default mode regions, suggesting selfless present-moment awareness instead of down regulating affective regions.[1]

A similar shift from "top-down" to "bottom-up" is also apparent in the regulation of pain, as we'll discuss in Neuro Note 11.2.

Imagine that you could experience a situation that provokes an unpleasant emotion, which currently costs you 4 hours of productivity—and 4 hours of happiness—and experience that unpleasant emotion for only a few minutes before you're right back to being in a positive emotional state, performing at the optimal level. How would that affect your performance as a leader? How would that affect your life?

As we'll explore more deeply in Chapters 10 and 11, our daily practice of mindfulness gradually removes the root cause of all negative emotions by helping us be free from the control of the thinking mind and its ego. But the key word in that statement is *gradually*. For most of us, unpleasant emotions, such as anger, fear, depression, and anxiety are going to continue to arise, at least to some degree, for the rest of our lives.

Practicing *mindfulness of emotions* by using the four steps below allows us to be free immediately, right in the present moment, from the problems and suffering that accompany unpleasant emotions when there is a lack of mindfulness. The practice also helps unpleasant emotions pass much more quickly.

With most emotions, practicing Step 3 will be all that's needed. However, to be free from the grip of a strong, unpleasant emotion when we're really caught in it, practicing all four steps is essential. Because anger can be the most destructive of emotions, we will use anger as the example.

Mindfulness of Emotions: SCIL

A helpful way to remember the four steps of the practice of mindfulness of emotions is to use the acronym SCIL. Mindfulness of emotions is indeed a great *skill*.

Step 1 : S = Stop

Whenever we notice anger arising within us, the first step in the practice of mindfulness of emotions is simply to stop for a moment so that we can effectively deal with the emotion. Taking a moment to stop is crucial for ensuring that the emotion doesn't escalate.

If another person is the perceived cause of the anger, this step is even more important. As long as we continue to see or interact with the perceived cause of the anger, we are only adding fuel to the fire. To have any chance of allowing the fire of anger to burn out, we clearly must not continue to add fuel to it.

When we continue to interact with the perceived cause of the anger, it is as though our house is burning down and instead of putting the fire out and saving our home, we focus on the cause of the fire. Unfortunately, by doing this, whether we discover and deal with the cause of the fire is meaningless because we would have nothing to return home to but a pile of burning ash. Clearly, the wise thing to do would be to first give our attention to the fire that is destroying our home and then, only after the fire has been taken care of, think about the cause of that fire.

Whenever possible, we should physically remove ourselves from the situation that gave rise to the anger. If we are interacting with another person, we can tactfully excuse ourselves by smiling and saying, "Please excuse me for a moment. I need to step out. Let's resume in about 5 minutes."

It is also very important that we refrain from speaking or acting while angry, other than to calmly remove ourselves from the perceived cause of the anger, because we have little or no conscious control over our actions or speech while the fight-or-flight response is engaged. If that automatic response has not yet completely faded away, our actions and speech are likely to do much more harm than good and to create even more problems.

Anger and other unpleasant emotions are not bad in and of themselves. For instance, the arising of anger can sometimes be a good indication that there is a real problem that needs to be dealt with. Although the arising of anger is certainly not necessary to recognize and deal with problems, the energy that anger brings to the mind and body can actually be used to help us do so.

However, to make use of the energy that anger brings to the mind and body in a way that is helpful rather than harmful, we must first allow the anger to be transformed into a more pleasant emotion and be firmly rooted in mindfulness. Once the anger has transformed, we can use the energy present in the mind and body to find rational, helpful solutions to any problems that need to be dealt with. In many cases, though, we will realize that there wasn't any real problem at all and that we simply overreacted to a situation. In those instances we will be especially grateful that we refrained from acting or speaking while angry.

STEP 2: C = CONTROL THE BREATH AND NAME THE EMOTION

Anger, and most of the other unpleasant emotions, are variations of the fight-or-flight response, which results from increased activation of the sympathetic nervous system (that system is almost always slightly active during our waking lives). The more active the sympathetic nervous system, the more the body releases hormones, such as adrenaline, norepinephrine, and cortisol (during prolonged activation), which result in the physical effects in the body, such as increased heart rate, shallow breathing, tightness, and perhaps even sweating.

The second step of the practice of mindfulness of emotions is to stop the fight-or-flight response from escalating any further and help it begin diminishing. There are two highly effective tools for stopping and reversing the fight-or-flight response. Each one can stop and reverse the response on its own. Together, they can be very powerful.

The first tool is to consciously control an autonomic function of the body, such as the breath. We simply intentionally slow down our breathing and breathe a little more deeply. As simple as this sounds, it is well known that consciously controlling the breathing quickly stops and even reverses the fight-or-flight response.

The second tool is using the inner voice to name the emotion that is present. Research conducted at the University of California, Los Angeles, by a neuroscientist named Matthew Lieberman and colleagues showed that naming the emotion present, which the authors call "affect labeling," interrupts amygdala activity, which is the part of the brain largely responsible for unpleasant emotions, while increasing activity in an area of the prefrontal cortex that is associated with the regulation of emotion. The results offer a possible explanation, at the neurobiological level, of how naming an emotion tends to reduce emotional reactivity.[2]

These two powerful tools—controlling the breath and naming the emotion—can be combined to become a super tool for short-circuiting the fight-or-flight response and allowing us to return to a positive emotional state more quickly.

The moment that we've ceased to interact with the perceived cause of the anger, we can begin to intentionally slow and deepen our breathing while naming the emotion. The practice could be something like this:

On the in breath: *There is anger.*

On the out breath: *I take care of the anger.*

The attitude of caring can be very helpful. It's perfectly natural for anger to arise. It happens to even the most saintly of people. Instead of judging ourselves when anger is present, we can simply recognize that it's okay for anger to arise and that we can have the attitude of caring for that anger just as we would care for another person who is dear to us.

We stay with Step 2 until we've noticed that the emotion is deescalating. In some instances, this may take only a couple of breaths. In other instances, we may need to practice with Step 2 for a couple of minutes before we can actually notice that the fight-or-flight response has been short-circuited.

STEP 3: I = INVESTIGATE THE EMOTION LIKE A MAD SCIENTIST

For most emotions, this step will be all that's necessary. Whether we're starting with Step 3 or we experienced some variation of the fight-or-flight response and are arriving here after Step 2, we do not need to control the breath with Step 3. We can just let the body breathe on its own and allow awareness of the body breathing to be our foundation for mindful self-awareness.

With Step 3 of the practice of mindfulness of emotions, we take an entirely different approach to an emotion such as anger. Instead of ignoring anger and pretending we're not angry, or fueling the anger by dwelling on negative thinking, we simply investigate the anger with curiosity, much like a mad scientist who is researching anger as it exists in his or her own body.

Once we've created some space and we have a bit of solitude, we can mentally note:

With the in breath: *There is anger.*

With the out breath: *What is anger like in the body?*

With this curious attitude we simply notice, nonjudgmentally, how anger manifests itself physically in the body. We may notice increased heart rate, shallower breathing, tense muscles in various places, butterflies in the stomach, or sweaty palms. We allow the physical manifestations of anger to be there and notice how they change with each in breath and out breath.

It can also be helpful to notice neutral sensations that have nothing to do with the emotion, such as the sensation of the feet touching the ground or the sit bones on a chair. The real-world information that we're receiving in the present moment most likely poses no threat at this point, so it helps us be free from the emotion.

This shift to being mindfully self-aware and investigating the anger can seem like absolute magic. It allows the emotion to unwind fairly quickly and helps us remove the more direct cause of the anger: being caught in our thinking.

Without mindfulness, emotions can escalate quickly and intensely, as follows. Something happens that triggers an emotion such as anger. The anger tends to fuel our thinking, which moves increasingly quickly and sucks us into the enticing drama it creates. That thinking then further stirs the pot of anger stew, strengthening the emotional response in the body. The two can continue to feed each other for hours and can result in a very strong emotional reaction.

By investigating anger in the body as it breathes in and out, we can stabilize awareness so that it is not pulled into the thinking that fuels the anger. As long as we're not caught up in the thinking that fuels the anger, the anger isn't getting the fuel it needs to persist and continues to unwind.

As the anger unwinds, the thoughts that fuel the anger start to settle down a bit. This makes it easier to stabilize awareness and thus see thoughts more objectively. We might even be able to smile at them. As we realize more and more space around the thinking, the anger unwinds even further. The escalation process we discussed above is now going in the complete opposite direction. The anger deescalates and can pass away fairly quickly.

Of course, it is quite likely that the thinking that fuels the anger will return soon and probably numerous times. But each time, we can simply apply Step 3 until awareness is stable and the emotion passes.

My favorite example of seeing this in action occurred while helping a friend of mine. She was quite upset, crying with moderate intensity. I guided her through this process for a few minutes, helping her create a solid foundation of awareness of her body breathing and the physical sensations of the sadness. Soon, she was no longer caught in the thinking that had been fueling her sadness.

About 3 or 4 minutes after beginning to practice mindfulness of emotions, her tears had slowed down. I noticed one starting to fall down her cheek and asked her what the tear felt like as it fell. She smiled. The tear touched her lip, and her smile grew. With her next out breath, she actually laughed. She was totally free in that moment.

In addition to helping us be free from unpleasant emotions such as anger right in the present moment, this practice of investigating emotions also has the nice side effect of helping us become much more aware of even very subtle physical sensations that result from the anger. The more aware we are of the subtle clues that let us know that anger is starting to arise, the easier it is to take care of the emotion before it escalates.

After practicing with Step 3 until the anger has been transformed, and our awareness is fairly stable, it is probably safe for us to return to interact with the person or situation that gave rise to the anger. However, if we have a few extra moments before we need to return, we could take those moments to immediately practice with Step 4.

STEP 4: L = LOOK DEEPLY

Once we are aware that the anger has been transformed, it is safe to investigate the causes of the anger. In fact, it is quite important that we do so. Each time anger arises because of a specific type of situation, there is at least some change in the brain that makes it more likely that anger will arise again whenever we encounter similar situations.

By looking deeply into the causes of anger and cultivating under-standing, we can prevent unhelpful changes in the brain, thereby reducing and potentially eliminating the likelihood that similar events will give rise to anger in the future. If, while looking into the causes of anger, we feel the emotion of anger arise even slightly, we should return to Step 3, mindfully investigating the anger until it fades once again.

When a person or event gives rise to anger, most of us perceive that person or event to be the sole cause of the anger. Deep inside we know better, but anger distorts our perspective severely. If we look deeply into any person or situation, we discover that there is never only one cause that gives rise to that person's actions or to an event but numerous causes and conditions.

For example, I once learned of a man who sat on a subway train and opened his paper, hoping to have a nice, quiet commute home. Within a few moments, he noticed two children running around. They were very loud and they repeatedly bumped into the man's newspaper. Each time the kids yelled out or bumped into his newspaper, the man felt his anger getting stronger and stronger.

Finally, the man reached a point where he couldn't take it anymore. He put his paper down and said quite angrily to the man who he assumed was the children's father, "Would you mind doing something about your kids? They are out of control!"

The other man took a few seconds to awaken from the daze he appeared to be in. He replied, "Huh? What did you say?"

The first man said, "Your kids are out of control and they're annoying the hell out of me. Would you mind doing something?"

The second man replied, "Oh, I'm so sorry. I hadn't noticed. I'm a bit out of it. We just came from the hospital. My wife just died."

The man with the newspaper surely would have reacted to the situation quite differently had he known from the beginning about the other man's wife. By having a broader understanding of the situation, instead of responding with anger, he likely would have responded with sympathy and compassion for the man who just lost his wife.

Of course, most of the events that give rise to anger do not have such simple explanations. Most situations require us to look deeply to see the causes and conditions that gave rise to the event. For instance, let's imagine that a man strikes us with a stick. Only a complete fool would get angry with the stick. This is because we can see that the stick is not the cause of the blow that we received but the man who swung the stick. Now, let's ponder, What caused the man to hit us?

Perhaps the man injured his brain in some way that caused him to do something he would never otherwise do. In that case, it would be just as foolish to be angry with the man as it is to be angry with the stick. In fact, we might even have compassion for the man and try to help him treat his injury.

Of course, in most cases, the situation will be even more complex. But the causes and conditions are there, and the same logic applies. Perhaps the man was raised in a culture of violence that conditioned him to be violent as well. He has worked hard to become a nice, nonviolent person, but today he had an absolutely terrible day. So, when we came along and bumped into him in a way that appeared to him to be deliberate, it was the last straw that he could bear and he snapped. Because he lacks mindfulness, he reacted unconsciously in anger, followed his programming, and struck us with the stick.

If we were to look very, very deeply, we would discover that there are literally an infinite number of causes and conditions that led to the man striking us with a stick. His bad day was the result of several things going wrong, each of which was the result of other causes and conditions. The man's violent reaction was also due in part to his violent upbringing. His parents were violent because that's how they were raised. They were raised that way because of certain causes and conditions, and so on for ages into the past.

Of course, this doesn't mean that there shouldn't be consequences for our actions. There certainly should be. A person who is violent may very well need to be removed from society for a time for the benefit of everyone. However, by realizing that there is not just one cause that gives rise to a situation but endless causes and conditions, we see that being angry with the man is just as foolish as being angry with the stick. Both are subject to causes and conditions.

The man's bad decision to hit us with the stick, made in the heat of anger, was only one cause among an infinite number of other causes and conditions. We see that without mindfulness, the man is subject to those causes and conditions in the same way the stick is. He's doing only what his brain has been programmed to allow him to do. For all practical purposes, this is no different than his brain having been injured.

We can see that the deeper cause of anger is our narrow perspective, our inability to see the entire picture. What is most important to realize is that when we see with a narrow perspective, and place blame on one cause or condition, we become angry. And, we are the ones who suffer from that anger in terms of poorer performance and unhappiness. Therefore, it is clearly in our best interest to broaden our perspective by looking deeply into reality. In this way, we remove the root cause of harmful emotions, gradually reducing the strength and frequency of such emotions.

One way to practice looking deeply into the cause of anger is to practice trading places with the person whom we perceive to be the cause of the anger. We can imagine ourselves being the other person, having lived her life exactly the way that she did up to the present moment. Although we may not know any details about her life, even a hypothetical life can help us broaden our perspective. We can see that no matter how her life has progressed, if we lacked mindfulness, had her genes, and had lived her life exactly the way that she did until this moment, we would act in the same frustrating way that she has.

Another contemplation, which I have found very powerful and has often brought me to tears, is to imagine the person who has caused difficulty for me as a five-year-old child. With this contemplation, we let go completely of the picture of the person that we currently have in the mind and instead visualize an innocent little child. We see the little child as so precious, full of childlike wonder, joy, and playfulness, and also very tender and easily molded by his or her surroundings. We see this sweet little child being treated in unloving ways that create the neurological foundations for increased fear, sadness, and low self-esteem.

As we look deeply in this way, we can begin to see the person who has caused us difficulty as that precious little child being molded by the world. The adult before us is only a larger version of that young child, a version in which the neural networks for anger, sadness, and low self-esteem have been reinforced and strengthened, resulting in strong tendencies to react negatively to many situations with unhelpful emotions and actions. Those tendencies have likely been transmitted for generations—both genetically and through environmental influence—by people who did not know how to take care of their own difficult emotions. Mindfulness gives us the power to put an end to this cycle.

Looking deeply into the causes of anger in these ways helps us gradually uproot some of the deeper causes of unpleasant emotions. Instead of blaming the stick that struck us, or the man who swung it, we become more aware of the deep root causes of such an event. As our understanding deepens, compassion tends to arise in our hearts more frequently. We begin to see the difficulties of others as our own difficulties.

We also see that the best way to help ourselves is to help others be free from the causes and conditions of difficult emotions. And, because of our broader understanding of the causes and conditions that give rise to actions and events, we are much more likely to be able to effect positive change. By helping us take more positive, meaningful action, the virtues of understanding and compassion can bring great joy and purpose into our lives.

A RIDE ON THE RIVER OF EMOTIONS

As we develop our emotional resilience with the practice of mindfulness, we begin to realize the absolute miracle of being free from the powerful grip of unpleasant emotions. We see that our emotions are just like a rapidly flowing river and sometimes more like powerful, thundering rapids. Without mindfulness, it can often seem as though we are caught in those rapids without even a flotation device. We are barely able to grasp a few precious breaths of air as our heads are continually pulled under the water and pounded relentlessly by the torrents.

However, the practice of mindfulness of emotions provides the lifesaving flotation device that allows us to keep our heads above the water. We can breathe easier as we realize that we are no longer in any danger. In fact, as our insight into the impermanent, flowing nature of emotions matures, strengthening our ability to remain mindful and take care of emotions, mindfulness becomes more like a kayak.

We are no longer afraid of being drowned by the rapids. Rather, we begin to see emotions as a natural part of life that we can ride and maneuver through just as an expert kayaker rides the rapids. We can ride the river of emotions with a fearless smile on our face. We realize a level of self-mastery that few people ever realize, giving us a tremendous advantage for achieving success as leaders and for realizing greater happiness in our lives.

REVIEW QUESTIONS

Using the analysis in this chapter, how much would you estimate unpleasant emotions cost your team each month?

How does mindfulness help significantly reduce the costs associated with being caught in unpleasant emotions?

How would you summarize each of the four steps of the practice of mindfulness of emotions?

S -

C -

I -

L -

10

THE WISDOM OF TRUE EXCELLENCE

Practicing mindfulness of emotions, as we discussed in the last chapter, allows us to be free from the grip of unpleasant emotions as they're occurring in the present moment. Step 4 of the practice also helps us begin the work of removing the deeper causes of unpleasant emotions. In the next two chapters, we'll explore some very special wisdom that can gradually remove the root cause of all unpleasant emotions.

This special wisdom also helps us remove the root cause of our habitual tendency to constantly veer from being mindfully self-aware toward being our thinking mind and the ego it creates. To develop this special wisdom, it is very, very helpful to practice mindfulness training while sitting still. This wisdom does not arise without stable inner awareness.

To develop the wisdom that is the foundation of leadership and personal excellence, we need to apply the stable and powerful awareness we develop in our daily practice toward the effort to investigate what we experience. When we investigate our experience with stable awareness, we discover the root cause of our habitual tendency to become the thinking mind and its ego. That root cause is a slight misunderstanding about how our world exists and how we operate in it.

THINGS AREN'T AS THEY SEEM

Perhaps the most intellectually intriguing aspect of mindfulness training is what happens when we investigate reality very closely. Gradually, this investigation leads to the realization that reality may be a little different than how we perceive it in our daily lives. In a way, reality is much like a two-sided coin.

On one side of the coin, there is the idea, created by our brain, that we are somehow separate from the world around us. This is actually a natural and important part of our cognitive development. We need to see the world in this way to communicate and even survive as a species. If we couldn't distinguish the separation between ourselves and the world around us—an ability even an amoeba apparently has—we wouldn't survive very long.

However, the idea of separation is only a conventional truth. As modern science has made very clear, there is another side of the coin that most people can grasp intellectually but very few ever directly realize. This is the side of interconnection, or interdependence, the truth that ultimately no thing is fundamentally separate from the world around it.

Imagine for a moment that you could see everything from the perspective of the nucleus of an atom. All you would see is vast empty space with tiny little bits of energy moving at incredible speeds, continuously flashing into and out of existence. You wouldn't be able to tell where a human body ends and the floor begins. You wouldn't be able to find objective separation between anything other than the little particles that make up atoms.

Quantum physics, the most successful physical theory created to date, suggests in many ways that even the tiny particles that we perceive as the discrete building blocks of matter are actually not separate either. An electron, for instance, is at once both a particle and a wave, and is not generally thought of as a discrete thing until it as actually measured. In a way, we create the electron as a separate particle via our effort to measure it.

As the well-known theoretical physicists David Bohm and Basil Hiley wrote, "Parts are seen to be in immediate connection, in which their dynamic relationships depend, in an irreducible way, on the state of the whole system. . . . Thus, one is led to a new notion of unbroken wholeness which denies the classical idea of analyzability of the world into separate and independently existent parts."[1] Much of quantum physics points to the truth that, ultimately, separateness is indeed an illusion.

Although it's a very complicated process, neuroscientists are starting to develop a good idea of how the illusion of a separate self is created in the brain.[2] If you'd like to learn more about how the sense of self is created, you might enjoy the book *The Self Illusion: How the Social Brain Creates Identity*, written by a neuroscientist named Dr. Bruce Hood, who is the director of the Bristol Cognitive Development Centre at the University of Bristol and a former research fellow at Cambridge University and University College London and professor at Harvard University.

Here's the problem. Most of us only ever see one side of the coin, the illusion of separateness. This is not to say that we are hallucinating, which means that we are seeing something that nobody else sees. No, we are seeing the same illusion that fools nearly every human on this planet. Below is an example of such an illusory perception.

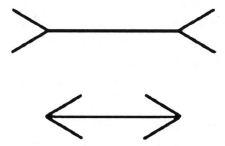

Nearly every person in the world perceives the top line in this example to be longer than the bottom line. However, when we measure the two lines, we see that in fact they are exactly the same length.

Because of the way our brain works, though, we still perceive the top line to be longer than the bottom one even after we have confirmed that the two lines are equal in length. The difference is that after measuring, we know better. We are no longer fooled by our illusory perception.

In the same way that we incorrectly see the top line in the example as being longer than the bottom one, the way that we perceive the world in general is also incorrect. We perceive everything we see as separate and distinct entities. Most important for our discussion here on the root cause of our tendency to operate from the perspective of being the thinking mind and the ego it creates is our perception that the mind and body are separate from the rest of the world.

This is another perceptual illusion created by the brain. Unfortunately, because of a slight misunderstanding about how reality actually exists, that illusory perception fools us. We feel very strongly that the mind and body are ultimately *me* or *mine* and fundamentally separate from the rest of the world.

Just as without a ruler we'll swear up and down that the top line in the diagram is longer than the bottom one, without closely examining reality we'll swear that the mind and body constitute a permanent, separate self. As a result, for most of our lives, we have been clinging to every part of that self—the body, sensations, thoughts, feelings, desires, and memories, collectively known as the ego—as being what we ultimately are.

This has resulted in a very strong habitual tendency to cling to and become all aspects of the body and mind. This habitual tendency compels us to cling to the thinking mind as our default mode of being, even when we're putting forth great effort to become and remain mindfully self-aware. The root of this whole process is our slight misunderstanding about how reality actually exists.

What would happen if we corrected this misunderstanding? What if we could see both sides of the coin of reality? What if we could see the world of separateness and operate in that world just like any other normal person in our daily lives but were no longer fooled by that illusion? What if we could see very clearly that ultimately, the mind and body are not a permanent, separate self?

When we realize this truth deeply enough, we remove the root cause of our habitual tendency to cling to and become the thinking mind and its ego: the mistaken identification with the body and mind as ultimately being what we are. This wisdom is what can allow us to eventually have the ability to remain mindfully self-aware as long as we wish.

AN INCREDIBLE DISCOVERY

Each one of us has a deep sense that there is some type of permanent, separate self that persists throughout our lives on Earth and perhaps even after the body dies. For instance, if we look at a picture of ourselves when we were five years old, we would surely identify the person in the photo as being *me*. We would say, "Yep, that's me. I was five then."

But that picture is of a little five-year-old. The mind, the body, and the personality have all changed dramatically since the age of five. Obviously, the physical body changes over the span of a human life. After leaving the womb, there is infancy, childhood, adolescence, adulthood, and then a slow process of decline, when the body wrinkles, hair turns gray or falls out, and so on. Not so obvious, though, is the fact that the body is changing every second. Each second millions of cells die and are replaced by new ones.

It is true that some cells don't die very quickly and may actually live for many years. In fact, some neurons are believed to live for the entire life span of the body. However, every one of the cells in our bodies is undergoing a constant process of change as the cell continuously replenishes and rebuilds itself with new food, water, and air. Each cell, and thereby our entire body, is like a portion of a continuously flowing river that appears to have a fixed shape but actually never consists of the same material for two consecutive seconds.

Although the body is continuously dying and being reborn in every moment (and perhaps, according to many quantum physicists, many, many times per second at the subatomic level), let's consider the generalization that the body is completely new every seven years, which is based on the average life span of the cells that make up the body. In other words, the body dies and is replaced by a completely new one every seven years. Thus, if we are 57 years old, we have already died eight times, and we are on our ninth new body.

We can reach two rather amazing conclusions from this simple understanding. First, the death of the body is nothing to fear. We've already experienced it numerous times. Second, the body is obviously not ultimately *me* or *mine*.

Returning to the thought of us identifying with the five-year-old in the picture, we can likely recall at least one vivid memory from that time. If we can bring this memory somewhat clearly into the mind, we can almost feel ourselves living that moment. It feels as though we really were that five-year-old, whose mind and body produced all sorts of thoughts and feelings that we could watch arise and pass away just as we do now.

Yet not one single piece of cellular matter—and thereby not one single cell—that makes up the body we call *me* today was there experiencing that moment we remember from when we were five.[3] Thus, neither our current brain, eyes, ears, nor anything else was there.

At this point we face a very interesting question. If not one single piece of cellular matter that makes up the body we call *me* today was there experiencing that moment when we were five, what was? In other words, what is it that observed the physical body and its thoughts and feelings undergo constant change when we were five, that is observing a completely new body and its thoughts and feelings arise and pass away now, and will be observing a completely new body that will feel like *me* when we are 20 years older?

✦

YOU'RE NOT WHAT YOU THINK

Most people seem to have at least a modicum of wisdom regarding the truth that the physical body as it exists here on planet Earth is not ultimately what we are. We identify with the body to some degree, but not entirely. We refer to the body as "my body," as though there is a self inside the body that is the owner of the body. In fact, many of us spend so much time in our heads that we've become quite disassociated with our bodies. As Sir Ken Robinson noted in his excellent first Technology, Entertainment, Design (TED) Talk, we often think of our bodies simply as the vehicles needed for "getting [our] heads to meetings."[4]

Most of us are fooled much more by our thinking than by our bodies. We tend to identify very strongly with our thinking, especially the voice inside our heads (or, for some of us, the various voices) and the sense of self, or ego, that the thinking mind creates. Intellectually, most of us know that we are not the thinking mind and the ego it creates. We know that thoughts are created by the brain, and that if there is no brain, there is no thinking. Nevertheless, we still live as though we are that voice in our heads that is constantly talking, analyzing, judging, criticizing, and so on. With mindfulness training, we can transform the intellectual understanding that we're not the thinking mind into *wisdom*.

For example, imagine that you are operating from the perspective of mindful self-awareness and you are observing the mind. Imagine that it is completely empty of thought (I know that sounds impossible, but it's actually quite common with extensive practice, especially when that is not made to be a goal). Now imagine that you observe a single thought arise in the mind. Perhaps it's an image of the cover of the best book you've ever read, *The Mindfulness Edge*. You see this image quite clearly. Then you see the image gradually dissolve, leaving you to observe a mind that is completely empty again.

Assuming you could do this, what does the observation tell you about your relationship to that thought?

The experience above shows us quite clearly that we are not our thinking. We were there observing an empty mind, we were there as we watched a thought arise and pass away, and we were still there after the thought had disappeared. The thought, then, is a fleeting phenomenon. It is not a permanent part of us.

It is also possible to notice this truth with the form of thinking that occurs as the voice in the mind. With training, that voice can go silent at times. We can rest in mindful self-awareness listening to a completely quiet mind, we can hear a thought arise, and we can hear it cease, leaving us once again listening to a completely silent mind.

Taking this a step further, it is quite clear that we are not the mind, the backdrop for thinking, either. We can observe the mind quite objectively, as though we're watching a television. We can know when the mind is empty and when it contains thought. The perception of this objective observation of the mind can seem like "The mind is over there, and I'm observing it from over here."[5]

These experiments, much like the thought experiment above involving the body, often raise some deep questions, such as "What was there observing things happen when I was five?" "What's observing the body and mind constantly change now?" "What is a permanent part of me?" and "Who am I?" I apologize, but these questions are not possible to answer with words and concepts. The aspect of ourselves that is aware of the body and mind transcends the mind and the words and concepts the brain creates. What we are ultimately is something we can truly know only through our own direct experience.

Because I am not a fan of disappointing people, I will share some really good news. By simply *being* mindful and self-aware, and seeing clearly what you are not, what you *are* gradually becomes increasingly clear. At some point, it becomes so clear that you will just *know*. You will not be able to describe it either, but you will certainly know how to *be* it. You will realize that you have been *being* it quite often.[6]

The most important aspect of this wisdom we are exploring, in terms of developing leadership excellence, including unconditional happiness, is to discover through our own direct experience that *we are clearly not the thinking mind*. This simple little insight—*I am not the thinking mind*—is actually incredibly powerful. The deeper this insight becomes, the less power the thinking mind and the ego have to suck us in. We continue to develop the sense that the thinking mind and whatever passes through it are over there, so to speak, like a heads-up display we can see out of the corner of the eye, and we're over here, observing the heads-up display we call the mind, much like the image in Figure 10.1 that was first introduced in Chapter 1.

We see whatever arises in the mind from a completely objective, third-person vantage point. As a result, we don't habitually cling to and become the thinking mind. If our wisdom were to become deep enough, we could reach a point where we are never pulled out of mindfulness by the thinking mind. We would be able to remain objectively self-aware as long we like, under even the most challenging situations.

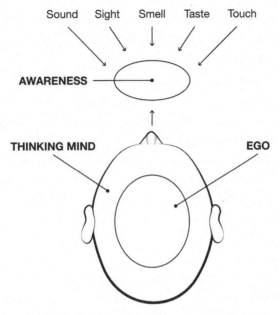

Figure 10.1   An Objective View of the Thinking Mind

Neuro Note 10.1: Mindfulness and an Objective View of the Self

As we have seen in Neuro Note 1.1, our minds are wandering quite often.[7] This state is characterized by self-generated and self-related thoughts[8] and related to a biased view.[9] In the brain this state of mind wandering is associated with activation in midline structures of the default mode network (DMN).[10]

As discussed in Neuro Note 1.3, mindfulness is related to a shift from this self-referential, mind-wandering modus to a more objective modus of being. Studies have shown that mindfulness training is associated with reduced mind wandering,[11] reduced bias,[12] and reduced brain activation in the DMN.[13]

Indeed, mindfulness is related to increased present-moment awareness, in particular of body sensations,[14] and increased brain activation and gray matter in the insula,[15] which is involved in body awareness.[16]

This insight is also the key to developing greater freedom from our conditioning and habits. As this wisdom that we are not our thinking becomes deeper, we recognize our conditioning and habits more quickly. We can eventually learn to objectively see our conditioned, habitual reactions to stimuli as they are arising, in the moment. It's as though there is more space around the thinking mind, ego, and conditioned reactions, somewhat like what we see in the image above. This is the highly revered "space between stimulus and response" that gives us the freedom to choose our response, which Dr. Stephen R. Covey has called "the greatest power" we can develop.

This space creates an effect that is somewhat like the difference between being in the same room with really loud, annoying music and hearing that same music from two miles away. When we're in the same room, the music has a lot of power to affect our emotions and actions. When the music is two miles away, it is barely audible and has no power over us. It doesn't bother us at all. With enough space around our conditioned thinking mind and ego, they have no power over us either.

WISDOM VERSUS KNOWLEDGE

It's very important that we move beyond the intellectual understanding that we're not the thinking mind and develop insight into that truth, which is wisdom. Intellectual understanding alone has very little effect on behavior and real-world, applicable skills. The difference between intellectual understanding and insight is simply a matter of experience.

For instance, let's imagine that you have two friends who have offered to give you a ride in their sports cars on curvy mountain roads. One friend, Joe, has read 125 books on the subject of driving a car and written his own book on how to drive a car. By Western standards, he would likely be called an expert on driving. However, Joe has never actually driven a car.

Samantha, on the other hand, has received only a brief explanation of driving from an experienced driver and has never read a book on how to drive a car. However, she has been driving every day for 15 years, including time as an amateur racecar driver, and she's never had an accident.

Whom would you rather ride with?

Clearly, riding with Samantha is the better choice. Although, intellectually, Joe understands quite well how to drive a car, he does not *know* how to drive a car. The actual experience of driving a car is different than the theory he has read. You may want to learn about the theory of driving from Joe, but if you're in a car on a curvy road, you would definitely prefer Samantha be behind the wheel.

The moment Samantha actually began driving a car, her intellectual understanding transformed into wisdom. There was an insight that arose within her: "Ah. . . . So this is what driving a car is like. I get it now."

Of course, the insight that arose from the first experience of driving a car was not yet very mature. There were still many aspects of driving a car that she had not yet directly experienced. But, as she continued to drive, her wisdom gradually became deeper. This wisdom is what gives us confidence in her car-driving skills.

In the same way, the more often and the more deeply we see through our own awareness that we are not the thinking mind and its ego, the more wisdom we develop and the greater the impacts we will see on our personal and professional performance.

THE INTERPLAY BETWEEN STABLE AWARENESS AND WISDOM

What we find with continued mindfulness training, both in our daily lives and while sitting still, is that there is a deep interconnection between wisdom and our ability to remain mindfully self-aware without being distracted by and pulled into the thinking mind. The more stable awareness is, the deeper the insight we have into the truth that we are not the thinking mind. With training, awareness becomes like a much brighter light with which to see our inner world.

This is somewhat similar to observing an object at night with a very bright, focused spotlight versus relying only on the light of the stars and moon. We see the object much more clearly with the spotlight, just as we see our inner world with greater clarity when we've trained awareness to be more stable in the present moment. This increased clarity in turn results in deeper insight.

The deeper the insight into the fact that we are not the thinking mind and its ego, the easier it is to remain mindfully self-aware without being distracted by and pulled into the thinking mind. The more easily we can remain mindfully self-aware, the more rapidly wisdom develops.

Wisdom and stable awareness continue to feed each other in this way, which results in the personal and professional benefits discussed in this book. Gradually, we are better able to realize mindful self-awareness on demand, anytime we like, with less effort. Eventually, mindful self-awareness can become our default mode of being.

REVIEW QUESTIONS

How would you describe, in a few sentences, the root cause of our habitual tendency to become the thinking mind instead of being mindfully self-aware?

How does mindfulness training allow us to gradually end our habitual tendency to become the thinking mind instead of being mindfully self-aware?

How would you describe the relationship between sustained mindful self-awareness and the development of wisdom?

11

EXTRAORDINARY LEADERSHIP PRESENCE AND THE FINAL PIECE OF THE PUZZLE OF UNCONDITIONAL HAPPINESS

The wisdom we discussed in Chapter 10 helps us realize every benefit for leadership excellence that we've discussed in this book, including unconditional happiness and extraordinary leadership presence, which are what we'll focus on in this chapter.

In Chapter 7, we discussed how simply by being free from comparative thinking, we can realize happiness during simple, mundane moments that make up the vast majority of our lives, at least for most people reading this book. But what about the times when life is really challenging?

When we're beginning our practice, there will be many, many moments when we revert back to our habitual tendency to cling to and be pulled around by unpleasant thoughts and emotions. We will still suffer. This suffering may arise as dissatisfaction during rather simple, neutral moments. In more challenging situations or when the pull of our thoughts and feelings is a bit stronger, we may experience varying degrees of other unpleasant mind states and emotions.

In very challenging situations, during the times in our lives that are not so neutral, when life is painful emotionally or physically, or when we're really pulled around by our thoughts and emotions, we can experience absolute mental and emotional anguish. We cannot leave out these more extreme moments of our lives. Although these moments may constitute only about five percent of life, they are part of the miracle of being human, and we can live them without having to suffer. Being skillful in how we deal with these more difficult periods of life is a key part of our effectiveness as leaders and our effectiveness in our personal lives.

To deal with the very difficult periods of life with cool, confident leadership presence, and to reach our potential to realize unconditional happiness in every moment, to be totally free from suffering, it is helpful to understand and cultivate an additional level of the wisdom we discussed in Chapter 10. This level of wisdom consists of some simple yet miraculously liberating insights into the causes of suffering. When we fully understand that suffering has a clearly identifiable cause, it becomes obvious that there is a way out.

When we remove oxygen from a fire, that fire is extinguished. In the same way, when we remove the root causes of suffering, we realize the perfection of the present moment. We realize complete satisfaction and peace. These insights into the cause of suffering—and the way out of it—result in the gradual liberation from every problem or fear that we could possibly imagine.

Pain Is Inevitable; Suffering Is Optional

Before we discuss the cause of suffering, we may want to investigate it a bit and pinpoint exactly what suffering really is. Of course, you might be thinking, "Who doesn't know what suffering is?" Everyone knows what suffering is, right? It's pain! Although at first this may appear to be only a matter of semantics, when we look more closely, we see that there is a clearly discernible difference between pain and suffering.

Pain is inevitable. As long as we are alive in a body with a properly functioning nervous system, we are going to experience pain to some degree. However, suffering, our negative reactivity to the pain, is quite optional. We can cultivate the ability to experience pain, both emotional and physical, without suffering.

The sensory nature of pain and the subjective nature of suffering become clear when we observe two people experiencing the same painful stimulus, such as touching something hot. When these two people touch the hot object, they both experience pain.

Although the painful stimulation is identical for both people, the degree to which they suffer may be quite different. Person one may be having a terrible day, be totally consumed by his negative thinking, and be very tense as a result. Thus, after burning his hand, he starts yelling profanity while he clutches his hand as though he is experiencing the worst pain imaginable. He suffers a great deal. On a pain scale where 10 is the worst pain, he might report pain of eight or nine.

Conversely, person two may be having a great day (perhaps she practices mindfulness—hint, hint). Her mind is collected and she is free of anxiety and tension. After she burns herself, she simply looks at her finger to assess the damage, sees that there isn't anything but a red mark, and calmly goes about what she is doing. Despite experiencing the exact same sensation as person one, she might report a one on the pain scale. She suffers very little, or not at all.

Neuro Note 11.1: Mind State Affects Pain Perception

It is well known that our state of mind affects how we experience pain. For example, in 2010 neuroscientist Chantal Berna and colleagues from Oxford University investigated how negative mood affects the experience of painful heat stimulation to the forearm. When participants were in a bad mood due to reading negative statements, such as "I feel worthless," and listening to sad music, they rated the pain as more unpleasant. In the brain this increase in pain was associated with increased brain activations in a wide network, including pain- and emotion-related brain regions, such as the insula and the amygdala.[1]

Thus, we can see that if pain doesn't bother us, we don't suffer. For instance, using an extreme example, let's imagine that we are tied down to a table and there is a giant, red-hot piece of metal being placed on our skin. This is very painful. However, imagine that despite the pain we feel, we have the ability to lie there and watch the metal touch our skin without it bothering us at all. We just calmly watch with a smile, enduring the pain, as though the metal were touching the table.

Because the pain doesn't bother us at all, there's no problem, is there? There is no suffering. Thus, we can see that suffering is a subjective phenomenon created in the mind. Suffering is struggling with, or being bothered by—experiencing varying degrees of dissatisfaction, stress, or anguish—what we experience.

Neuro Note 11.2: How Mindfulness Facilitates a Reduction in Suffering

Pain research with experienced mindfulness practitioners supports the argument that pain is inevitable but suffering is optional and that through mindfulness you can opt out of the latter. At the behavioral level, several studies have shown that during a state of mindfulness, experienced mindfulness practitioners perceive pain as less unpleasant but not as less intense. That is, the sensory aspect of pain is unchanged, while the emotional aspect of pain, the suffering aspect, is reduced.[2]

In the brain a matching pattern of brain activity is observed: Experienced mindfulness practitioners have increased brain activation in brain regions that process the sensory aspects of pain, including the posterior insula and the thalamus, but decreased brain activity in cognitive, evaluative, and regulative brain regions, including the lateral prefrontal cortex.[3] In addition, neuroscientist Joshua Grant and colleagues reported decreased functional connectivity between the dorsal anterior cingulate cortex and the lateral prefrontal cortex, regions that are involved in pain processing and cognitive evaluative and regulative processes, respectively.[4] This pattern suggests bottom-up processing.

On the contrary, short-term mindfulness practitioners typically show reduced pain unpleasantness *and* pain intensity.[5] In the brain, the activation pattern of pain reduction in beginning mindfulness practitioners is quite the opposite of that of experienced mindfulness practitioners and includes decreased brain activation in regions involved in processing the sensory aspects of pain, including the primary somatosensory cortex, and increased activation in cognitive, regulatory brain regions, including the lateral prefrontal cortex.[6] This brain activation pattern suggests top-down processing.

We have seen this pattern of top-down control in beginning mindfulness practitioners and bottom-up processing in experienced practitioners previously in the emotion regulation study of Véronique Taylor and colleagues (Neuro Note 9.1).[7]

As neuroscientist Joshua Grant stated when discussing the research cited in Neuro Note 11.2 in an interview for *Scientific American* with Tom Ireland, "It seems [mindfulness] practitioners were able to remove or lessen the [aversion to] the stimulation—and thus the stressing nature of it—by altering the connectivity between two brain regions which are normally communicating with one another. They certainly don't seem to have blocked the experience. Rather, it seems they refrained from engaging in thought processes that make it painful."[8]

Of special note in the research discussed above is the fact that the mindfulness practitioners were not making any special effort to achieve some peaceful state of mind. The research suggests that their brains have been rewired in a way that changes their perception of pain.

Imagine that you could go through the rest of your life without ever struggling with or being bothered by *anything*. No matter what happens, whether it's physical pain, workplace pressures or crises, or emotional pain, it no longer pulls you from your perspective of mindful self-awareness against your will. You are at peace in the face of even the most challenging moments in life, and you respond skillfully in a way that inspires confidence in everyone around you. This is the ultimate in leadership presence, a quality we saw in First Lieutenant Raymond Beaudoin when his life and the lives of his men were on the line (see Chapter 5). Imagine how effective you could be as a leader if you developed this type of extraordinary presence.

This ability to be at peace under any circumstances—which is also the final piece of the puzzle of unconditional happiness—is a possibility for all of us. It is the fruit of cultivating deep insight into the causes of suffering and the way out. If the idea of developing extraordinary leadership presence and living a deeply satisfying life that is free of suffering sounds appealing, then we should certainly look into why things bother us. To understand the way out of suffering, it is essential that we clearly see exactly how suffering comes about.

A TASTE OF LIBERATION

Although the cause of suffering is actually a sort of chain reaction that involves quite a few steps, this chain of events can be summarized and clearly understood as the immediate cause and the root cause. The immediate cause of suffering is that which immediately precedes the arising of dissatisfaction, stress, or anguish. It's what takes us from a state of satisfaction and peace to states of varying degrees of misery. This immediate cause of suffering is *a lack of space around a desire.*

To understand how this lack of space around a desire results in suffering, let's consider two examples that encompass the three types of experience—unpleasant, neutral, and pleasant. The first example involves the desire to get rid of an unpleasant experience, which is called aversion. In lieu of the extreme example of having a hot piece of metal burn our skin, let's start with something a little more subtle, such as having an itch.

Let's imagine that we are sitting in mindfulness peacefully when a rather noticeable itch arises in the middle of the back. We don't like the itch, which isn't necessarily a problem. It is perfectly natural to dislike something. But if we identify with this feeling of dislike, aversion will arise.

This desire to get rid of what we don't like is also quite natural. Unfortunately, if we don't see the desire objectively and there is no space around it, we condemn ourselves to suffer until we gratify the desire. It's as though we cling to and become the desire, and we are consumed with aversion. The body becomes tense, which strengthens the desire to get rid of the itch, which creates further stress. We will have no peace until we scratch the itch and it is gone once and for all.

Furthermore, because the mind is easily conditioned into habits, clinging to one desire conditions us to cling to and become the next one. Thus, the peace that we realize from scratching is only temporary. When the next itch arises, we'll be stuck right back in suffering again.

In the alternative, let's imagine that the same itch arises. We don't like it. The desire to get rid of it arises. However, instead of clinging to the desire to get rid of the itch and allowing it to take control, we investigate how the mind and body are reacting to it by taking the perspective of mindful self-awareness.

We can start by simply mentally noting the desire: "There is a desire to get rid of the itch." With this simple shift, we see the desire objectively, and some space opens up around it. As we observe the mind and body carefully, we become aware of how desire and the compulsion to act manifest in the body via contracted muscles. We see that by simply becoming aware of the contracted muscles and letting them uncontract, the physical sense of compulsion fades. The desire itself also fades away.

With mindfulness, we realize that if we see the desire to get rid of the itch objectively and have some space around it, there is no problem. We can sit in mindfulness totally at peace with an itch in the middle of the back. When we realize this peace, we also realize a taste of liberation, the cessation of suffering.

The insight arises that when we cling to and become the desire to get rid of something, we suffer and that the suffering ceases as soon as we become mindfully self-aware and investigate how the desire manifests in the body. We also realize that if we simply objectively observe the desire in mindful self-awareness, and allow the physical sense of compulsion in the body to unwind, the desire fades away on its own. We don't have to struggle with or get rid of anything.

Once the desire has ceased, it no longer matters whether we scratch the itch or not. We have peace either way. In this case, since an itch can do us no harm, we can simply leave it be until it fades away on its own. If the sensation that gave rise to the desire to get rid of something was an indicator that harm was about to occur, we could do our best to remedy the situation with greater calm and grace and a clearer mind.

A desire is nothing more than an impulse to take action. Letting go of a desire does not mean that we don't take action. It means that we are not forced to act by the desire, which is what tends to happen when we lack mindfulness. As insight increases the strength of mindfulness in us, freeing us from our tendency to cling to mental phenomena, we develop more space around desires, which gives us the ability to respond to experiences based on wise reflection rather than blindly reacting based on desire. Desires are no longer our masters.

More Fully Enjoying What's Pleasant

Now let's consider an example of how a lack of space around the desire to have a pleasant experience causes suffering. Imagine that we are at work in the afternoon, which is often a relatively neutral experience. We are doing rather monotonous work, such as reviewing some spreadsheet that we don't normally enjoy, but because we are practicing mindfulness, we are actually quite content performing this task.

Suddenly, we remember that we are going to be eating pizza, our favorite food, for dinner tonight. Next, the thought arises: "I really like pizza." If there is no space around this thought, it gives rise to the desire to have the pizza. The mouth begins to water. We really want to have that pizza.

As long as there is no space around the desire to have the pizza, we have condemned ourselves to suffer, haven't we? The work that we were enjoying just a moment ago becomes a tedious obstacle, keeping us from the pleasure that awaits us at dinner. The time cannot pass quickly enough. We are pulled along unconsciously toward the future like a fish on a hook. There is a general feeling of dissatisfaction that won't be alleviated until we eat that pizza. We may think, "Once I get that pizza in my mouth, my life will be complete!"

If for some reason we don't get the pizza we were expecting, we'll be quite upset. It may even put us in a bad mood for the rest of the night. And, unfortunately, even if we do get the pizza, it won't live up to our expectations. The satisfaction that comes from eating pizza is very short-lived.

Also, by clinging to the desire to eat the pizza, we have conditioned the mind to seek happiness by gratifying its desires. Thus, within a short time after eating the pizza, a void will arise that yearns to be filled. This will give rise to the desire for something else. If we don't see that desire objectively and there is no space around it, we will have begun once again the whole process of suffering while waiting to gratify a desire and then being disappointed when gratifying that desire provides only temporary satisfaction.

Instead, let's return to the point where the thought arose of having pizza for dinner. This thought gives rise to thinking, "I really like pizza." This gives rise to the desire to have that pizza. However, when we notice that we're starting to be controlled by the desire to have the pizza, we investigate it by practicing mindfulness.

We can start by simply mentally noting the desire: "There is a desire to eat pizza." This creates some space, allowing us to see the desire objectively, in mindful self-awareness. As we observe the mind and body carefully, we become aware of how clinging to that desire and the resulting compulsion to act manifests in the body via contracted muscles. We see that simply by becoming aware of the contracted muscles and letting them uncontract, the physical sense of compulsion fades.

The space around the desire then gradually increases, allowing the desire to fade away. It may arise again in a few minutes if we lose our mindful perspective of self-awareness, but we just investigate it once more and allow the physical sense of compulsion to unwind, which in turn allows the desire itself to fade away on its own.

By objectively observing the desire with mindful self-awareness, some space opens up around it, and we are immediately freed from the suffering that would have resulted if there were no space around it. Our afternoon of work is now another opportunity to realize complete satisfaction instead of being a tedious obstacle that keeps us from experiencing the pleasure of eating pizza.

Also, we will have peace of mind whether or not we get the pizza. If we get it, fine. If not, no big deal. In fact, we'll most likely enjoy the pizza even more because we'll be more able to be fully present for the experience instead of thinking about what's next while we're eating.

It can be very exciting just to understand the immediate cause of suffering, and how suffering ceases when we become and remain mindfully self-aware and realize the space around the desires that arise within us. If we truly understand these two points, we may see a very bright light at the end of the proverbial tunnel!

We see that by cultivating the ability to recognize desires and ensure there is ample space around them or that they have completely passed before we take action, we can go through the rest of our lives with extraordinary leadership presence and without having to suffer. We can live our lives with peace of mind no matter what life throws at us. Also, we begin to see our suffering as an opportunity to learn how to be liberated. Thus, instead of running away from suffering, we courageously face it head-on and investigate it.

THAT DARN WISDOM AGAIN

However, the excitement that arises when we understand suffering, its cause, and its cessation is a very fleeting feeling. We must go beyond just understanding this as a theory. Because we have been conditioned to cling to our desires for a very long time, we need to practice recognizing desires and letting go of our tendency to cling to them and directly realize the peace and freedom that result when there is some space around a desire. If we only understand a theory about how remaining mindfully self-aware results in peace, we will not go very far in breaking our conditioned habit of clinging.

It's kind of like a person has been carrying a worthless 150-pound piece of iron on his back for his whole life. He thinks that this piece of iron is a prized possession. If we were to tell him that if he only set his piece of iron down, he would realize great peace and ease, he would likely say, "Well, that's a great theory. Maybe I'll try that sometime." But it won't be until he actually puts the piece of iron down that he realizes the peace of letting it go and the foolishness of carrying it around all the time.

In the same way, as we begin to practice investigating suffering when it arises, we will begin to realize directly for ourselves that when we fail to see desires objectively with mindful self-awareness, we suffer. We also see that by mindfully investigating desires, and seeing them objectively, the suffering immediately stops and there are peace and satisfaction instead. The more deeply we realize these insights, the more we will see the foolishness of clinging to desires and the less often we will cling. We will come to see clinging to desires as no different from sticking our hand in a fire. We know that sticking our hand in a fire is very painful, so most of us tend not to go around doing this.

THE ROOT CAUSE OF SUFFERING

Our ability to remain free from the immediate cause of suffering—a lack of space around desires—grows stronger when we remove the deeper root cause of suffering. This root cause of suffering is the same root cause of the habitual tendency to cling to and become the thinking mind and its ego, which we discussed in the previous chapter. The root cause of suffering is the mistaken identification with the body and mind as ultimately being what we are.

Let's look at how correcting this mistaken belief and seeing clearly that the body and mind are not ultimately *me* or *mine* helps us to be free from suffering and thereby realize both extraordinary leadership presence and unconditional happiness. If we realized deeply enough that the mind and body are not ultimately *me* or *mine*, we would no longer be fooled by the perception created by the brain telling us that the mind and body are ultimately what we are. The habitual tendency to identify with the body and mind as ultimately being *me* or *mine* would gradually fade away.

Thus, the chain reaction that leads to suffering could no longer occur. Instead of habitually reverting to the perspective of being the mind and body against our will, we would be able to remain mindfully self-aware. If we had the ability to maintain this perspective of mindfulness whenever we wanted to, we would see the body and the mind objectively, and we would no longer habitually identify with them as ultimately being *me*.

If we don't identify with the body as ultimately being *me* or *mine*, whenever we experience a sensation such as an itch or a thought about having pizza, we do not identify with that sensation as being *me* or *mine* either. There is some space around the sensation, and our perception is less like "I have an itch" and more like "There is an itch." It's almost as though "The itch is over there, and I'm over here observing it happen."

If we don't identify with a sensation as happening to *me*, then a feeling of like or dislike almost certainly doesn't even arise, because a feeling of like or dislike for something depends on some type of personal experience with that thing.[9] If a feeling of like or dislike doesn't arise, then the desires to get something we don't have, hold on to something we do have, or get rid of something, don't arise either. If there is no desire, suffering is not able to arise. The immediate cause of suffering—a lack of space around desire—simply doesn't exist.

When our wisdom is deep enough, we no longer struggle with experience. If we choose to, because we think it's skillful, we can identify with any aspect of the mind and body at any time. But we're no longer forced to do that by our conditioning.

We can operate from the perspective of mindful self-awareness at will, even in very challenging situations, and thereby remain perfectly at peace. We are able to respond to even the most challenging moments in life without all the negative internal garbage that arises when we cling to the thinking mind and its desires. Instead of blindly reacting to our experience based on desires, we respond based on wise reflection and an almost automatic reflex to do what's best for all involved in a given situation. We realize both extraordinary leadership presence and the subtle yet extraordinary happiness that does not depend on anything outside ourselves.

REVIEW QUESTIONS

What is the difference between pain and suffering?

How does freedom from suffering result in extraordinary leadership presence?

How would you describe the immediate cause of suffering?

How does mindfulness training allow you to gradually become free from all suffering?

12

ADVANCED-LEVEL TRAINING

Although the ideas covered in the last two chapters become self-evident to anyone who closely examines our world and how we operate in it, the ideas can appear quite radical because they challenge the status quo view of the world that many of us have held for most of our lives. Some people state that they flat-out disagree with the idea that the mind and body are not ultimately what we are. Ironically, this can actually be a good thing.

These ideas are not meant to become some philosophy that we simply *believe* in. Making a philosophy out of the notion that we are not ultimately the body and mind is not very helpful and can actually be harmful in some cases. Transformation doesn't result from adopting a new philosophy. Transformation is the result of seeing the truth for ourselves. This happens automatically when we look closely at ourselves, and at the world, with sufficiently stable awareness.

The ideas around the wisdom of true excellence were offered not to convince anyone that we should believe something but to help us understand why we should bother to look and see for ourselves that we are not the thinking mind. When we understand the incredible benefits that result from directly realizing that we are not the thinking mind, we have a much greater motivation to develop the wisdom that fuels both leadership and personal excellence.

The exercises offered in this chapter are designed to help you develop the wisdom of true excellence. These exercises are called advanced, not because they are necessarily any more complex than the beginner- and intermediate-level exercises. They are considered advanced because they are not easy to practice without at least some training under our belts. If our awareness has not yet become sufficiently stable, these exercises will not bear much fruit.

However, please don't feel like you must train for years before you can begin practicing with these advanced-level exercises. Although some stability of awareness is certainly required, we don't need to have superpowers of attentional control to develop wisdom. A little bit of stability of awareness can lead to a little bit of wisdom. That little bit of wisdom makes it easier to sustain mindful self-awareness, which in turn makes it easier to develop deeper wisdom.

Whether you feel that you're ready to begin practicing with the advanced-level exercises, you can certainly read this chapter now if you like. Understanding this level of practice can help improve your practice regardless of the level you're currently at.

THE BEST MOVIE EVER

Each of the advanced-level exercises picks up where the last intermediate-level exercise in Chapter 9 left off.

With this first exercise, we're shifting the balance of our awareness. Now, we're going to explore the practice of allowing the mind itself to become the foundation of awareness. Just as with the body breathing, which has been the foundation until now, the idea is not to focus on the mind to the point where we're excluding everything else. We just make the effort to know what's happening in the mind.

Watching the mind for a while is pretty entertaining. It's a lot like a really good movie, but better. In even the best movies, one can often guess what's coming next, which spoils the suspense. With the mind, however, you really never know what's going to come up next. If you approach this exercise with that type of anticipation, it will likely be very easy and enjoyable.

I recommend setting a timer for at least 10 minutes for this exercise. You can start with the intermediate-level exercise, with the following transition about halfway through.

Gradually allow the mental noting of "In" and "Out" to become quieter and quieter in your mind until your inner voice is silent, and you're simply watching the body breathe, aware of the muscles in your body, but still open to whatever passes through your awareness.

You will likely notice that as you maintain this refined awareness of the body breathing, you are also aware of the mind. You may notice that thoughts are among the sensations that pass through your awareness. You may notice that you can observe the mind, without losing awareness of the body breathing, almost as though you are watching a television screen. If you're not sure whether you're aware of the mind, you could mentally question, "Is there any thinking now?" The moment that question is posed, you will likely be quite aware of what's happening in the mind.

For the remainder of this exercise the practice is to keep that attitude alive, "Is there any thinking now?" which allows you to observe and listen to the mind as though you are sitting and watching a movie. You will likely still be subtly aware of the body breathing and other sensations that pass through awareness. This is fine.

In fact, if you find that you are being pulled into your thinking and becoming distracted more often than when the body breathing was the foundation of awareness, you may find it helpful to shift the balance of awareness back to the body for a while, until your awareness is a little more stable. Once you feel fairly stable again, you can explore shifting the balance back to observing the mind with the attitude of "Is there any thinking now?"

Just sit, observe, and listen to the show. Sometimes the mind will be busy. Sometimes it may be pretty quiet and still. There is no good or bad here, no right or wrong. The practice is just to sit, observe, and listen to the show. You're learning to rest in the awareness of the mind.

BRUTAL, COMPASSIONATE HONESTY

This and the subsequent advanced-level practices are all simply variations on advanced-level exercise 1 that will help you work with the body and mind, learn from them, and continue to develop the wisdom of excellence discussed in previous chapters.

During our time sitting still in mindfulness, observing the body and mind, we become increasingly familiar with the incredible richness and variety of thoughts, states of mind, and emotional states. Thoughts can range from wonderfully altruistic to fiercely selfish, from incredibly exciting to truly depressing, and even from epiphanies to useless blabbering about nothing. The list goes on and on. States of mind and emotional states are equally as diverse.

Oftentimes, people who are beginner- or intermediate-level practitioners work to achieve some special state of mind through their mindfulness practice. They've heard about bliss, boundless compassion, or a clear mind, and they want those things. I certainly did when I was at that stage. I wanted all of it. But it is actually this very wanting that keeps us from realizing the true goal.

During our sitting-still practice, it doesn't matter what thought or state is present. It could be lovely. It could be terrible. Our job is simply to recognize what's there with brutal honesty. If a thought arises about serving the homeless, we simply acknowledge it and allow that thought to arise and pass away on its own, without judging it or adding on to it. If a thought arises about slapping an annoying person, we simply acknowledge it and allow that thought to arise and pass away on its own, without judging it or adding on to it (and certainly without acting on it).

The practice is not about achieving some special state. Special states are dependent on conditions that aren't always within our control. The practice is about developing the ability to be free from any struggle with whatever state we're experiencing, or what's happening right now, whether it's pleasant, unpleasant, or neutral. This incredible freedom allows us to experience every aspect of life with peace of mind.

While we're gradually developing the wisdom that results in that freedom from struggle, we can—and should—fake it until we make it, so to speak. During our sitting-still practice, our effort should be to nonjudgmentally recognize whatever is happening right now— pleasant, unpleasant, or neutral—both within us and around us. Then we do that again right now, then right now, and so on. In any moment we can do that, we're no longer struggling with what is happening. We are free.

Over time, we develop the wisdom that these thoughts and states are not *me* or *mine*. We see, through our own experience, that they are phenomena that we can observe arise and pass away. The more clearly we see that, the less effort we have to apply to nonjudgmentally recognize and accept whatever thought or state we're currently experiencing. This ability gradually becomes our natural response to our inner world, as well as the outer world.

The ability to realize the freedom described above starts with brutal honesty. We must learn to be completely honest about whatever thought or state is present—pleasant, unpleasant, or neutral. But this honesty isn't so brutal. It's actually a basis for great compassion.

When we learn to accept whatever is rising within us without judging or trying to get rid of it, we begin to develop compassion for ourselves. We see in a whole new light all those thoughts and mind states that we used to beat ourselves up over. We realize that each one of these thoughts and mind states is just a result of our programming—our genetics and life experiences up to this moment in time—and that each one is completely out of our control. We start to see how much suffering we've created because of our constant self-judgment and self-punishment, and compassion arises. When we can have compassion like this for ourselves, it is much easier to have compassion for others.

INVESTIGATION OF PHENOMENA

As we continue to deepen our advanced practice of being aware of the mind, and seeing it objectively, we are gradually better able to sustain that awareness, and rest in it, without being caught by thinking. This is a good sign that we're ready to begin practicing with an essential element of mindfulness training: investigation of phenomena.

Up to this point, we have likely been pretty passive with how we observe the thoughts that arise in the mind. We simply watch them come and go.

You might notice that sometimes there is a thought pattern, or some variation of it, that comes up multiple times. You might lose your equanimity here and wish for the thought pattern to go away. A powerful antidote to this is to intentionally think that thought and really look closely at it.

With a visual image, it may seem as though you're taking a thought that is kind of on the fringes of awareness, and you're moving it to front and center of awareness, looking right at it. Once you're looking right at it, holding it up to the light of awareness and seeing it objectively, you can stop thinking it intentionally and allow it to just be there until it passes away on its own.

Assuming your awareness is stable, this simple practice can allow you to see the exact instant that a thought ceases in the mind, which results in the insight "The thought is impermanent. It's not what I am." Depending on the level of energy in the mind, you might find that this insight gives rise to a lot of joy. You may also find that the mind then becomes very tranquil and collected, and that you have a deep sense of equanimity toward whatever you're experiencing.

This powerful insight into the truth that we are not our thinking is what gradually chips away at our habitual tendency to cling to our thinking and lose the perspective of mindful self-awareness.

You can apply the same spirit of investigation to the inner voice in your head. If that voice keeps talking, you can intentionally say something in the mind while listening to it. For instance, "This mindfulness stuff is a bunch of crap," "Mindfulness training is the most important thing I can do," "My boss is a big, fat poopy head," or "I have the best boss in the world." Whatever the idea is, say it with some volume (in the mind only, not vocalized), while listening to it, and then really notice the silence once you've completed whatever sentence you say. This can help you hear the voice in your head quite objectively and see very clearly that it is not what you are.

FEARLESSNESS

At first, you may want to practice with the previous exercise of investigating thinking only a couple of times during a session of sitting still in mindfulness. However, as you become more comfortable with the practice, you might find that you are comfortable enough with your stability of mindfulness that you want to investigate many, or even all, of the thoughts that arise during your training session.

When you become more comfortable investigating thoughts in general, you may discover that you are developing a subtle yet powerful sense of fearlessness. You realize that there is nothing that comes up in the mind that has any power over you. You see with greater clarity that sense of "The mind (the source of all fear, and all other suffering) is over there, and I'm over here observing it." You see thoughts so objectively—even thoughts that used to provoke fear—that you can smile at their presence.

While the wisdom is developing that allows you to have that type of fearlessness, you can fake it until you make it, just as we discussed in the section above, "Brutal, Compassionate Honesty." If there's a thought hanging around in the mind that you really don't want there, or are perhaps even afraid of, you can bring it up intentionally and look right at it. You then discover that the thought that was causing the fear has absolutely no power over you. It's just a natural part of this show called *Being Human*.

(Note: Although people who have had severe trauma can engage in the exercise described above on their own, I highly recommend that anyone who has experienced such trauma begin this exercise when practicing in the presence of a skilled teacher, preferably someone who is also a licensed counselor. Bringing up trauma can be very frightening at first and potentially dangerous in rare cases. Over time, though, it can also be incredibly liberating and healing. As one's confidence builds, she or he may eventually no longer need the presence of a teacher or counselor to engage in this exercise.)

✨

MANAGING CHANGE

As we spend more time sustaining awareness in the present moment, and investigating with curiosity the phenomena that pass through that sustained awareness, another simple yet very powerful insight emerges: Everything changes.

Of course, we all know this intellectually. But we often don't live as though we know it, do we? We often resist, or even fear, change—like a downturn in the economy or rapidly changing market conditions—when it threatens us.

Mindfulness training helps us become very comfortable with change and even embrace it. During all moments of practice, and especially while sitting still, we gradually transform our intellectual understanding that "Everything is always changing" into wisdom.

As our awareness becomes more stable, we see with increasing clarity that everything that arises in awareness soon passes away. Instead of only intellectually acknowledging that a thought, sound, or sensation that we experienced a few moments ago is no longer present, we see the exact moment—with clarity and in great detail—when a phenomenon ceases to be.

This can be one of your advanced-level exercises. Simply pay extra attention to the exact moment that things cease. When does the out breath end? When does the in breath end? When does a sound end? When does a tactile sensation, a smell, or perhaps even a taste end?

Practicing in this way, it might seem as though the experience of dwelling in mindfulness is like observing a flowing river pass by. There is a constant flow of breathing, sensations, thoughts, mind states, and emotions. They just keep arising and passing away, ceaselessly. Gradually, you discover that you are part of this flow.

Entering this flow is actually a very pleasant and often liberating experience. Joy often arises. As you gain some experience with actually enjoying the experience of change, you can start to apply this practice to more areas of your life, including your work life. With practice, you can start to enter in the flow of change in more demanding situations and realize that you experience the same joy. You can gradually reprogram your response to change from trying to avoid it to seeing it as something you truly enjoy. You can actually thrive in change, which makes life much more pleasant and can dramatically improve your performance as a leader.

SEEING OPPORTUNITIES NO ONE ELSE SEES

This advanced-level practice allows us to experience freedom from suffering by facing pain head-on. We commit to sitting absolutely still, not moving a single muscle, unless there is a life-threatening emergency.

This is quite counterculture, isn't it? We are conditioned to avoid unpleasant experiences at all costs and do whatever we can to ensure that we are comfortable.

This exercise is not about intentionally seeking out pain. The idea here is to commit to not run away from physical or emotional pain. Instead, we investigate it, as though we're scientists researching the experience of being in our own bodies. Anytime we notice that something bothers us, it should be a wonderful reminder to us: "Hey, let's look into this a bit and learn how to be at peace in any situation!"

When an unpleasant experience, such as an itch, arises, don't just get rid of it, out of habit. Take full advantage of the opportunity to see how you create suffering and how you can be free from it. Instead of allowing the mind to blabber away about how unpleasant something is, you can take an entirely different perspective.

You can simply notice, "How are the mind and body reacting to this? Is there a feeling of dislike? Is there a desire to get rid of the itch?"

When you look into this, you might notice that there is a desire to get rid of the itch in the mind. You might make it fully conscious by intentionally saying in the mind, "I want to get rid of the itch," while listening to that sentence and listening to the silence that follows it.

You might notice that you are clinging to that desire, which has resulted in some muscles contracting in various parts of the body. You can simply let those muscles uncontract and continue with the curious attitude of "How are the mind and body reacting to this itch?" This allows you to see that if instead of focusing on the itch you shine your awareness on the mental and physical reactions to the itch, you can experience unpleasantness without having to suffer. You know the itch is there, but it no longer bothers you.

At first, this exercise takes willpower. You might have to really work at your commitment to bear with unpleasant experiences patiently. However, the practice of investigating your reactions to unpleasant situations can quickly become a profound source of happiness and freedom.

You gradually realize through your direct experience that you can be with even the most unpleasant of experiences without suffering. You know that no matter what life throws at you, you have a refuge that allows you to deal with it with confidence and peace of mind. You simply make the shift from being the thinking mind and its ego to being the awareness that knows the thinking mind for what it is: a wonderful tool that is not in control of you.

Gradually you can learn to respond to all of your experiences in this way, which frees you from suffering and allows you to increasingly see opportunities where you used to see only problems. In some cases, this can allow you to see opportunities that no one else sees.

JUST LISTENING

A very liberating practice is to spend a portion of your time practicing while sitting still to make the concerted effort to really listen, both inwardly and outwardly. You may notice as soon as you intentionally listen to anything, you are listening both inwardly and outwardly. You can hear sounds in the room, and you can also hear the voice that seems to always be chattering away in your head.[1]

For most of us, this is likely the aspect of the mind with which we are most identified. We really feel as though that voice in our heads is *me*. That's why it can be so powerful to take some time to intentionally listen to it. When we really listen deeply, it becomes increasingly clear that we are not that voice in our heads. We are what's listening to that voice.

To engage in this practice you might simply decide to just listen at some point during a session of sitting-still training. You could gently remind yourself with the inner voice to "Just listen" to that same inner voice. How long can you just listen before you start talking to yourself again?

If you wake up at some point and realize that you're lost in conversation with yourself (sounds a bit like we're all crazy, doesn't it?), you could just nonjudgmentally recognize that you're lost—it's totally normal—and then gently ask with the inner voice, "Is there any talking now?" and just listen for the answer.

Sometimes just the clarity of the end of the word *now* can yield a pleasant insight into the truth that the voice in our heads is a temporary phenomenon that we can hear come and go. It's not what we are.

For the remainder of the time training with this exercise, simply keep alive the attitude of "Is there any talking now?" and just listen.

THE POWER OF DOING NOTHING

Perhaps the most challenging practice of all is to sit still and do absolutely nothing. Quite naturally, we likely think that to realize benefits from mindfulness training, we have to be *doing* something. Common ideas among many practitioners include the needs to pay attention, notice the breath, or let go of thinking. For most people, these will be necessary parts of the training to be mindfully self-aware.

One of the most powerful moves we can make in our sitting-still practice, though, is the move toward doing absolutely nothing at all. We just sit. As advanced practitioners, we spend a lot of time during our sitting-still practice doing absolutely nothing other than occasionally reminding ourselves with a gentle inner voice that we're "just sitting," or "doing nothing."

This practice is so powerful because it yields an amazing insight. The practice of *doing nothing* allows us to discover that being mindfully self-aware is actually our natural state. We don't have to *do* anything to be mindfully self-aware.

The insight eventually arises that in terms of advancing our practice of sitting still, there is nothing we have to achieve. We're not working to create some better version of our brain. The rewiring of the brain that occurs as a result of spending more time being mindfully self-aware is more like allowing a brain that has become unhealthy to return to its natural healthy state.

Although engaging in this exercise is certainly not easy—the tendency to become the thinking mind or feel the need to do something is extremely powerful for most of us—it is very, very simple. During periods of your time spent sitting still, commit to doing absolutely nothing. Occasionally, you can gently remind yourself with "just sitting" or "doing nothing" or asking, "What's happening now?" without making any effort to look for an answer.

If you get caught up in thinking, once you wake up to mindful self-awareness, you might like to make fully conscious the last thought that was present until it fades away on its own. The rest of the time, simply sit and do nothing.

This practice helps us discover that although there are many things we can do to train to be mindfully self-aware, actually *being* mindfully self-aware is our natural state. It can be effortless. This insight then informs our actions in daily life. We discover that so much of what we used to find very difficult in life becomes much easier, or even effortless. An activity may be very physically demanding, but in the mind it seems to require no effort. We just do it. To be most precise, it is just done.

Review Questions

How does the advanced-level practice of "Brutal, Compassionate Honesty" help you become a more compassionate leader?

How does the advanced-level practice of "Fearlessness" help you become a fearless leader?

How does the advanced-level practice of "Seeing Opportunities No One Else Sees" allow you to do just that?

13

THE FOUNDATIONS OF WISDOM

PHYSICAL TRAINING FOR CHARACTER

One of the first ideas shared in this book is that everything we do, or fail to do, begins in the mind (or, more precisely, in the brain that creates the mind). However, one of the biggest takeaways from scientists who explore neuroplasticity is that our behaviors, our thought patterns, and even what we pay attention to all affect the brain.

Upon first reading the title of this chapter, you might envision a workout regimen designed to somehow facilitate leadership excellence. Although I'm certainly a huge proponent of keeping the body physically fit, this chapter of the book is not about physical fitness. It's about being much more intentional about our speech and the behaviors in which we engage; making the effort to spend more time acting and speaking in ways that can change the brain positively and improve our ability to sustain mindful self-awareness; and refraining from acting and speaking in ways that undermine that ability.

Traditionally, mindfulness training has always been taught as having three essential components. We have already thoroughly discussed the first two components: stabilizing awareness and applying that stable awareness to develop wisdom. The third component, the behavioral component that we'll explore in this chapter, can actually be viewed as the foundation of the entire practice. (This component is not as "sexy" as the other two components, so I usually don't introduce it until people are already sold on mindfulness training. I'm assuming that if you've gotten this far into the book, you see some benefit to mindfulness training.)

We cannot develop wisdom without stable awareness, and we cannot develop stable awareness without a foundation of wise speech and behavior. Wise speech and behavior are in accordance with the truth of our interconnectedness and thus take into account equally the well-being of both ourselves and others. When we engage in unwise speech and behavior—behavior that is more self-centered than other centered—we reinforce the habitual tendency to cling to the thinking mind and its ego, which makes it much more difficult to sustain mindful self-awareness than it needs to be.

Conversely, consistently speaking and acting wisely helps us break free from being controlled by the thinking mind and its ego and makes it significantly easier to become and remain mindfully self-aware. Thus, I call the practices outlined in this chapter the *Foundations of Wisdom*.

Consistently communicating and acting wisely requires us to be more aware of very subtle aspects of our interaction with the world around us. Engaging in the practices outlined in this chapter results in paying attention to elements of speech and behavior, and the results of both, that we may have never paid attention to before. So the Foundations of Wisdom are mindfulness practices that allow our overall mindfulness training to permeate many more moments of our lives.

Another interesting benefit to practicing with the Foundations of Wisdom (which may not seem like a benefit at first) is that these practices can really create a healthy struggle that helps us build even stronger character than we may already have. We may often find ourselves in a minor battle between our aspirations to adhere to the Foundations of Wisdom or simply to follow our desires, or whims, and do what's easy. Although this struggle can be a bit annoying, it helps us improve our ability to do the right thing even when it's hard to do so and at very subtle levels of speech and behavior.

These Foundations of Wisdom are not meant to be "thou shalt not" commandments which, if violated, will result in our eternal damnation (although better safe than sorry, eh?). Rather, they greatly assist us in seeing for ourselves how unwise actions and speech affect the mind and the ability to become and remain mindfully self-aware. As with everything else offered in this book, we shouldn't just blindly believe that the Foundations of Wisdom significantly affect the mind. We should practice with them and see for ourselves.

The Foundations of Wisdom also help us refrain from unwise actions and speech while we are deepening our realization of how those actions and ways of speaking result in suboptimal outcomes as leaders and in our lives in general. Therefore, using the Foundations of Wisdom can help us improve performance and reduce much of our suffering as soon as we begin practicing with them. They are kind of like training wheels that help us act and speak with great virtue until doing so becomes our natural response to life during every moment.

THE FOUNDATIONS OF WISDOM

In the pages that follow, you'll find the Foundations of Wisdom that are most essential for enhancing your mindfulness training and explanations of how they help. This list constitutes what I consider the bare minimum for having a strong foundation for mindfulness training. However, you could certainly add to this list if you like, and I encourage you to do so.

After reading the Foundations of Wisdom, please take some time to reflect on the five values you feel are most essential for being the type of leader you want to be (these may include one or more of the Foundations of Wisdom). These are your personal core values.

A very powerful practice is to recite out loud each day (perhaps during a break at work) the five Foundations of Wisdom and your personal core values (again, there may be some overlap), which helps remind you to actually live the values that are so important to you. Leaders who consistently live their values and the Foundations of Wisdom are those whom we tend to call *authentic* leaders of strong character. These types of leaders build tremendous trust with team members and inspire others to live authentically, with strong character, as well.

Another element of this practice is to outline a couple of key behaviors for each value that indicate you're living up to that value. At the end of each day (perhaps in place of a moment of TV or another nonessential activity), you can take a minute to review the Foundations of Wisdom, your personal core values, and their associated behaviors and note any gaps between who you aspire to be and who you actually were that day. There's no need to beat yourself up over your short-comings. Just note the gaps and renew your aspiration to live those values going forward.

FOUNDATION OF WISDOM 1—INTEGRITY

Because living with integrity is an essential element of mindfulness training and leadership excellence, I aspire to:

- *State the truth without exaggerating*
- *Refrain from omitting the truth*
- *Live my core values*
- *Do what I say I'm going to do*

Integrity is a trait that many people and organizations list as a core value, and with good reason. Living with integrity, especially as defined by the four behaviors above, helps us to build deep bonds of trust with the people around us. Trust is an absolutely essential component of healthy, productive relationships.

Engaging in the behaviors listed above is also extremely helpful for breaking the habit of continuously becoming the thinking mind and its ego. This is especially true when we state something that isn't true, or exaggerate or omit truth, which we usually do as an act of some variation of self-defense. We're trying to protect our reputation, or a view, or somehow make ourselves look better. All of this mental activity reinforces the habitual tendency to operate from the ego instead of being mindfully self-aware.

Failing to live our core values, or failing to do things we've explicitly said we're going to do, tends to create a general sense of unrest in the mind. The thought patterns that come up because of that unrest can be quite powerful and can include patterns of self-doubt, disappointment, depression, or even self-hatred. These powerful thought patterns can all easily pull us into egocentrism and make becoming and remaining mindfully self-aware much more challenging.

FOUNDATION OF WISDOM 2—SKILLFUL COMMUNICATION

Because skillful communication is an essential element of mindfulness training and leadership excellence, I aspire to:

- *Prioritize listening over talking*
- *Speak in ways that are helpful*
- *Refrain from offering opinions unless asked to do so or it is absolutely necessary*
- *Be mindful while using electronic devices*

Because effective communication is such a key element of interpersonal relationships, especially for leaders, we'll explore several ideas for more effective communication here, in addition to the behaviors listed above.

As you progress with practicing mindfulness during the activities on the list you created in Chapter 7, and with your sitting-still practice, you will likely find that mindfulness is starting to become stronger when communicating. You might find that you're more present with people when you're speaking with them. You might find that you're more aware of your own thoughts when you're listening to someone or preparing a response. And, especially if you're practicing mindfulness of emotions, you may find that you're less likely to speak, or click the *send* button on an e-mail, when you're caught in an unpleasant emotion.

Practicing with this Foundation of Wisdom helps to make communication an intentional part of your mindfulness training. Generally, the core effort is very simple. When communicating with others, you practice being fully present by applying mindfulness and you practice listening very deeply. As Dr. Stephen Covey put it in *The 7 Habits of Highly Effective People*, you seek to understand before seeking to be understood.

This effort can dramatically improve your communication. Working to listen to and more fully understand others, instead of focusing on what you want to say, is one of the most powerful things you can do in any situation but especially as a leader. The better you listen to team members, the more empowered and cared for they feel and the better able you are to capitalize on the intelligence and ideas of those team members.

This shift from focusing on talking to focusing on listening is also a powerful mindfulness practice. The more caught up we are in what we want to say, the more caught up we are in the thinking mind and ego. Conversely, the effort to just listen is a simple way to shift to being mindfully self-aware. With practice, we discover that whenever we're listening outwardly we're also listening inwardly, and we can hear our own thinking more objectively.

The "Just Listening" exercise outlined in Chapter 12 involves doing nothing but sitting still and listening both inwardly and outwardly. That practice can further strengthen your ability to listen to others. And, practicing with this Foundation of Wisdom can help strengthen that exercise.

SPEAK IN WAYS THAT ARE HELPFUL

If we don't have something helpful to say, something that would add value over silence and doesn't attack someone personally, it's probably better to say nothing. This type of restraint can prevent the degradation of a relationship. It also helps us refrain from the egocentric inner dialogue that makes being mindfully self-aware more difficult than it needs to be. Additionally, this practice can help us speak less and do more listening, which is very conducive to sustaining mindful self-awareness.

Refrain from Offering Opinions Unless Asked to Do So or It Is Absolutely Necessary

This is a good general rule to follow for effective leadership whenever we're hoping to get the best ideas from team members. The moment we, as leaders, state an opinion, we're very likely to steer thinking away from ideas that are contrary to that opinion. These may be the very ideas that we need to hear to arrive at the best solutions.

Also, the more often we express opinions, the more entrenched we become in those opinions. This can make letting go of egocentric thinking and becoming and remaining mindfully self-aware much more challenging. Opinions are one of the most ego-charged thoughts we carry around in our minds.

Be Mindful while Using Electronic Devices

One of the most common questions I receive during the workshops and training programs I offer is "What effect do our devices have on our ability to be mindful?" This question is so important today that there's actually an entire conference series, called Wisdom 2.0, dedicated to discussing how we can keep wisdom alive in the digital age.[1]

We are certainly facing problems in this digital age. Many people are in an almost constant state of anxiety, people don't seem to be present with each other while interacting, and people's attention spans appear to be rapidly dwindling.[2]

The problem isn't with the devices themselves. Smartphones and tablets and laptop computers are all very useful devices that can help us in many ways. The problem is our relationship to the devices. It seems that many of us are addicted to them, compelled by the neurotransmitter dopamine to seek the pleasure of the opioid neurotransmitter we receive when we interact with them, as Dr. Susan Weinschenk wrote in an article for *Psychology Today*.[3] Have you ever seen a person driving on a freeway at 55 miles per hour or faster, with a child in the backseat of the car, pick up a smartphone and not only read a text but also reply to it? That extremely dangerous act sounds quite similar to the risky behavior a person addicted to crack cocaine might engage in to get another hit.

We need to change our relationship with our devices. It can start with some hard rules about when and where we check e-mail or text messages, doing so only during deliberately scheduled times, when we're not walking or operating a vehicle, and when we're not interacting with a real person who is right in front of us.

Actually, you can make device use one of your mindfulness practices. You just need to change the way you interact with the device. Instead of multitasking, rushing to complete whatever task you're engaged in with the device, caught in your thinking in a state of mild to moderate anxiety, you can interact with devices in a much healthier way. Before using a device, pause for at least one breath, and remind yourself to be mindful while using the device. Simply keep your awareness alive to what the device feels like and what's happening in the body. It may be helpful to note occasionally in the mind, "Texting" or "Typing," to reestablish mindfulness.

CONFLICT MANAGEMENT

Conflict is likely inevitable in the workplace. How we deal with conflict is a crucial element of the emotional climate of our teams. The first step is to remember that conflict isn't a bad thing in and of itself.

Disagreements can be very valuable because they can prevent bad ideas from being executed, and they can help refine good ideas. In fact, many great leaders invite or even demand dissenting opinions about ideas they suggest. For instance, if you've proposed an idea, you could make a rule that the meeting doesn't end until you've heard at least three ideas from team members about why that idea won't work or how it could be improved.

Conflict becomes problematic when we're not skillful in how we deliver a message, and we contribute to the arising of an unpleasant and unproductive emotion for a team member. When we notice that we've played a part in upsetting a team member, it's usually a very good use of time to help resolve the issue as soon as possible. It's clearly the kind thing to do; it's helpful for maintaining healthy, productive relationships; and it helps a team member get back to an optimal state for performance, thereby increasing productivity.

The most powerful communication tool I'm aware of for resolving conflict is known as Nonviolent Communication (NVC) and was developed by Dr. Marshall Rosenberg. This tool is a wonderful mindfulness practice and is much more effective when we have a solid foundation in mindfulness training. In a way, the tool actually helps us guide someone else through the practice of mindfulness of emotions in a skillful, kind, empathetic way. By helping another person feel heard and become more aware of the emotion that is present for him, we help him create some space around that emotion.

The essence of the approach is to break free from any tendency we might have to defend ourselves or judge another person when we've contributed to an unpleasant emotion for her. Instead, the intention is to truly understand her point of view, give her a chance to clearly identify the emotion that's present (or was present when the interaction occurred) and to express why she feels that way, and offer a potential solution. The process is defined in four steps:

1. Making objective observations
2. Identifying emotions
3. Identifying the needs or desires or expectations that weren't met
4. Identifying a request that would meet the need, desire, or expectation

For instance, let's presume you made a comment in a meeting—"The idea we're about to discuss might make Jim lose the little hair he has left"—that was intended to lighten the mood but clearly offended the controller, Jim. The conversation afterward (or right then if it seems appropriate) might go something like the following:

You: *(Guessing at what Jim is feeling)* Jim, are you feeling irritated because you would have liked me to not make sarcastic comments about you?

Jim: Yes. That was a little rude.

You: I apologize, Jim. Would you like me to commit to refraining from joking about your appearance?

Jim: Not just me. I don't think you should joke about anyone's appearance.

You: *(Realizing that we've clarified Jim's request and that it is very reasonable)* I will be much more aware of that in the future, and make every effort to refrain from joking about the physical appearance of you or anyone else.

Notice how we're not taking responsibility for the emotion that Jim is experiencing. We are taking responsibility for what we said and how it failed to meet a very legitimate human need: not to be belittled in front of other people. By taking just a few seconds to acknowledge the emotion Jim was experiencing, identify the need that wasn't met, help Jim feel truly heard, and agree to a request to meet that need in the future, we can help transform the emotional climate in the meeting.

Although there is clearly a template for the process of NVC, it's not meant to be a rigid framework. It's just a guide. The most important first step in resolving conflict is to ensure that the other person feels truly heard and understood. This requires us to have both the aspiration and the ability to listen and observe without making any judgments and objectively state exactly what's happening. In other words, it requires mindfulness (often defined as nonjudgmental awareness).

This nonjudgmental, objective observation is also the key to getting our needs met. For instance, let's apply the NVC approach with a potential business partner who has been late for three of the last 10 meetings we've had and has contributed to the emotion of anger arising within us.

An obviously unskillful approach would be to say something like, "Sara, you are always late. That is really unprofessional." There's no need to attack Sara as a person. That is going to cause her to become defensive immediately. Likewise, stating that she is "always late" will cause her to become defensive because it's simply not true. She can immediately argue that. If she's defensive, she's much less likely to be willing to hear us out, much less compromise with us.

The NVC approach avoids creating any defensiveness because it involves only stating facts, our needs, and how we feel when our needs are not met. There's nothing for the other person to defend.

With the NVC approach, we might start by applying the approach to understand why she's been late. Maybe there's something deeply troublesome happening in her life. If there is, we could really deepen our relationship by having compassion for her instead of harming it by assuming she's just unprofessional.

Assuming that there isn't a strong argument for why Sara has been late, we would say something like "Sara, you have been late three out of the last 10 meetings we've had. I'm feeling a little frustrated about this. I have an expectation that people I do business with show up on time for meetings, and when that doesn't happen I feel frustrated."

We could pause for a moment and then make a request: "Would you be willing to commit to being on time for our meetings going forward?

With this approach, there is a much better chance that Sara will hear us out and a much better chance that our needs will be met. We haven't pushed her to have to defend herself, so we haven't closed her off from empathy. This, in combination with expressing the emotion we feel, improves the likelihood that Sara will be able to empathize with us. If she can empathize with us, it's much more likely that she will be open to a reasonable request.

The NVC approach can also be extended to help two team members who are not getting along to resolve their differences. We can instruct the two parties in the structure of NVC and mediate a conversation where we help uncover facts, needs, emotions, and possible resolutions. Although it is by no means easy to do this, it is certainly worth the effort. Resolving interpersonal conflicts can significantly improve the emotional climate of a team.

THE POWER OF EMPATHY

For the purposes of brevity, the two examples above of the NVC process are clearly quite sanitized versions of reality. Effectively resolving conflict almost always takes longer than a minute or two, and there is often a lot more subtlety and nuance to the conversations we have while applying the NVC approach. In fact, we can often spend a good deal of time on the first two steps alone. It can take time to help someone understand the root emotion. It can be a lot like peeling an onion.

The first time I practiced the first two steps in the process, which are very similar to a practice called *reflective listening*, I spent 10 minutes listening deeply to a peer talk about an issue she was dealing with in her life. I listened with my full attention until she paused. Then I reflected back a brief summary of what I heard and what emotion I thought she was feeling. She would either correct me if I was incorrect and then go deeper once she felt understood, or if I was correct, she just went deeper right away.

Each time I reflected what I heard and what I thought she was feeling, she went a little deeper and opened up a little more. After about 10 minutes, it was clear that she had resolved her own issue. There was a natural pause. I asked her, "Is there anything more you'd like to share about that?"

She smiled and said, "No. Thank you."

It became so obvious to me that there is a lot of power inherent in the ability to just listen deeply and empathize. I didn't offer any advice or otherwise try to fix her. I just listened and helped her feel heard and understood. This allowed her to uncover the solution for herself. This is so much more empowering and satisfying than trying to solve people's problems.

In our busy lives, spending 10 minutes may sound like a long time to just listen to another person. But I can't think of a better investment of time than to deepen so significantly our relationships with the people we see every day. Relationships are so much more important both personally and professionally than most of the things we have on our to-do lists.

To better understand the approach to listening, and the many other nuances of the NVC approach, I highly, highly recommend the best-selling book *Nonviolent Communication*. I'm extremely confident that you will find that book one of the best investments you make. Following is an example from that book of just how powerful this approach can be and how to apply it in a challenging situation.

While presenting the NVC approach to 170 Palestinian men in a mosque at Dheisheh Refugee Camp in Bethlehem, Dr. Rosenberg noticed some murmuring in the audience. The translator told him that the men were commenting that Dr. Rosenberg was an American. Just a few seconds later, a man stood up and yelled, "Murderer!"

His shout was echoed by several others who yelled, "Assassin!" "Child killer!" "Murderer!"

Dr. Rosenberg was fortunate to have had some clues as to why the men would feel that way. On his way to the refugee camp, he had seen several empty tear gas canisters that had recently been fired into the camp. Each canister was clearly marked with the words "Made in the USA." He was aware of the anger many refugees felt toward the United States for supplying Israel with weapons.

This awareness helped him focus his attention not on self-defense but on understanding what the man who first yelled at him was feeling and needing. Thus, he addressed the man with compassion.

He asked, "Are you angry because you would like my government to use its resources differently?" He was just guessing. But he was making a sincere effort to understand the man.

The man replied, "Damn right I'm angry! You think we need tear gas? We need sewers, not your tear gas! We need housing! We need to have our own country!"

"So you're furious and would appreciate some support in improving your living conditions and gaining political independence?" Dr. Rosenberg asked.

"Do you know what it's like to live here for 27 years the way I have with my family, children, and all? Have you got the faintest idea what that's been like for us?"

"Sounds like you're feeling very desperate and you're wondering whether I or anybody else can really understand what it's like to be living under these conditions. Am I hearing you right?"

"You want to understand? Tell me, do you have children? Do they go to school? Do they have playgrounds? My son is sick! He plays in open sewage! His classroom has no books! Have you seen a school with no books?"

"I hear how painful it is for you to raise your children here. You'd like me to know that what you want is what all parents want for their children—a good education, opportunity to play and grow in a healthy environment . . ."

"That's right! The basics! Human rights. Isn't that what you Americans call it? Why don't more of you come here and see what kind of human rights you're bringing here!"

"You'd like more Americans to be aware of the enormity of the suffering here and to look more deeply at the consequences of our political actions?" Dr. Rosenberg clarified.

The dialogue lasted for roughly 20 minutes. The man continued to express deep pain, and Dr. Rosenberg continued to listen deeply and identify the emotion and the need wrapped up in each statement. He didn't agree or disagree. He just listened with compassion.

Once the man had fully expressed his pain and felt truly heard and understood, he was able to hear Dr. Rosenberg explain why he was visiting the camp. About an hour later, the man who so recently saw Dr. Rosenberg as a murderer, and verbally attacked him, invited him to have a Ramadan dinner at his home.[4]

FOUNDATION OF WISDOM 3—WISE CONSUMPTION

Because wise consumption is an essential element of mindfulness training and leadership excellence, I aspire to:

- *Consume only what I need to consume to be healthy and productive and to develop as a human being*

- *Refrain from consuming things that cause anxiety*
- *Refrain from consuming things that inhibit mindfulness*

Most of us have heard that "we are what we eat." We can easily take this a step further. As we explored in Chapter 10, what we habitually refer to as the self—the body, the thinking mind, and the ego—is composed entirely of things that come from outside that self. Quite literally, we are what we consume.

Unfortunately, many of us consume things on a regular basis that are not so good for us. Many of the movies, TV programs, apps, websites, books, and magazines that we consume induce anxiety, fuel certain opinions, or simply distract us from doing what's actually important. Much of the food and drink we consume provides little or no nutritional benefit and, in many cases, actually leads to a less healthy body and mind.

The negative effects on our physical and emotional well-being that result from unwise consumption are compounded by the negative effects on our ability to become and remain mindfully self-aware. So much of what we consume reinforces the powerful seeking inside of us that is constantly looking for what's next, what's bigger, or what's better. We are bombarded with messages telling us that we're not good enough, what we have isn't good enough, and we don't have enough of what we do have.

This habitual tendency to look elsewhere for satisfaction is one of the most powerful aspects of the conditioning that fuels the habitual tendency to operate from the thinking mind and its ego. Breaking this vicious cycle by practicing with this foundation of wisdom is one of the most important things we can do to improve our mindfulness training and uncover more of the benefits we receive from the practice.

Some of the things we consume, such as alcohol or other intoxicating drugs, immediately and directly impede our ability to be mindfully self-aware. When we're intoxicated, we have little or no conscious control over our actions and speech, much less over our awareness. Many careers, indeed many lives, have been ruined because of actions taken while under the influence of some intoxicating drug.

This matter is so important that it's probably best never to consume intoxicants. However, this may be a huge, perhaps insurmountable step for some of us. If that's the case, we may just start by never consuming enough of an intoxicating drug to actually become intoxicated, perhaps limiting alcohol consumption to one drink every 2 hours or so during social events.

The first step to practicing with this foundation of wisdom is simply to pay more attention to what we're consuming. At its core, this practice is another powerful exercise in mindfulness. We're doing our best to create some space between the stimulus of an enticing thing that we don't actually need and that can be quite detrimental and the habitual reaction just to go ahead and consume it.

You might find it helpful to have a question that you use to filter your decisions about what you'll consume. For example, before you consume something, you could pause for one breath and simply ask in the mind, "Is what I'm about to consume something I actually need to be healthy, or productive, or to grow as a human being, or is it only something that I want? Am I in charge of my behaviors, or am I being controlled by my desires?"

Of course, you may find that many times desires certainly are in control. You'll fail to adhere to this foundation of wisdom. This is okay, and it's quite natural. When you fail temporarily, you can simply renew your aspiration to keep practicing. Gradually, you'll find that desires lose their power over you. You'll also realize that this freedom results in happiness and self-mastery that is infinitely more rewarding than the brief pleasure you experience when you blindly follow and gratify desires.

There is also a direct link between practicing with this foundation of wisdom and reducing expenses in an organization. As the practice of being much more deliberate about what you consume permeates more and more of your life, you'll likely find that you're being much more deliberate about what you consume at work. You may find that you're less wasteful and that you much more carefully consider whether an expenditure or other application of resources is really necessary to best serve all of your stakeholders.

FOUNDATION OF WISDOM 4—GENEROSITY

Because generosity is an essential element of mindfulness training and leadership excellence, I aspire to always give more value than I receive.

The effort to be generous, to always give more value than we receive, may be the most powerful secret to worldly success there is. When customers feel that we provide them greater value than we receive from them, they want to do business with us again, and they're very likely to refer other people to us. When team members feel that we provide them greater value (helping them grow, valuing them as human beings, being committed to their well-being, etc.) than we receive from them, they're much more likely to go the extra mile to serve the team or organization.

This practice of giving more value than we receive doesn't mean that we don't receive the value we need. It simply means that instead of being greedy, and trying to win as much as we can in the short term, we focus on receiving what we actually need and giving much more than we receive. If we do this consistently, over the long term, we'll end up receiving much more than we would have if we focused on the short term.

The practice of generosity is also very powerful in terms of training the mind. Each generous act can chip away at our self-centered tendencies and reduce the power that the thinking mind and ego have to suck us in. This is because generosity is perfectly aligned with the truth of how interdependent we are, so it subtly reinforces the wisdom that is so helpful for breaking the habit of becoming and operating from the thinking mind and the ego.

Although this may not always be the best idea for worldly success, you might like to experiment with completely selfless generosity in matters that wouldn't put your family or business at risk of harm. Perhaps you could commit to giving your time or something else of value to someone, once per week, without any thought of what you might receive in return. Throughout this process, notice the effects on the mind, paying special attention to the mind after completing the generous act.

FOUNDATION OF WISDOM 5—KINDNESS

Because kindness is an essential element of mindfulness training and leadership excellence, I aspire to:

- *Be kind to all conscious beings, including myself*
- *Respect the belongings of others*

For this Foundation of Wisdom, kindness simply means refraining from harming and, whenever possible, finding a way to contribute to the well-being of others. Although in the corporate world kindness has often been viewed as weakness, nothing could be further from the truth. Only the truly strong are able to be kind in difficult situations. Similar to generosity, this ability to be kind even when it's not easy to do so is a key element to building the healthy, productive relationships that are essential for long-term success, especially as leaders.

There are, of course, many forms that such kindness can take. In general, our actions affect a person directly, affect people who are important to a person, or affect the belongings of a person. It is important to consider each of these.

RESPECT THE BELONGINGS OF OTHERS

There are several levels to the idea of respecting the belongings of others. The most obvious is that we should not take anything from anyone that is not freely given to us. Stealing is clearly not a kind thing to do and can cause suffering for others. Stealing also has significant, adverse effects on the mind. Much like dishonesty, stealing results in all sorts of thoughts that are egocentric, revolving around the foolish endeavors of preserving and defending the false sense of self and justifying its actions. These thought patterns are not conducive to becoming and remaining mindfully self-aware.

We can certainly refine our efforts to respect the belongings of others and consider much subtler aspects of how we interact with those belongings. For instance, a fruitful practice to follow is to refrain from picking up or even touching the property of others without their permission. Many people are quite annoyed when someone walks into their office or home and starts picking things up, especially when those things are very valuable.

By making the effort to refrain from touching the property of others without their permission, we can, at a minimum, avoid annoying people. This is also another way to allow mindfulness to permeate many more moments of our lives. With this practice, each time we encounter the property of others, we are pulled out of habit and reminded to be much more intentional about what we're doing. This awakens us and requires us to remain awake.

BE KIND TO ALL CONSCIOUS BEINGS

Although many of us may not value the lives of certain living beings, such as mosquitoes, rats, or cockroaches, and we may not care one bit whether they are experiencing fear, pain, or peace, we almost certainly do care about our own happiness. We may have never made the connection before being introduced to the practice of mindfulness, but how we treat even the most insignificant little flea has a great deal to do with our own happiness because our attitude affects our ability to become and remain mindfully self-aware.

The mind is a very habitual, easily conditioned computer of sorts, as we discussed earlier. The more we do something, the more likely it is that we repeat that behavior in the future and the easier it will be to do so. If we continuously act with aversion and aggression toward the world around us, even by killing annoying insects, we are conditioning the mind to act with aversion as an unconscious reaction to all experience. This is an extremely significant obstacle to becoming mindfully self-aware, which requires a curious, nonjudgmental attitude.

We are able to realize complete freedom from our habitual tendency to become the thinking mind and the ego only when we are able to accept all the thoughts and feelings that arise in the mind and body, rather than try to escape from them or annihilate them. This is not very easy to do, even if we have been practicing for some time and have excellent virtue. If we continue to condition the mind to react to the world around us with aversion, we are making a difficult task much more difficult than it needs to be.

If you are truly committed to leadership excellence, and to your own happiness, you would be extremely well served to put effort into this foundation of wisdom. As you begin to cultivate the attitude of kindness toward even the most insignificant of creatures, you will gradually notice significant change in the mind. You will find that you can peacefully coexist with your own thoughts and feelings much more easily, which is essential for success with mindfulness training.

EXERCISES IN KINDNESS

Kindness is such an important element of mindfulness training that, traditionally, taking some time each day to practice generating kindness or compassion has always been a key element of the training, especially for people who experience a lot of aversion. The exercise below can be practiced during one of your sitting-still practice sessions, whether or not you are feeling aversion toward another person.

EXERCISE 1 *Start with the beginner sitting-still practice for a moment or two. If you are alone, once you are no longer dwelling in aversion, choose two or three people whom you like. For each person, visualize sending him or her the energy of kindness for three breaths each. (Or, if you have trouble with visualization, you could simply give rise to the thought "May you be happy and well.") Then, do the same for a few people toward whom you feel relatively neutral. Then, do the same for the person toward whom you were feeling aversion. You could follow this by offering kindness for yourself for a few breaths.*

You could then widen your circle of kindness and visualize sending the energy of kindness to everyone at once in your city for three breaths. You could continue in the same way with all the people in your state or province, your country, and even the entire world.

EXERCISE 2 *When around other people, you can also visualize sending kindness to the people with whom you are sharing space, either individually or as a group. If you have trouble with visualization, you could simply give rise to the thought "May you be happy and well" as you look at people. Making this a habit, especially before interacting with people, can be incredibly powerful. It is a wonderful, joyful way to coexist with those around us. And, projecting the energy of kindness toward those with whom we are interacting improves our chances for a positive encounter, which can help strengthen our relationships with others and improve our effectiveness as leaders.*

Naturally, it is a bit more difficult to be kind when we are actually interacting with other beings. While you are developing your practice of kindness, you will likely fall short of your intentions many times. When this happens, you should recognize that you have done something unkind and kindly accept any thoughts or feelings that arise as a result. Once those thoughts and feelings have faded away, you can reestablish your intention to be kind to all conscious beings. You could start by apologizing to whomever you treated unkindly, without making any excuses for your actions.

YOUR PERSONAL CORE VALUES

Per the instructions from earlier in this chapter, please take some time to reflect on your core values. Once you feel that you're clear on them, please write in the space below any of your core values, along with the associated behaviors, that are not listed in the Foundations of Wisdom.

REVIEW QUESTIONS

How does the practice of integrity facilitate your ability to become and remain mindfully self-aware?

Why is nonviolent communication so helpful for resolving conflict and getting your needs met?

What are three reasons why practicing with the Foundations of Wisdom and your personal core values is so helpful for facilitating leadership excellence?

How can practicing mindful consumption help reduce expenses for your team?

Why is generosity so powerful for long-term success in business?

So that you can have quick access to a list for review, write below the five Foundations of Wisdom your personal core values (there may be some overlap), and their associated behaviors:

1. *Because living with integrity is an essential element of mindfulness training and leadership excellence, I aspire to:*
   a. *State the truth without exaggerating and without omitting the truth*
   b. *Live my core values*
   c. *Do what I say I'm going to do*

2.
   a.
   b.
   c.

3.
   a.
   b.
   c.

4.
   a.
   b.
   c.

5.
   a.
   b.
   c.

6.
   a.
   b.
   c.

7.

    a.

    b.

    c.

8.

    a.

    b.

    c.

9.

    a.

    b.

    c.

10.

    a.

    b.

    c.

Write out a description of how you'll remind yourself to review the list above each morning and evening, and note any gaps between who you want to be and who you actually were the previous day:

14

DISCOVERING INCREDIBLE MEANING AT WORK AND IN YOUR TIME AWAY FROM WORK

There are many reasons you may choose to begin and maintain some form of mindfulness training. You may want to have better business acumen, to increase your emotional intelligence, to be more innovative, to have greater leadership presence, or simply to be happier. Most likely, you'd like to have a combination of all of those things. It's also quite possible that you've made a connection between what you'd most like to achieve, or becoming the ideal version of yourself, and how mindfulness can help you get there.

As we discussed in Chapter 7, the most important thing you can do to realize whatever benefits you'd like to realize as a result of mindfulness training is to let go of any goals while you're practicing and living your daily life (practice and daily life are synonymous when you practice well).

However, it can be very helpful, especially when you're first starting to practice, to take a moment every day to remind yourself why you're engaging in mindfulness training. When you're reminded of how mindfulness training can help you achieve what is most important to you, you're more likely to put appropriate effort into the practice that day.

You might like to take a moment to copy the following statement—or something similar that resonates with you—fill in the blanks, and then keep it someplace you can review once a day during your first few weeks or months of training:

Aware that _____ *are my top priorities as a leader and/or in life, and that mindfulness training can help me significantly with these priorities, I am committed to practicing mindfulness during the activities below, taking* _____ *minutes to train while sitting still in the morning and afternoon, and making the effort to be mindfully self-aware whenever I'm not actively engaged in planning or analyzing or otherwise intentionally thinking.*

- _____
- _____
- _____
- _____
- _____

A PURPOSEFUL PARADIGM SHIFT

I'd like to propose one more reason—perhaps the most important reason of all—to engage in some form of mindfulness training, which you might like to add to the statement above as part of your daily reminders. Mindfulness training can help you realize deep meaning in your time at work and your time away from work, without having to add anything to your schedule.

A rather amazing paradigm shift—which we partially introduced in Chapter 7—occurs when we begin to practice mindfulness training during routine daily activities. Without mindfulness training, we tend to rush through most of our mundane daily activities, seeing them as boring wastes of time, in our hopes of getting on to the more exciting moments of our days. As a result, we skip over many, many moments of every day, building up anxiety, changing our brains in ways that are not conducive to leadership excellence, and feeling dissatisfaction in our rush to the future.

By practicing mindfulness during those mundane daily activities, we can transform them into opportunities to unwind the buildup of anxiety in our bodies, to realize satisfaction right in the present moment, and to change our brains in ways that facilitate leadership excellence. Just understanding that this is possible, and realizing even a small taste of these fruits of the practice, helps us see that every moment of our lives is incredibly important, and not one moment should be taken for granted. We see that every moment can be filled with deep meaning and purpose.

When we look even more deeply into the effects of mindfulness training on ourselves and those around us, we find that mindfulness training can actually help us live the most meaningful life that we could possibly live. This, in addition to how mindfulness training allows us to realize one of the primary goals of life—happiness—is why I often call the practice the "ultimate success habit."

What is the most meaningful thing we could possibly accomplish in our lives? Is it being rich and famous? Is it being the head of a powerful nation? Although these surely have appeal for some of us, we have the ability to live a life of much deeper meaning than either of those. What if we could put an end to poverty, violence, and other preventable suffering in our world? What if we could save the world, so to speak?

Can there possibly be a greater achievement than being the person who saves the world? This is the greatest movie plotline of all. And wouldn't it be the ultimate epithet? "Here lies Susan Jones. She was the successful chief executive officer of a large company. She is also credited with having ended poverty, violence, and other preventable suffering. Mrs. Jones saved the world."

Although you may be laughing at the idea of being able to save the world and dismissing it as pure fantasy, I'm confident you would agree that if it could be done, saving the world is far and away the most meaningful thing, in the conventional sense, that we could possibly do with our lives. This raises the more important question: How could we possibly go about saving the world?

At first, we might think of the nearly endless list of preventable problems in our world—including poverty, hunger, homelessness, crime, terrorism, and war—and think of how we might be able to tackle just one of those issues. After only a few moments of analysis, we'd likely conclude that the problem is very complex. We'd likely need a team of people to put together a plan for tackling the problem. Then, we'd likely give up on the idea because we'd realize that we have to go to work tomorrow.

Fortunately, there are already many teams and organizations working on solving each of the problems mentioned above. These organizations are necessary for making rapid progress in the right direction. Taking time to help one of these organizations can be an extremely rewarding use of our time, allowing us to realize the joy of serving our communities.

However, as important as the work is of the various organizations striving to end the many problems we see in our world, the absolute most important thing we can do to end those problems doesn't require any team or organization. You can do what's most important for saving the world while you're walking to the bathroom at work.

To help illustrate this point, let's consider the following hypothetical situation. Imagine that you have the same life goal as I do, and you want to create the conditions for a permanent end to poverty, violence, and other preventable suffering in your lifetime. So when a magical genie appears to you and offers you a couple of wishes, you wish that:

1. Everyone on the planet is given equal amounts of food, shelter, and money, and
2. Every weapon on the planet would disappear.

That would be wonderful, wouldn't it? (Unless you like to hunt. Then it would suck. But please play along for a moment if you're a hunter.) No one would be hungry, no one would be homeless, and it would be very hard for people to hurt each other.

But how long would those effects last? What would the situation on the planet be like 50 years from the time our wishes were granted, or 100 years from that time?

What we overlooked in our attempt to save the world is the most important variable of all: the human mind. Even if it were possible to have our hypothetical wishes granted, the effects of those wishes would be very temporary if we did nothing to change the condition of the minds of the billions of humans who live on this planet.

All the greedy, selfish people would still be greedy and selfish. Those people would find new ways to hoard food, money, and shelter for themselves, just as they do now. All the angry, violent people would still be angry and violent. Those people would find new ways to oppress, subjugate, or otherwise harm people around them, just as they do now. Within 50 years (or perhaps sooner) of having our wishes granted, the situation on our planet would return to exactly the way it is today.

For there to be a permanent end to poverty, violence, and other preventable suffering in the world, every person on the planet would need to be completely free from the poisons of anger and greed. Every person would need to have a deep capacity for unconditional kindness, compassion, and generosity.

This is where it becomes very clear that the practice of mindfulness is quite miraculous! The practice of mindfulness allows us to see through the illusion of separateness, which is the root cause of anger, hate, and greed, and to see the truth of interdependence. With each moment of practice, our insight into this truth deepens our capacity for unconditional kindness, compassion, and generosity. When our insight becomes strong enough, we see that although, conventionally speaking, we're all separate people interacting with each other, ultimately, we are so interconnected with those around us that they are no more separate from us than our own heart.

Could you imagine a world full of people who see both sides of the coin of reality? If all people realized that their neighbor is no more separate from them than their own heart, we wouldn't put our own needs above the needs of others. We would see our needs and the needs of others as equally important. We would be able to love each other unconditionally. Treating each other with kindness, compassion, and generosity would be the only way we could imagine interacting. Only people with brain illnesses would act otherwise.

As selfishness disappeared, all the symptoms of that selfishness— poverty, hunger, homelessness, crime, terrorism, war, and so on— would disappear as well. We would share with those who are in need not because of some form of imposed communism, but because we *want* to. We wouldn't be able to imagine committing an act of violence or another crime that harmed others to benefit only ourselves.

In addition to helping us eradicate many of the social problems we've created, mindfulness training, and the wisdom that develops because of the practice, can help us eradicate the suffering that arises from elements of life that we'll never be able to eliminate, such as pain and illness. Although pain and all illness will always be part of the experience of being human, the practice of mindfulness allows us to experience pain and illness without having to suffer (see Chapters 11 and 12) and to see more quickly how our experience of pain and illness can actually help us grow and be better able to serve others.

SAVING THE WORLD ON YOUR WAY
TO THE BATHROOM

Of course, the first step toward helping all people realize the benefits of mindfulness is to realize the benefits of mindfulness ourselves. As Gandhi said, we must be the change we want to see in the world. This may be the greatest act of leadership we can undertake: leading others, by our example, toward a future free of preventable suffering.

By putting effort into our own practice of mindfulness, we will become happier, more successful, kinder, more compassionate, and more gener- ous. Developing those qualities is the most powerful way there is to attract people to the practice of mindfulness. People are naturally attracted to others who are happy, loving, and successful because we all want to be happy and successful, and we all want to be loved. If our own practice is strong, we are also much better able to skillfully help those who ask about the practice of mindfulness. We can speak to them from our own experience, versus only offering ideas about the practice.

When we help others develop their own practice, they can in turn help others who are attracted to their happiness, kindness, and success. Those people can in turn help others, and so on. Little by little, we can move in the direction of a world inhabited only by people who have replaced the poisons of greed, anger, and other selfishness with the treasures of kindness, compassion, and generosity.

Is this going to happen quickly? It's not very likely. The process described above of transforming every human mind on the planet will likely take hundreds or even thousands of years. What's most important to remember, though, is that the most important aspect of working to save the world, and in fact the only way to ensure that a permanent end to poverty, violence, and other preventable suffering is brought about, is to practice mindfulness to the best of our ability.

This is not to say that we should not engage in acts of social service. Serving others with our time and resources can bring us great joy and can definitely speed up the process of saving the world.

Rather, the point here lies in the wonderful truth that when we engage in mindfulness training, every moment of our lives can be infused with the deepest meaning possible, even in our current roles, whether or not we are currently engaged in an act of helping others. Mindfulness can transform any moment into a moment of helping others. In any moment that we're practicing mindfulness—even walking to the bathroom at work—we're actually doing the most important thing we could possibly do to save the world. In any moment of being mindfully self-aware, we're living the most meaningful life possible.

At first, this might just be a conceptual framework that inspires us to practice. However, we eventually start to realize very deeply how meaningful each moment of life is when we're not caught in the thinking mind and its ego. We cannot describe the realization in words. We just know. There is a subtle yet liberating intuition that the most meaningful life we could possibly live is achieved right now, in this moment, simply by being mindfully self-aware.

As with everything else offered in this book, I hope you don't believe the ideas above. Rather, I hope you test things out and realize for yourself the effects of engaging in mindfulness training. If you continue to practice, I have no doubt you will gradually discover that being mindfully self-aware is the greatest gift you can offer to yourself, to your organization, and to the world.

REVIEW QUESTIONS

How can mindfulness training help you live the most meaningful life possible?

How can mindfulness training help you save the world on your way to the bathroom?

AFTERWORD

Thank you for reading this book.

We hope that you enjoyed it and found it very valuable and that you are already finding practical ways to integrate mindfulness training into your daily life. Doing so is a gift to you and to everyone you will ever meet.

If you have any questions about the practice of mindfulness, please feel free to reach out to us at www.TheMindfulnessEdge.com.

We also hope that you enjoyed the journey through the mindful brain and that it was useful for you to hear what neuroscience has to say about the profound change in being that mindfulness training can initiate. If you want to read more scientific literature about the neuroscience of mindfulness, we highly recommend the two overview articles of Tim's colleagues Britta Hölzel et al. and Yi-Yuan Tang et al.[1] If you are ready to deal with more complex models of how mindfulness works, we also recommend the papers by David Vago and David Silbersweig and Antoine Lutz and colleagues.[2] For an up-to-date overview of mindfulness research, we recommend the website of the American Mindfulness Research Association (https://goamra.org).

If you'd like to get this book in the hands of more people, there are two actions you can take. First, and most obvious, please share your copy of the book with someone who you think will benefit from reading it, or recommend the book to him or her.

Second, please take a moment to post a review online at Amazon .com, Barnes & Noble, Goodreads, or wherever else people are looking for books these days. Your review improves the chances that the book will be read by another person.

Thanks for spreading the word!

INTRODUCTION TO NEUROSCIENCE

DR. GARD

How We Study the Brain

The brain can be studied in several ways. The most widely used methods to study the brain, and certainly the mindful brain, are electroencephalography (EEG) and magnetic resonance imaging (MRI). EEG is used to measure electrical activity of the brain by sticking up to 256 electrodes on the scalp. Although the timing of EEG is very precise, it is not very helpful for determining where exactly in the brain activity occurs.

An MRI machine, on the other hand, can quite precisely locate where in the brain activity takes place. Besides measuring brain function, it can also be used to measure the structure of the brain. You may have already been in an MRI scanner in the hospital. It is a very large machine that looks like a giant donut on its side, with a table that slides into its hole. The massive outer part contains a very strong magnet (often 3 tesla), which is about 60,000 times stronger than the magnetic field of the earth. Once put inside the opening of an operating MRI machine, you'll hear beeping and hammering noises, a little bit like minimalist techno music.

The MRI scanner works as follows. The human body, including the brain, consists of a lot of water (H_2O), which is made up of two hydrogen atoms (H). The protons of the hydrogen atoms spin around their axes like spin tops, but the spin axes of all the protons randomly point in different directions. When put into the strong magnetic field of the MRI scanner, the spin axes align with the magnetic field. Then a radio wave at the resonance frequency of the protons is sent into the body, which causes the spin axes to flip. When the radio wave is switched off, the spin axes move back to their aligned state with the magnetic field. While moving back, they emit a radio wave that is recorded and used to create the MRI image.

To know exactly where in the brain the radio signal is coming from, so-called gradient coils are used to slightly alter the magnetic field and hence the resonance frequency of the hydrogen protons in different slices of the brain. The loud noises that you hear inside the scanner are caused by the vibration of these gradient coils when rapid pulses of electricity are passed through them to change the magnetic field.[1]

WHAT CAN WE SEE IN THE BRAIN?

NEURONS

Using different sequences of radio frequency pulses in the MRI scanner, we can create images that display different properties of the brain. The core components of the brain are neurons (nerve cells). The brain consists of on average 86 billion neurons that connect to each other and form networks that enable us to perceive, respond, think, experience emotions, and be otherwise human. Neurons generally consist of the cell body, dendrites, axon, and axon terminals. The dendrites are branches of the cell body that connect to other neurons and receive signals from them. The axon, also called the nerve fiber, is the long and thin tail of the neuron and transmits electrical impulses to other neurons. At the end of the axon branches, there are axon terminals that connect to dendrites of other neurons. The connection between axon and dendrite, where the electrical impulse is transmitted through chemicals called neurotransmitters, is called the synapse.[2]

STRUCTURAL MRI AND GRAY MATTER

On structural MRI images of the brain, we can distinguish between gray matter and white matter. The gray matter is mostly made up of the cell bodies, dendrites, axon terminals, synapses, and tiny blood vessels called capillaries. The gray matter is located in the outer layer of the brain (cerebral cortex) and in clusters of nerve cell bodies, deeper inside the brain (nuclei). Using the computer metaphor, the gray matter is the place where the computations take place; it's the switchboard of the brain. When gray matter is measured with MRI, it is expressed in terms of gray matter density, volume, or cortical thickness.

STRUCTURAL MRI AND WHITE MATTER

White matter consists mostly of myelinated axons and glia cells. Myelin is a fatty substance that is part of the glia cells and is wrapped around the axons forming a myelin sheath. Myelin is white, hence "white matter," and its function is to isolate the axons and to speed up electric signal transmission through them. Speaking in terms of the computer metaphor, the axons, or nerve fibers, in the white matter can be viewed as the wires of the brain. Bundles of these myelinated nerve fibers are called neural tracts or pathways and connect distant areas of the brain. These neural tracts can be imaged with an MRI technique called diffusion tensor imaging (DTI) that is based on the principle that water diffuses or moves more rapidly along these bundles.

FUNCTIONAL MRI AND BRAIN ACTIVATION

Functional MRI (fMRI) is used to measure brain activity indirectly by detecting activity related changes in blood flow. When neurons fire and transmit signals, oxygen and glucose are required, which are supplied through increased blood flow to active areas. The so-called blood-oxygen-level-dependent (BOLD) contrast that is most often used in fMRI measures the changes in brain activation–related blood flow based on the different magnetic properties of oxygen-rich and oxygen-poor blood. With fMRI, several images of brain activation are made in intervals of typically 1 to 3 seconds so that a time series or movie of brain activation is created. Average brain activations between tasks, events, and groups can then be compared.

FUNCTIONAL CONNECTIVITY

Based on the information about how brain activation fluctuates over time in several brain regions, we can calculate how strongly correlated the activation is in these regions or how strongly the brain regions are functionally connected. In other words, functional connectivity refers to how much brain regions talk to each other.

NETWORK ANALYSIS

Based on this functional connectivity data, we then can study complex communication patterns between several or all brain regions by using network or graph analytical methods. Networks do not only exist inside the brain, but they also exist outside of the brain, for example, a social network. With graph theoretical methods, we can calculate all kinds of properties of a network, for example, how many friends you have and how quickly news travels from one person in your network to another person. Similar methods are used to understand brain networks.[3]

AREAS OF THE BRAIN INVOLVED IN MINDFULNESS

Using the methods described above, the regions in Figure A.1 have been identified as being involved in mindfulness.

Side (lateral) and middle (medial) view of the brain with schematically indicated brain regions that are involved in mindfulness and mentioned throughout the book: The anterior cingulate cortex is part of the salience network and plays a role in attention. The lateral prefrontal cortex is part of the central executive network and involved in regulating emotions and cognitions. The medial prefrontal cortex and

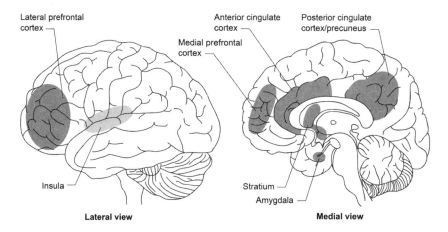

Figure A.1   Brain regions involved in mindfulness
Copyright © David Vago and Fritz Gard. Used with permission.

the posterior cingulate cortex and the adjacent precuneus are part of the default mode network and associated with mind-wandering. The amygdala is part of the salience network and plays a role in emotions. The insula plays a role in (body) awareness and the striatum in habits.

NOTES AND RESOURCES

INTRODUCTION

1. *Mindfulness training* refers to a set of practices that help one be mindful on demand and more often. The definition I use for *being mindful* is "being nonjudgmentally aware of what is being experienced—including thoughts and emotions—in the present moment." It is an adaptation of the most common functional definition of mindfulness, created by Jon Kabat-Zinn. The definition I use makes explicit the idea implied in Kabat-Zinn's definition that mindfulness is an awareness that includes self-awareness.

2. Dr. Gard—Gray matter is mostly made up of the cell bodies of nerve cells or neurons, dendrites (branches of the cell body that make connections to other neurons and receive signals from them), axon terminals (the club-shaped endings by which axons—another type of branch from the cell body—make connections with dendrites), and tiny blood vessels called capillaries. The gray matter is located in the outer layer of the brain (cerebral cortex) and in clusters of nerve cell bodies, deeper inside the brain (nuclei) (Kalat 2015).

Kalat, James W. 2015. *Biological Psychology.* 12th ed. Boston: Cengage Learning.

3. Draganski, Bogdan, Christian Gaser, Volker Busch, Gerhard Schuierer, Ulrich Bogdahn, and Arne May. 2004. "Neuroplasticity: Changes in Grey Matter Induced by Training." *Nature* 427 (6972): 311–2. doi:10.1038/427311a.

4. Dr. Gard—The 2004 juggling study by Draganski and colleagues was the first study to show that training really can change the brain in terms of gray matter. This study not only showed that training juggling for three months results in increases in gray matter in brain regions that are associated with the processing and storage of complex visual motion, it also showed that after not juggling for another three months, gray matter decreased in these brain areas. So you can train your brain, but if you don't use it, you may lose it. The clear link between brain and behavior in this study was strengthened by the finding that the jugglers who had a greater change in juggling performance also had a greater change in brain gray matter.

5. Lövdén, Martin, Elisabeth Wenger, Johan Mårtensson, Ulman Lindenberger, and Lars Bäckman. 2013. "Structural Brain Plasticity in Adult Learning and Development." *Neuroscience & Biobehavioral Reviews* 37 (9): 2296–310. doi:10.1016/j.neubiorev.2013.02.014.; Valkanova, Vyara, Rocio Eguia Rodriguez, and Klaus P. Ebmeier. 2014. "Mind over Matter—What Do We Know about Neuroplasticity in Adults?" *International Psychogeriatrics* 26 (6): 891–909. doi:10.1017/s1041610213002482.

6. Scholz, Jan, Miriam C. Klein, Timothy E. J. Behrens, and Heidi Johansen-Berg. 2009. "Training Induces Changes in White-Matter Architecture." *Nature Neuroscience* 12 (11): 1370–1. doi:10.1038/nn.2412.

7. When I use the word *mind*, I'm referring to the activity of the brain. Here, Dr. Gard elaborates on the relationship between mind and brain. Dr. Gard—The mind–body problem, or the mind–brain problem, refers to the philosophical problem of what the relationship between the mind and the brain is. Two main views on this problem exist: dualism and monism. Dualism is the view that the mind and brain are of different nature and thus not identical. This view was defended by sixteenth-century philosopher René Descartes. Monism is the view that mind and brain consist of the same substance. This view knows several forms, of which the identity view is the most accepted among neuroscientists today. According to this view, mental processes and brain activity are identical, so it is assumed thoughts are brain activity and brain activity is thoughts (Kalat 2015).

Kalat, James W. 2015. *Biological Psychology.* 12th ed. Boston: Cengage Learning.

8. Woollett, Katherine, and Eleanor A. Maguire. 2011. "Acquiring 'the Knowledge' of London's Layout Drives Structural Brain Changes." *Current Biology* 21 (24): 2109–14. doi:10.1016/j.cub.2011.11.018.

9. In 2005, there were 75 scholarly articles published on the topic of mindfulness. In 2010, that number reached 436. In 2014, it was 1,063. So much research has been compiled, in fact, that an association has been formed to keep track of it all and support further research efforts, called the American Mindfulness Research Association (https://goamra.org/). The number of published articles in 2005 was based on a search in Web of Science using the query "TOPIC:(mindfulness), Timespan:2005, Search language=Auto." The same query but with Timespan:2010 and 2014 was used for the respective years.

10. Fox, Kieran C. R., Savannah Nijeboer, Matthew L. Dixon, James L. Floman, Melissa Ellamil, Samuel P. Rumak, Peter Sedlmeier, and Kalina Christoff. 2014. "Is Meditation Associated with Altered Brain Structure? A Systematic Review and Meta-Analysis of Morphometric Neuroimaging in Meditation Practitioners." *Neuroscience and Biobehavioral Reviews* 43 (June): 48–73. doi:10.1016/j.neubiorev.2014.03.016.;

Hölzel, Britta K., James Carmody, Mark Vangel, Christina Congleton, Sita M. Yerramsetti, Tim Gard, and Sara W. Lazar. 2011. "Mindfulness Practice Leads to Increases in Regional Brain Gray Matter Density." *Psychiatry Research: Neuroimaging* 191 (September): 36–43. doi:10.1016/j.pscychresns.2010.08.006.

11. Dr. Gard—The field of cognitive neuroscience is still quite young. Functional magnetic resonance image (fMRI) was first used to study brain activation in the early 1990s (Belliveau et al. 1991). The field that investigates the neural mechanisms of mindfulness, the so-called contemplative neuroscience, is in its infancy. It was only in 2005 that the brain structure of mindfulness practitioners was studied for the first time (Lazar et al. 2005), and the first studies investigating the effects of mindfulness-based interventions on brain structure are from 2010 and 2011 (Hölzel et al. 2011; Tang et al. 2010). Although what we have learned so far about the neural mechanisms of mindfulness is amazing, it is important to realize that in this very young field, much of the interpretations of the findings are speculative. Many studies don't directly relate brain findings to self-report or behavioral measures, and, because of study designs that are not optimal, it is not always clear whether the findings are exclusive to mindfulness. These problems are actually quite normal when a field is young. With ongoing research, firmer conclusions can be drawn in the future. With this note of cautious optimism in mind, I hope that you'll enjoy learning how mindfulness might rewire your brain and that you become as excited by the findings in the field of contemplative neuroscience as I have become.

Belliveau, J. W., D. N. Kennedy Jr., R. C. McKinstry, B. R. Buchbinder, R. M. Weisskoff, M. S. Cohen, J. M. Vevea, T. J. Brady, and B. R. Rosen. 1991. "Functional Mapping of the Human Visual Cortex by Magnetic Resonance Imaging." *Science* 254 (5032): 716–9. doi:10.1126/science.1948051.

Hölzel, Britta K., James Carmody, Mark Vangel, Christina Congleton, Sita M. Yerramsetti, Tim Gard, and Sara W. Lazar. 2011. "Mindfulness Practice Leads to Increases in Regional Brain Gray Matter Density." *Psychiatry Research: Neuroimaging* 191(1): 36–43. doi:10.1016/j.pscychresns.2010.08.006.

Lazar, Sara W., Catherine E. Kerr, Rachel H. Wasserman, Jeremy R. Gray, Douglas N. Greve, Michael T. Treadway, Metta McGarvey et al. 2005. "Meditation Experience Is Associated with Increased Cortical Thickness." *Neuroreport* 16 (17): 1893–7. doi:10.1097/01.wnr.0000186598.66243.19.

Tang, Yi-Yuan, Qilin Lu, Xiujuan Geng, Elliot A. Stein, Yihong Yang, and Michael I. Posner. 2010. "Short-Term Meditation Induces White Matter Changes in the Anterior Cingulate." *Proceedings of the National Academy of Sciences of the United States of America* 107 (35): 15649–52. doi:10.1073/pnas.1011043107.

CHAPTER 1

1. Michelson, Albert A., and Morley, Edward W. 1887. "On the Relative Motion of the Earth and the Luminiferous Ether." *The American Journal of Science* 34 (203): 333–45.
2. I highly recommend this thought-provoking book that explores the incredible world of special and general relativity and quantum mechanics in a fun, easy-to-read format.
3. Shunryu Suzuki-roshi was a highly respected mindfulness teacher. An excellent book that I highly recommend was created from a collection of his talks: *Zen Mind, Beginner's Mind.*
4. Quoted by James Franck in Seelig, *Albert Einstein,* (1954), 84.
5. Please note that this image and the others like it are not intended to have any biological correlation to brain structure. They are intended to provide a very simple visual aid for understanding the relationship between awareness and the mind. Also, this image has a serious shortcoming. Awareness is actually nonlocal and certainly not fixated inside the head. The most accurate representation of how things actually are would be to put all the sense objects, including the thinking mind and its ego, inside the brain, because that is where our relationship with those things is created. Awareness would transcend the boundaries of the physical body and not be bound by artificial constructs such as physical location. However, that more accurate image would be very difficult to create in a way that wouldn't confuse people or distract them with metaphysical questions. Thus, I elected to focus on what is most useful, which is seeing clearly that we can have an objective, third-person awareness of the thinking mind and the ego it creates.
6. Killingsworth, Matthew A., and Daniel T. Gilbert. 2010. "A Wandering Mind Is an Unhappy Mind." *Science* 330 (6006): 932. doi:10.1126/science.1192439.
7. Smallwood, Jonathan, and Jonathan W. Schooler. 2015. "The Science of Mind Wandering: Empirically Navigating the Stream of Consciousness." *Annual Review of Psychology* 66 (January): 487–518. doi:10.1146/annurev-psych-010814–015331.
8. Dr. Gard—Please note that mind wandering is not all bad. It has, for example, been shown to facilitate creative problem solving (Baird et al. 2012). Matt and I suggest, however, that you be intentional about mind wandering, and don't allow mind wandering to be your default mode of operating in the world.

Baird, Benjamin, Jonathan Smallwood, Michael D. Mrazek, Julia W. Y. Kam, Michael S. Franklin, and Jonathan W. Schooler. 2012. "Inspired by Distraction: Mind Wandering Facilitates Creative Incubation." *Psychological Science* 23 (10): 1117–22. doi:10.1177/0956797612446024.

9. Killingsworth, Matthew A., and Daniel T. Gilbert. 2010. "A Wandering Mind Is an Unhappy Mind." *Science* 330 (6006): 932. doi:10.1126/science.1192439;

Mrazek, Michael D., Jonathan Smallwood, Michael S. Franklin, Jason M. Chin, Benjamin Baird, and Jonathan W. Schooler. 2012. "The Role of Mind-Wandering in Measurements of General Aptitude." *Journal of Experimental Psychology: General* 141 (4): 788–98. doi:10.1037/a0027968.

10. Vago, David R. 2014. "Mapping Modalities of Self-Awareness in Mindfulness Practice: A Potential Mechanism for Clarifying Habits of Mind." *Annals of the New York Academy of Sciences* 1307 (January): 28–42. doi:10.1111/nyas.12270; Hafenbrack, Andrew C., Zoe Kinias, and Sigal G. Barsade. 2014. "Debiasing the Mind through Meditation: Mindfulness and the Sunk-Cost Bias." *Psychological Science* 25 (2): 369–76. doi:10.1177/0956797613503853.

11. Mason, Malia F., Michael I. Norton, John D. Van Horn, Daniel M. Wegner, Scott T. Grafton, and C. Neil Macrae. 2007. "Wandering Minds: The Default Network and Stimulus-Independent Thought." *Science* 315 (5810): 393–5. doi:10.1126/science.1131295; Christoff, Kalina, Alan M. Gordon, Jonathan Smallwood, Rachelle Smith, and Jonathan W. Schooler. 2009. "Experience Sampling during fMRI Reveals Default Network and Executive System Contributions to Mind Wandering." *Proceedings of the National Academy of Sciences of the United States of America* 106 (21): 8719–24. doi:10.1073/pnas.0900234106.

12. Greicius, Michael D., Ben Krasnow, Allan L. Reiss, and Vinod Menon. 2003. "Functional Connectivity in the Resting Brain: A Network Analysis of the Default Mode Hypothesis." *Proceedings of the National Academy of Sciences of the United States of America* 100 (1): 253–8. doi:10.1073/pnas.0135058100; Buckner, Randy L., Jessica R. Andrews-Hanna, and Daniel L. Schacter. 2008. "The Brain's Default Network: Anatomy, Function, and Relevance to Disease." *Annals of the New York Academy of Sciences* 1124 (March): 1–38. doi:10.1196/annals.1440.011; Raichle, Marcus E. 2015. "The Brain's Default Mode Network." *Annual Review of Neuroscience* 38 (July): 433–47. doi:10.1146/annurev-neuro-071013-014030; Raichle, Marcus E., Ann Mary MacLeod, Abraham Z. Snyder, William J. Powers, Debra A. Gusnard, and Gordon L. Shulman. 2001. "A Default Mode of Brain Function." *Proceedings of the National Academy of Sciences of the United States of America* 98 (2): 676–82. doi:10.1073/pnas.98.2.676.

13. In the 1999 Warner Brothers film *The Matrix*, the majority of humans are asleep and experience a reality that is simulated by a computer program. People in this program can do only what they are programmed to do. It is only when people unplug from the matrix that they can transcend the program. Similarly, when we wake up with mindfulness, we can transcend the programming that results from our genetics and social conditioning.

14. Graybiel, Ann M. 2008. "Habits, Rituals, and the Evaluative Brain." *Annual Review of Neuroscience* 31 (July): 359–87. doi:10.1146/annurev.neuro.29.051605.112851.

15. Ashby, F. Gregory, Benjamin O. Turner, and Jon C. Horvitz. 2010. "Cortical and Basal Ganglia Contributions to Habit Learning and Automaticity." *Trends*

in Cognitive Sciences 14 (5): 208–15. doi: 10.1016/j.tics.2010.02.001; Braunlich, Kurt, and Carol Seger. 2013. "The Basal Ganglia." *Wiley Interdisciplinary Reviews: Cognitive Science* 4 (2): 135–48. doi:10.1002/wcs.1217; Graybiel, Ann M. 2008. "Habits, Rituals, and the Evaluative Brain." *Annual Review of Neuroscience* 31 (July): 359–87. doi:10.1146/annurev.neuro.29.051605.112851; Ostlund, S. B., and B. W. Balleine. 2005. "Lesions of Medial Prefrontal Cortex Disrupt the Acquisition but Not the Expression of Goal-Directed Learning." *The Journal of Neuroscience*, 25(34), 7763–7770. doi:10.1523/JNEUROSCI.1921–05.2005; Yin, Henry H., and Barbara J. Knowlton. 2006. "The Role of the Basal Ganglia in Habit Formation." *Nature Reviews Neuroscience* 7 (6): 464–76. doi:10.1038/nrn1919.

16. Traditionally, *mindfulness* and *self-awareness*, although two separate words, are often used together. Thus, I have elected to combine them in this text for the sake of simplicity and clarity. When I use the word *traditionally* in this text, I'm referring to a specific tradition of practice, which I explain here. Mindfulness is not something that some person invented. It is an inherent human quality. Most spiritual traditions include mindfulness practices, as do many psychological therapies. However, a man named Siddhartha Gautama, who lived around 500 BC, was one of the first people to discover that intentionally spending more time being mindful results in numerous benefits. He focused on the benefits of reducing suffering and wrongdoing and increasing happiness and virtue. Gautama, often referred to as the "Buddha," which means "awakened one," was essentially a psychologist. He created a very in-depth, scientific approach to training and mastering the mind over a period of roughly 45 years. The path was eventually written down in great detail in what is known as the Pāli (an ancient Indian language) canon. This is why many of the modern teachings on mindfulness training refer to Buddhist psychology. It's not because Gautama created or was even the first to apply mindfulness training but because the training methodologies were so detailed and thorough. Also of note, the path Gautama offered is not traditionally thought of as a religion by people who actually practice but rather a method of training the mind that people of any religious background can use.

17. Hafenbrack, Andrew C., Zoe Kinias, and Sigal G. Barsade. 2014. "Debiasing the Mind through Meditation: Mindfulness and the Sunk-Cost Bias." *Psychological Science* 25 (2): 369–76. doi:10.1177/0956797613503853; Mason, Malia F., Michael I. Norton, John D. Van Horn, Daniel M. Wegner, Scott T. Grafton, and C. Neil Macrae. 2007. "Wandering Minds: The Default Network and Stimulus-Independent Thought." *Science* 315 (5810): 393–5. doi:10.1126/science.1131295; Christoff, Kalina, Alan M. Gordon, Jonathan Smallwood, Rachelle Smith, and Jonathan W. Schooler. 2009. "Experience Sampling during fMRI Reveals Default Network and Executive System Contributions to Mind

Wandering." *Proceedings of the National Academy of Sciences of the United States of America* 106 (21): 8719–24. doi:10.1073/pnas.0900234106.

18. Mrazek, Michael D., Michael S. Franklin, Dawa T. Phillips, Benjamin Baird, and Jonathan W. Schooler. 2013. "Mindfulness Training Improves Working Memory Capacity and GRE Performance While Reducing Mind Wandering." *Psychological Science* 24 (5): 776–81. doi:10.1177/0956797612459659. Seelig, Carl. 1954. *Albert Einstein; Eine Dokumentarische Biographie.* Zurich, Switzerland: Europa Verlag.

19. Hafenbrack, Andrew C., Zoe Kinias, and Sigal G. Barsade. 2014. "Debiasing the Mind through Meditation: Mindfulness and the Sunk-Cost Bias." *Psychological Science* 25 (2): 369–76. doi:10.1177/0956797613503853; Mason, Malia F., Michael I. Norton, John D. Van Horn, Daniel M. Wegner, Scott T. Grafton, and C. Neil Macrae. 2007. "Wandering Minds: The Default Network and Stimulus-Independent Thought." *Science* 315 (5810): 393–5. doi:10.1126/science.1131295.

20. Arkes, Hal R., and Catherine Blumer. 1985. "The Psychology of Sunk Cost." *Organizational Behavior and Human Decision Processes* 35 (February): 124–40. doi:10.1016/0749–5978(85)90049–4.

21. Brewer, Judson A., Patrick D. Worhunsky, Jeremy Gray, Yi-Yuan Tang, Jochen Weber, and Hedy Kober. 2011. "Meditation Experience Is Associated with Differences in Default Mode Network Activity and Connectivity." *Proceedings of the National Academy of Sciences of the United States of America* 108 (50): 20254–9. doi:10.1073/pnas.1112029108.

22. Taylor, Véronique A., Véronique Daneault, Joshua Grant, Geneviève Scavone, Estelle Breton, Sébastien Roffe-Vidal, Jérôme Courtemanche et al. 2013. "Impact of Meditation Training on the Default Mode Network during a Restful State." *Social Cognitive and Affective Neuroscience* 8 (1): 4–14. doi:10.1093/scan/nsr087; Kilpatrick, Lisa A., Brandall Y. Suyenobu, Suzanne R. Smith, Joshua A. Bueller, Trudy Goodman, J. David Creswell, Kirsten Tillisch, Emeran A. Mayer, and Bruce D. Naliboff. 2011. "Impact of Mindfulness-Based Stress Reduction Training on Intrinsic Brain Connectivity." *Neuroimage* 56 (February): 290–8. doi:10.1016/j.neuroimage.2011.02.034; Wells, Rebecca E., Gloria Y. Yeh, Catherine E. Kerr, Jennifer Wolkin, Roger B. Davis, Ying Tan, Rosa Spaeth et al. 2013. "Meditation's Impact on Default Mode Network and Hippocampus in Mild Cognitive Impairment: A Pilot Study." *Neuroscience Letters* 556 (November): 15–19. doi:10.1016/j.neulet.2013.10.001; Jang, Joon H., Wi H. Jung, Do-Hyung Kang, Min S. Byun, Soo J. Kwon, Chi-Hoon Choi, and Jun S. Kwon. 2010. "Increased Default Mode Network Connectivity Associated with Meditation." *Neuroscience Letters* 487 (3): 358–62. doi:10.1016/j.neulet.2010.10.056; Hasenkamp, Wendy, and Lawrence W. Barsalou. 2012. "Effects of Meditation Experience on Functional Connectivity of Distributed Brain Networks." *Frontiers*

in Human Neuroscience 6 (March): 1–14. doi:10.3389/fnhum.2012.00038; Manna, Antonietta, Antonio Raffone, Mauro G. Perrucci, Davide Nardo, Antonio Ferretti, Armando Tartaro, Alessandro Londei, Cosimo Del Gratta, Marta O. Belardinelli, and Gian L. Romani. 2010. "Neural Correlates of Focused Attention and Cognitive Monitoring in Meditation." *Brain Research Bulletin* 82 (1–2): 46–56. doi:10.1016/j.brainresbull.2010.03.001; Josipovic, Zoran, Ilan Dinstein, Jochen Weber, and David J. Heeger. 2011. "Influence of Meditation on Anti-Correlated Networks in the Brain." *Frontiers in Human Neuroscience* 5 (January): 1–11. doi:10.3389/fnhum.2011.00183.

23. Bornemann, Boris, Beate M. Herbert, Wolf E. Mehling, and Tania Singer. 2015. "Differential Changes in Self-Reported Aspects of Interoceptive Awareness through 3 Months of Contemplative Training." *Frontiers in Psychology* 5 (January): 1–13. doi:10.3389/fpsyg.2014.01504; Bornemann, Boris, and Tania Singer. 2015. "Taking Time to Get in Touch with Our Body: Heart Beat Perception Accuracy Increases Linearly over Nine Months of Contemplative Training." Paper presented at the International Convention of Psychological Science, Amsterdam, Netherlands, March; Fox, Kieran C., Pierre Zakarauskas, Matt Dixon, Melissa Ellamil, Evan Thompson, and Kalina Christoff. 2012. "Meditation Experience Predicts Introspective Accuracy." *PLoS ONE* 7 (9): e45370. doi:10.1371/journal.pone.0045370; Sze, Jocelyn A., Anett Gyurak, Joyce W. Yuan, and Robert W. Levenson. 2010. "Coherence between Emotional Experience and Physiology: Does Body Awareness Training Have an Impact?" *Emotion* 10 (6): 803–14. doi:10.1037/a0020146.

24. Fox, Kieran C., Pierre Zakarauskas, Matt Dixon, Melissa Ellamil, Evan Thompson, and Kalina Christoff. 2012. "Meditation Experience Predicts Introspective Accuracy." *PLoS ONE* 7 (9): e45370. doi:10.1371/journal.pone.0045370.

25. Lazar, Sara W., Catherine E. Kerr, Rachel H. Wasserman, Jeremy R. Gray, Douglas N. Greve, Michael T. Treadway, Metta McGarvey et al. 2005. "Meditation Experience Is Associated with Increased Cortical Thickness." *Neuroreport* 16 (17): 1893–7. doi:10.1097/01.wnr.0000186598.66243.19; Hölzel, Britta K., Ulrich Ott, Tim Gard, Hannes Hempel, Martin Weygandt, Katrin Morgen, and Dieter Vaitl. 2008. "Investigation of Mindfulness Meditation Practitioners with Voxel-Based Morphometry." *Social Cognitive and Affective Neuroscience* 3 (1): 55–61. doi:10.1093/scan/nsm038; Farb, Norman A. S., Adam K. Anderson, Helen Mayberg, Jim Bean, Deborah McKeon, and Zindel V. Segal. 2010. "Minding One's Emotions: Mindfulness Training Alters the Neural Expression of Sadness." *Emotion* 10 (1): 25–33. doi:10.1037/a0017151; Farb, Norman A. S., Zindel V. Segal, and Adam K. Anderson. 2013. "Mindfulness Meditation Training Alters Cortical Representations of Interoceptive Attention." *Social Cognitive and Affective Neuroscience* 8 (1): 15–26.

doi:10.1093/scan/nss066; Gard, Tim, Britta K. Hölzel, Alexander T. Sack, Hannes Hempel, Sara W. Lazar, Dieter Vaitl, and Ulrich Ott. 2012. "Pain Attenuation through Mindfulness Is Associated with Decreased Cognitive Control and Increased Sensory Processing in the Brain." *Cerebral Cortex* 22 (11): 2692–702. doi:10.1093/cercor/bhr352.

26. Craig, A. D. 2002. "How Do You Feel? Interoception: The Sense of the Physiological Condition of the Body." *Nature Reviews Neuroscience* 3 (8): 655–66. doi:10.1038/nrn894; Craig, A. D. 2003. "Interoception: The Sense of the Physiological Condition of the Body." *Current Opinion in Neurobiology* 13 (4): 500–5. doi:10.1016/S0959–4388(03)00090–4; Craig, A. D. 2009. "How Do You Feel—Now? The Anterior Insula and Human Awareness." *Nature Reviews Neuroscience* 10 (1): 59–70. doi:10.1038/nrn2555; Critchley, Hugo D., Stefan Wiens, Pia Rotshtein, Arne Öhman, and Raymond J. Dolan. 2004. "Neural Systems Supporting Interoceptive Awareness." *Nature Neuroscience* 7 (2): 189–95. doi:10.1038/nn1176.

27. Farb, Norman A. S., Zindel V. Segal, Helen Mayberg, Jim Bean, Deborah McKeon, Zainab Fatima, and Adam K. Anderson. 2007. "Attending to the Present: Mindfulness Meditation Reveals Distinct Neural Modes of Self-Reference." *Social Cognitive and Affective Neuroscience* 2 (4): 313–22. doi:10.1093/scan/nsm030.

28. Frankl, Viktor E. (1946) 2006. *Man's Search for Meaning.* Boston: Beacon Press.

29. Covey, Stephen R. 2013. *The 7 Habits of Highly Effective People: Powerful Lessons in Personal Change.* 25th anniversary ed. New York: Simon & Schuster.

30. Boyatzis, Richard E. 1982. *The Competent Manager: A Model for Effective Performance.* New York: John Wiley & Sons.

31. Hasenkamp, Wendy, Christine D. Wilson-Mendenhall, Erica Duncan, and Lawrence W. Barsalou. 2012. "Mind Wandering and Attention during Focused Meditation: A Fine-Grained Temporal Analysis of Fluctuating Cognitive States." *Neuroimage* 59 (1): 750–60. doi:10.1016/j.neuroimage.2011.07.008.

32. Seeley, William W., Vinod Menon, Alan F. Schatzberg, Jennifer Keller, Gary H. Glover, Heather Kenna, Allan L. Reiss, and Michael D. Greicius. 2007. "Dissociable Intrinsic Connectivity Networks for Salience Processing and Executive Control." *Journal of Neuroscience* 27 (9): 2349–56. doi:10.1523/jneurosci.5587–06.2007.

33. Seeley, William W., Vinod Menon, Alan F. Schatzberg, Jennifer Keller, Gary H. Glover, Heather Kenna, Allan L. Reiss, and Michael D. Greicius. 2007. "Dissociable Intrinsic Connectivity Networks for Salience Processing and Executive Control." *Journal of Neuroscience* 27 (9): 2349–56. doi:10.1523/jneurosci.5587–06.2007; Corbetta, Maurizio, and Gordon L. Shulman. 2002. "Control of Goal-Directed and Stimulus-Driven Attention in the Brain." *Nature Reviews Neuroscience* 3 (3): 201–15. doi:10.1038/nrn755.

34. Hasenkamp, Wendy, Christine D. Wilson-Mendenhall, Erica Duncan, and Lawrence W. Barsalou. 2012. "Mind Wandering and Attention during Focused Meditation: A Fine-Grained Temporal Analysis of Fluctuating Cognitive States." *Neuroimage* 59 (1): 750–60. doi:10.1016/j.neuroimage.2011.07.008.

35. Gard, Tim, Britta K. Hölzel, Alexander T. Sack, Hannes Hempel, Sara W. Lazar, Dieter Vaitl, and Ulrich Ott. 2012. "Pain Attenuation through Mindfulness Is Associated with Decreased Cognitive Control and Increased Sensory Processing in the Brain." *Cerebral Cortex* 22 (11): 2692–702. doi:10.1093/cercor/bhr352; Grant, Joshua A., Jérôme Courtemanche, and Pierre Rainville. 2011. "A Non-Elaborative Mental Stance and Decoupling of Executive and Pain-Related Cortices Predicts Low Pain Sensitivity in Zen Meditators." *Pain* 152 (1): 150–6. doi:10.1016/j.pain.2010.10.006.

36. Brefczynski-Lewis, J. A., A. Lutz, H. S. Schaefer, D. B. Levinson, and R. J. Davidson. 2007. "Neural Correlates of Attentional Expertise in Long-Term Meditation Practitioners." *Proceedings of the National Academy of Sciences of the United States of America* 104 (27): 11483–8. doi:10.1073/pnas.0606552104.

CHAPTER 2

1. As we'll discuss later in the chapter, we can certainly transcend our hardwiring with self-awareness and mental agility, so there could certainly be a higher percentage of leaders who can create and sustain profitable organizations over the long term.

2. Taylor, Jim. 2013. "Cognitive Biases Are Bad for Business: Do You See Irrationality in Your Company?" *The Power of Prime* (blog). *Psychology Today*. https://www.psychologytoday.com/blog/the-power-prime/201305/cognitive-biases-are-bad-business.

3. Krantz, Matt. 2014. "The 11 Brands You're Paying up For." *USA Today Money*, November 5. http://americasmarkets.usatoday.com/2014/11/05/the-11-brands-youre-paying-up-for.

4. Sun, Sai, Ziqing Yao, Jaixin Wei, and Rongjun Yu. 2015. "Calm and Smart? A Selective Review of Meditation Effects on Decision Making." *Frontiers in Psychology* 6: 1–11. doi:10.3389/fpsyg.2015.01059.

5. Kirk, Ulrich, Jonathan Downar, and P. Read Montague. 2011. "Interoception Drives Increased Rational Decision-Making in Meditators Playing the Ultimatum Game." *Frontiers in Neuroscience* 5: 1–11. doi:10.3389/fnins.2011.00049.

6. Bolton, Gary E., and Rami Zwick. 1995 "Anonymity versus Punishment in Ultimatum Bargaining." *Games and Economic Behavior* 10: 95–121. doi:10.1006/game.1995.1026; Güth, Werner, Rolf Schmittberger, and Bernd Schwarze. 1982. "An Experimental Analysis of Ultimatum Bargaining." *Journal of Economic Behavior and Organization* 3 (4): 367–88. doi:10.1016/0167–2681

(82)90011–7; Kirk, Ulrich, Jonathan Downar, and P. Read Montague. 2011. "Interoception Drives Increased Rational Decision-Making in Meditators Playing the Ultimatum Game." *Frontiers in Neuroscience* 5: 1–11. doi:10.3389/fnins.2011.00049.

7. Sanfey, Alan G., James K. Rilling, Jessica A. Aronson, Leigh E. Nystrom, and Jonathan D. Cohen. 2003. "The Neural Basis of Economic Decision-Making in the Ultimatum Game." *Science* 300 (5626): 1755–8. doi:10.1126/science.1082976.

8. Craig, A. D. 2002. "How Do You Feel? Interoception: The Sense of the Physiological Condition of the Body." *Nature Reviews Neuroscience* 3 (8): 655–66. doi:10.1038/nrn894.

9. Dr.Gard—Furthermore, rational nonpractitioners, that is, those who accept more than 85 percent of unfair offers, had increased brain activation in the dorsolateral prefrontal cortex, which could indicate cognitive control over emotions. Rational mindfulness practitioners, on the other hand, had increased brain activation in the somatosensory cortex and posterior superior temporal cortex, regions that are involved in body awareness and perspective taking, respectively (Behrens et al. 2008; Craig 2002; Hampton, Bossaerts, and O'Doherty 2008).

Behrens, Timothy E., Laurence T. Hunt, Mark W. Woolrich, and Matthew F. S. Rushworth. 2008. "Associative Learning of Social Value." *Nature* 456 (7219): 245–9. doi:10.1038/nature07538.

Craig, A. D. 2002. "How Do You Feel? Interoception: The Sense of the Physiological Condition of the Body." *Nature Reviews Neuroscience* 3 (8): 655–66. doi:10.1038/nrn894.

Hampton, Alan N., Peter Bossaerts, and John P. O'Doherty. 2008. "Neural Correlates of Mentalizing-Related Computations during Strategic Interactions in Humans." *Proceedings of the National Academy of Sciences of the United States of America* 105 (18): 6741–6. doi:10.1073/pnas.0711099105.

10. Lazar, Sara W., Catherine E. Kerr, Rachel H. Wasserman, Jeremy R. Gray, Douglas N. Greve, Michael T. Treadway, Metta McGarvey et al. 2005. "Meditation Experience Is Associated with Increased Cortical Thickness." *Neuroreport* 16 (17): 1893–7. doi:10.1097/01.wnr.0000186598.66243.19.

11. Please note that the 2005 Lazar study was a cross-sectional study. In other words, instead of comparing people before and after mindfulness training to see whether there were changes in their brains, the researchers compared 20 people who had about 10 years of daily mindfulness practice with 15 people who did not practice mindfulness. Thus, it could have been possible that only people who have a thicker insula in the first place were interested in and able to practice mindfulness for 10 years.

12. Fox, Kieran C. R., Savannah Nijeboer, Matthew L. Dixon, James L. Floman, Melissa Ellamil, Samuel P. Rumak, Peter Sedlmeier, and Kalina Christoff. 2014.

"Is Meditation Associated with Altered Brain Structure? A Systematic Review and Meta-Analysis of Morphometric Neuroimaging in Meditation Practitioners." *Neuroscience and Biobehavioral Reviews* 43 (June): 48–73. doi: 10.1016/j.neubiorev.2014.03.016; Tang, Yi-Yuan, Britta K. Hölzel, and Michael I. Posner. 2015. "The Neuroscience of Mindfulness Meditation." *Nature Reviews Neuroscience* 16 (4): 213–25. doi:10.1038/nrn3916; Hölzel, Britta K., Sara W. Lazar, Tim Gard, Zev Schuman-Olivier, David R. Vago, and Ulrich Ott. 2011. "How Does Mindfulness Meditation Work? Proposing Mechanisms of Action from a Conceptual and Neural Perspective." *Perspectives on Psychological Science* 6 (6): 537–59. doi:10.1177/1745691611419671.

13. Sze, Jocelyn A., Anett Gyurak, Joyce W. Yuan, and Robert W. Levenson. 2010. "Coherence between Emotional Experience and Physiology: Does Body Awareness Training Have an Impact?" *Emotion* 10 (6): 803–14. doi:10.1037/a0020146.

14. Fox, Kieran C., Pierre Zakarauskas, Matt Dixon, Melissa Ellamil, Evan Thompson, and Kalina Christoff. 2012. "Meditation Experience Predicts Introspective Accuracy." *PLoS ONE* 7 (9): e45370. doi:10.1371/journal.pone.0045370.

15. Bornemann, Boris, and Tania Singer. 2015. "Taking Time to Get in Touch with Our Body: Heart Beat Perception Accuracy Increases Linearly over Nine Months of Contemplative Training." Paper presented at the International Convention of Psychological Science, Amsterdam, Netherlands, March.

16. Dr. Gard—It should be noted that this high-quality study had a large sample size (N = 160), a longitudinal design, and a long (39 weeks) intervention. Other studies with small sample sizes did not find increased interoceptive accuracy in mindfulness practitioners (Khalsa et al. 2008; Melloni et al. 2013; Nielsen and Kasezniak 2006; Parkin et al. 2013).

Khalsa, Sahib S., David Rudrauf, Antonio R. Damasio, Richard J. Davidson, Antoine Lutz, and Daniel Tranel. 2008. "Interoceptive Awareness in Experienced Meditators." *Psychophysiology* 45 (4): 671–7. doi:10.1111/j.1469-8986.2008.00666.x.

Melloni, Margherita, Lucas Sedeño, Blas Couto, Martin Reynoso, Carlos Gelormini, Roberto Favaloro, Andrés Canales-Johnson, Mariano Sigman, Facundo Manes, and Agustin Ibanez. 2013. "Preliminary Evidence about the Effects of Meditation on Interoceptive Sensitivity and Social Cognition." *Behavioral and Brain Functions* 9 (December): 47. doi:10.1186/1744-9081-9-47.

Nielsen, Lisbeth, and Alfred W. Kasezniak. 2006. "Awareness of Subtle Emotional Feelings: A Comparison of Long-Term Meditators and Nonmeditators." *Emotion* 6 (3): 392–405. doi:10.1037/1528-3542.6.3.392.

Parkin, Lucy, Ruth Morgan, Anna Rosselli, Maxine Howard, Alicia Sheppard, Davy Evans, Amy Hawkins et al. 2013. "Exploring the Relationship between Mindfulness and Cardiac Perception." *Mindfulness* 5 (3): 298–313. doi:10.1007/s12671–012–0181–7.

17. Wenk-Sormaz, Heidi. 2005. "Meditation Can Reduce Habitual Responding." *Alternative Therapies in Health and Medicine* 11 (2): 42–58.

18. Stroop, J. Ridley. 1935. "Studies of Interference in Serial Verbal Reactions." *Journal of Experimental Psychology* 18 (6): 643–62.

19. Chan, Davina, and Marjorie Woollacott. 2007. "Effects of Level of Meditation Experience on Attentional Focus: Is the Efficiency of Executive or Orientation Networks Improved?" *Journal of Alternative and Complementary Medicine* 13 (November): 651–7. doi:10.1089/acm.2007.7022; Moore, Adam, and Peter Malinowski. 2009. "Meditation, Mindfulness and Cognitive Flexibility." *Consciousness and Cognition* 18 (1): 176–86. doi:10.1016/j.concog.2008.12.008; Teper, Rimma, and Michael Inzlicht. 2013. "Meditation, Mindfulness and Executive Control: The Importance of Emotional Acceptance and Brain-Based Performance Monitoring." *Social Cognitive and Affective Neuroscience* 8 (1): 85–92. doi:10.1093/scan/nss045.

20. Kozasa, Elisa H., João R. Sato, Shirley S. Lacerda, Maria A. M. Barreiros, João Radvany, Tamara A. Russell, Liana G. Sanches, Luiz E.A.M. Mello, and Edson Amaro Jr. 2012. "Meditation Training Increases Brain Efficiency in an Attention Task." *Neuroimage* 59 (July): 745–9. doi:10.1016/j.neuroimage.2011.06.088.

21. MacDonald, Angus W., Jonathan D. Cohen, V. Andrew Stenger, and Cameron S. Carter. 2000. "Dissociating the Role of the Dorsolateral Prefrontal and Anterior Cingulate Cortex in Cognitive Control." *Science* 288 (5472): 1835–8. doi:10.1126/science.288.5472.1835.

22. Teper, Rimma, and Michael Inzlicht. 2013. "Meditation, Mindfulness and Executive Control: The Importance of Emotional Acceptance and Brain-Based Performance Monitoring." *Social Cognitive and Affective Neuroscience* 8 (1): 85–92. doi:10.1093/scan/nss045.

23. Ashby, F. Gregory, Benjamin O. Turner, and Jon C. Horvitz. 2010. "Cortical and Basal Ganglia Contributions to Habit Learning and Automaticity." *Trends in Cognitive Sciences* 14 (5): 208–15. doi: 10.1016/j.tics.2010.02.001; Braunlich, Kurt, and Carol Seger. 2013. "The Basal Ganglia." *Wiley Interdisciplinary Reviews: Cognitive Science* 4 (2): 135–48. doi:10.1002/wcs.1217; Graybiel, Ann M. 2008. "Habits, Rituals, and the Evaluative Brain." *Annual Review of Neuroscience* 31 (July): 359–87. doi:10.1146/annurev.neuro.29.051605.112851; Yin, Henry H., and Barbara J. Knowlton. 2006. "The Role of the Basal Ganglia in Habit Formation." *Nature Reviews Neuroscience* 7 (6): 464–76. doi:10.1038/nrn1919.

24. Gard, Tim, Maxime Taquet, Rohan Dixit, Britta K. Hölzel, Bradford C. Dickerson, and Sara W. Lazar. 2015. "Greater Widespread Functional Connectivity of the Caudate in Older Adults Who Practice Kripalu Yoga and

Vipassana Meditation than in Controls." *Frontiers in Human Neuroscience* 9 (March): 1–12. doi:10.3389/fnhum.2015.00137.

25. Jansen, Arthur S. P., Xay V. Nguyen, Vladimir Karpitskiy, Thomas C. Mettenleiter, and Arthur D. Loewy. 1995. "Central Command Neurons of the Sympathetic Nervous System: Basis of the Fight-or-Flight Response." *Science* 270 (5236): 644–6; Kalat, James W. 2015. *Biological Psychology.* 12th ed. Boston: Cengage Learning.

26. Schwabe, Lars, and Oliver T. Wolf. 2011. "Stress-Induced Modulation of Instrumental Behavior: From Goal-Directed to Habitual Control of Action." *Behavioural Brain Research* 219 (2): 321–8. doi:10.1016/j.bbr.2010.12.038; Schwabe, Lars, and Oliver T. Wolf. 2013. "Stress and Multiple Memory Systems: From 'Thinking' to 'Doing.'" *Trends in Cognitive Sciences* 17 (2): 60–8. doi:10.1016/j.tics.2012.12.001.

27. Graybiel, Ann M. 2008. "Habits, Rituals, and the Evaluative Brain." *Annual Review of Neuroscience* 31 (July): 359–87. doi:10.1146/annurev.neuro.29.051605.112851.

28. Levenson, Robert W., Paul Ekman, and Matthieu Ricard. 2012. "Meditation and the Startle Response." *Emotion* 12 (3): 650–8.

29. Botvinick, Matthew M., Jonathan D. Cohen, and Cameron S. Carter. 2004. "Conflict Monitoring and Anterior Cingulate Cortex: An Update." *Trends in Cognitive Sciences* 8 (12): 539–46. doi:10.1016/j.tics.2004.10.003; Botvinick, Matthew M., Jonathan D. Cohen, and Cameron S. Carter. 2004. "Conflict Monitoring and Anterior Cingulate Cortex: An Update." *Trends in Cognitive Sciences* 8 (12): 539–46. doi:10.1016/j.tics.2004.10.003; Seeley, William W., Vinod Menon, Alan F. Schatzberg, Jennifer Keller, Gary H. Glover, Heather Kenna, Allan L. Reiss, and Michael D. Greicius. 2007. "Dissociable Intrinsic Connectivity Networks for Salience Processing and Executive Control." *Journal of Neuroscience* 27 (9): 2349–56. doi:10.1523/jneurosci.5587–06.2007.

30. Dajani, Dina R., and Lucina Q. Uddin. 2015. "Demystifying Cognitive Flexibility: Implications for Clinical and Developmental Neuroscience." *Trends in Neurosciences* 38 (9): 571–8. doi:10.1016/j.tins.2015.07.003.

31. Kelley, William M., Dylan D. Wagner, and Todd F. Heatherton. 2015. "In Search of a Human Self-Regulation System." *Annual Review of Neuroscience* 38 (July): 389–411. doi: 10.1146/annurev-neuro-071013–014243.

32. Hofmann, Wilhelm, Kathleen D. Vohs, and Roy F. Baumeister. 2012. "What People Desire, Feel Conflicted About, and Try to Resist in Everyday Life." *Psychological Science* 23 (6): 582–8. doi:10.1177/0956797612437426.

33. Fox, Kieran C. R., Savannah Nijeboer, Matthew L. Dixon, James L. Floman, Melissa Ellamil, Samuel P. Rumak, Peter Sedlmeier, and Kalina Christoff. 2014. "Is Meditation Associated with Altered Brain Structure? A Systematic Review and Meta-Analysis of Morphometric Neuroimaging in Meditation Practitioners." *Neuroscience and Biobehavioral Reviews* 43 (June): 48–73. doi: 10.1016/j.

neubiorev.2014.03.016; Tang, Yi-Yuan, Britta K. Hölzel, and Michael I. Posner. 2015. "The Neuroscience of Mindfulness Meditation." *Nature Reviews Neuroscience* 16 (4): 213–25. doi:10.1038/nrn3916; Hölzel, Britta K., Sara W. Lazar, Tim Gard, Zev Schuman-Olivier, David R. Vago, and Ulrich Ott. 2011. "How Does Mindfulness Meditation Work? Proposing Mechanisms of Action from a Conceptual and Neural Perspective." *Perspectives on Psychological Science* 6 (6): 537–59. doi:10.1177/1745691611419671.

CHAPTER 3

1. Spencer, Lyle. 2001. "Improvement in Service Climate Drives Increase in Revenue." Paper presented at the meeting of the Consortium for Research on Emotional Intelligence in Organizations, Cambridge, Massachusetts, April 19.
2. Williams, Daniel. 1995. *Leadership for the 21st Century: Life Insurance Leadership Study.* Boston: Hay Group.
3. Lewis, Thomas, Fari Amini, and Richard Lannon. 2000. *A General Theory of Love.* New York: Random House.
4. Friedman, Howard S., and Ronald E. Riggio. 1981. "Effect of Individual Differences in Nonverbal Expressiveness on Transmission of Emotion." *Journal of Nonverbal Behavior* 6 (2): 96–104. doi:10.1007/BF00987285.
5. Kelly, Janice R., and Sigal G. Barsade. 2001. "Mood and Emotions in Small Groups and Work Teams." *Organizational Behavior and Human Decision Processes* 86 (1): 99–130. doi:10.1006/obhd.2001.2974.
6. Tee, E. Y. 2015. "The Emotional Link: Leadership and the Role of Implicit and Explicit Emotional Contagion Processes across Multiple Organizational Levels." *The Leadership Quarterly* 26 (4): 654–70. doi:10.1016/j.leaqua.2015.05.009.
7. Di Pellegrino, G., L. Fadiga, L. Fogassi, V. Gallese, and G. Rizzolatti. 1992. "Understanding Motor Events: A Neurophysiological Study." *Experimental Brain Research* 91 (1): 176–80. doi:10.1007/BF00230027; Ferrari, Pier F., and Gaicomo Rizzolatti. 2014. "Mirror Neuron Research: The Past and the Future." *Philosophical Transactions of the Royal Society of London. Series B, Biological Sciences* 369 (1644): 20130169. doi:10.1098/rstb.2013.0169.
8. Iacoboni, Marco, and Mirella Dapretto. 2006. "The Mirror Neuron System and the Consequences of Its Dysfunction." *Nature Reviews Neuroscience* 7 (12): 942–51. doi:10.1038/nrn2024.
9. Shamay-Tsoory, Simone G. 2011. "The Neural Bases for Empathy." *The Neuroscientist* 17 (1): 18–24. doi:10.1177/1073858410379268.
10. Dr. Gard—Please note that recently the point has been made that there might not be a causal link between the mirror neuron system and empathy (Lamm and Majdandžić 2015).

Lamm, Claus, and Jasminka Majdandžić. 2015. "The Role of Shared Neural Activations, Mirror Neurons, and Morality in Empathy—A Critical Comment." *Neuroscience Research* 90: 15–24. doi:10.1016/j.neures.2014.10.008.

11. Bachman, Wallace. 1988. "Nice Guys Finish First: A SYMLOG Analysis of U.S. Naval Commands. In *The SYMLOG Practitioner: Applications of Small Group Research*, edited by Richard Brian Polley, A. Paul Hare, and Phillip J. Stone. New York: Praeger.

12. © 2015 Daniel Goleman, PhD, and Richard Boyatzis, PhD. Distributed by the Hay Group. All rights reserved, with permission from Hay Group.

13. Baer, Ruth A., Gregory T. Smith, and Kristin B. Allen. 2004. "Assessment of Mindfulness by Self-Report: The Kentucky Inventory of Mindfulness Skills." *Assessment* 11 (3): 191–206. doi:10.1177/1073191104268029; Baer, Ruth A., Gregory T. Smith, Jaclyn Hopkins, Jennifer Krietemeyer, and Leslie Toney. 2006. "Using Self-Report Assessment Methods to Explore Facets of Mindfulness." *Assessment* 13 (1): 27–45. doi:10.1093/clipsy.bpg015; Bao, Xueming, Song Xue, and Feng Kong. 2015. "Dispositional Mindfulness and Perceived Stress: The Role of Emotional Intelligence." *Personality and Individual Differences* 78 (May): 48–52. doi:10.1016/j.paid.2015.01.007; Brown, Kirk W., and Richard M. Ryan. 2003. "The Benefits of Being Present: Mindfulness and Its Role in Psychological Well-Being." *Journal of Personality and Social Psychology* 84 (4): 822–48. doi:10.1037/0022–3514.84.4.822; Schutte, Nicola S., and John M. Malouff. 2011. "Emotional Intelligence Mediates the Relationship between Mindfulness and Subjective Well-Being." *Personality and Individual Differences* 50 (7): 1116–9. doi:10.1016/j.paid.2011.01.037; Sinclair, Helen, and Janet Feigenbaum. 2012. "Trait Emotional Intelligence and Borderline Personality Disorder." *Personality and Individual Differences* 52 (6): 674–9. doi:10.1016/j.paid.2011.12.022; Wang, Yu, and Feng Kong. 2014. "The Role of Emotional Intelligence in the Impact of Mindfulness on Life Satisfaction and Mental Distress." *Social Indicators Research* 116 (3): 843–52. doi:10.1007/s11205–013–0327–6.

14. Bao, Xueming, Song Xue, and Feng Kong. 2015. "Dispositional Mindfulness and Perceived Stress: The Role of Emotional Intelligence." *Personality and Individual Differences* 78 (May): 48–52. doi:10.1016/j.paid.2015.01.007; Schutte, Nicola S., and John M. Malouff. 2011. "Emotional Intelligence Mediates the Relationship between Mindfulness and Subjective Well-Being." *Personality and Individual Differences* 50 (7): 1116–9. doi:10.1016/j.paid.2011.01.037; Wang, Yu, and Feng Kong. 2014. "The Role of Emotional Intelligence in the Impact of Mindfulness on Life Satisfaction and Mental Distress." *Social Indicators Research* 116 (3): 843–52. doi:10.1007/s11205–013–0327–6.

15. Peña-Sarrionandia, Ainize, Moïra Mikolajczak, and James J. Gross. 2015. "Integrating Emotion Regulation and Emotional Intelligence Traditions: A Meta-Analysis." *Frontiers in Psychology*, 6 (February): 1–27. doi:10.3389/fpsyg.2015.00160.

16. Bao, Xueming, Song Xue, and Feng Kong. 2015. "Dispositional Mindfulness and Perceived Stress: The Role of Emotional Intelligence." *Personality and Individual Differences* 78 (May): 48–52. doi:10.1016/j.paid.2015.01.007.

17. Hölzel, Britta K., Sara W. Lazar, Tim Gard, Zev Schuman-Olivier, David R. Vago, and Ulrich Ott. 2011. "How Does Mindfulness Meditation Work? Proposing Mechanisms of Action from a Conceptual and Neural Perspective." *Perspectives on Psychological Science* 6 (6): 537–59. doi:10.1177/1745691611419671; Tang, Yi-Yuan, Britta K. Hölzel, and Michael I. Posner. 2015. "The Neuroscience of Mindfulness Meditation." *Nature Reviews Neuroscience* 16 (4): 213–25. doi:10.1038/nrn3916.

18. Roemer, Lizabeth, Sarah K. Williston, and Laura G. Rollins. 2015. "Mindfulness and Emotion Regulation." *Current Opinion in Psychology* 3: 52–7. doi:10.1016/j.copsyc.2015.02.006.

19. Jha, Amishi P., Elizabeth A. Stanley, Anastasia Kiyonaga, Ling Wong, and Lois Gelfand. 2010. "Examining the Protective Effects of Mindfulness Training on Working Memory Capacity and Affective Experience." *Emotion* 10 (1): 54–64. doi: 10.1037/a0018438.

20. Taylor, Véronique A., Joshua Grant, Véronique Daneault, Geneviève Scavone, Estelle Breton, Sébastien Roffe-Vidal, Jérôme Courtemanche, Anaïs S. Lavarenne, and Mario Beauregard. 2011. "Impact of Mindfulness on the Neural Responses to Emotional Pictures in Experienced and Beginner Meditators." *Neuroimage* 57 (4): 1524–33. doi:10.1016/j.neuroimage.2011.06.001.

21. Zeidan, Fadel, Katherine T. Martucci, Robert A. Kraft, Nakia S. Gordon, John G. McHaffie, and Robert C. Coghill. 2011. "Brain Mechanisms Supporting the Modulation of Pain by Mindfulness Meditation." *Journal of Neuroscience* 31 (14): 5540–8. doi:10.1523/JNEUROSCI.5791–10.2011.

22. Veehof, Martine M., Maarten-Jan Oskam, Karlein M. G. Schreurs, and Ernst T. Bohlmeijer. 2011. "Acceptance-Based Interventions for the Treatment of Chronic Pain: A Systematic Review and Meta-Analysis." *Pain* 152 (3): 533–42. doi:10.1016/j.pain.2010.11.002.

23. Hofmann, Stefan G., Alice T. Sawyer, Ashley A. Witt, and Diana Oh. 2010. "The Effect of Mindfulness-Based Therapy on Anxiety and Depression: A Meta-Analytic Review." *Journal of Consulting and Clinical Psychology* 78 (2): 169–83. doi:10.1037/a0018555; Piet, Jacob, and Esben Hougaard. 2011. "The Effect of Mindfulness-Based Cognitive Therapy for Prevention of Relapse in Recurrent Major Depressive Disorder: A Systematic Review and Meta-Analysis." *Clinical Psychology Review* 31 (6): 1032–40. doi:10.1016/j.cpr.2011.05.002.

24. Hoge, Elizabeth A., Eric Bui, Luana Marques, Christina A. Metcalf, Laura K. Morris, Donald J. Robinaugh, John J. Worthington, Mark H. Pollack, and Naomi M. Simon. 2013. "Randomized Controlled Trial of Mindfulness Meditation for Generalized Anxiety Disorder: Effects on Anxiety and Stress Reactivity." *Journal of Clinical Psychiatry* 74 (8): 786–92. doi:10.4088/JCP.12m08083.

25. Barrett, Lisa F., Batja Mesquita, Kevin N. Ochsner, and James J. Gross. 2007. "The Experience of Emotion." *Annual Review of Psychology* 58 (January): 373–403. doi:10.1146/annurev.psych.58.110405.085709; Sayers, W. Michael, J. David Creswell, and Adrienne Taren. 2015. "The Emerging Neurobiology of Mindfulness and Emotion Processing." In *Handbook of Mindfulness and Self-Regulation*, edited by Brian D. Ostafin, Michael D. Robinson, and Brian P. Meier. New York: Springer.

26. Ochsner, Kevin N., and James J. Gross. 2005. "The Cognitive Control of Emotion." *Trends in Cognitive Sciences* 9 (5): 242–9. doi:10.1016/j.tics.2005.03.010; Sayers, W. Michael, J. David Creswell, and Adrienne Taren. 2015. "The Emerging Neurobiology of Mindfulness and Emotion Processing." In *Handbook of Mindfulness and Self-Regulation*, edited by Brian D. Ostafin, Michael D. Robinson, and Brian P. Meier. New York: Springer.

27. Sayers, W. Michael, J. David Creswell, and Adrienne Taren. 2015. "The Emerging Neurobiology of Mindfulness and Emotion Processing." In *Handbook of Mindfulness and Self-Regulation*, edited by Brian D. Ostafin, Michael D. Robinson, and Brian P. Meier. New York: Springer.

28. Chiesa, Alberto, Alessandro Serretti, and Janus C. Jakobsen. 2013. "Mindfulness: Top-Down or Bottom-Up Emotion Regulation Strategy?" *Clinical Psychology Review* 33 (1): 82–96. doi:10.1016/j.cpr.2012.10.006; Gard, Tim. 2014. "Different Neural Correlates of Facing Pain with Mindfulness: Contributions of Strategy and Skill: Comment on 'Facing the Experience of Pain: A Neuropsychological Perspective' by Fabbro and Crescentini." *Physics of Life Reviews* 11 (3): 564–6. doi:10.1016/j.plrev.2014.07.003; Tang, Yi-Yuan, Britta K. Hölzel, and Michael I. Posner. 2015. "The Neuroscience of Mindfulness Meditation." *Nature Reviews Neuroscience* 16 (4): 213–25. doi:10.1038/nrn3916.

29. Sources for the Campbell's story included an interview I conducted with Doug Conant and the following: Conant, Douglas R. 2011. "Secrets of Positive Feedback." *Harvard Business Review*, February 16. https://hbr.org/2011/02/secrets-of-positive-feedback/; Duncan, Roger Dean. 2014. "How Campbell's Soup's Former CEO Turned the Company Around." *Hit the Ground Running* (blog), September 18. http://www.fastcompany.com/3035830/hit-the-ground-running/how-campbells-soups-former-ceo-turned-the-company-around; Gerdeman, Dina. 2013. "Pulling Campbell's out of the Soup." Harvard Business

School. March 23. http://hbswk.hbs.edu/item/pulling-campbells-out-of-the-soup; Campbell Soup Company. n.d. "About Campbell." Accessed November 11, 2015. http://www.campbellsoup.com/about-us/.

CHAPTER 4

1. Hölzel, Britta K., Sara W. Lazar, Tim Gard, Zev Schuman-Olivier, David R. Vago, and Ulrich Ott. 2011. "How Does Mindfulness Meditation Work? Proposing Mechanisms of Action from a Conceptual and Neural Perspective." *Perspectives on Psychological Science* 6 (6): 537–59. doi:10.1177/1745691611419671.

2. Hoge, Elizabeth A., Eric Bui, Luana Marques, Christina A. Metcalf, Laura K. Morris, Donald J. Robinaugh, John J. Worthington, Mark H. Pollack, and Naomi M. Simon. 2013. "Randomized Controlled Trial of Mindfulness Meditation for Generalized Anxiety Disorder: Effects on Anxiety and Stress Reactivity." *Journal of Clinical Psychiatry* 74 (8): 786–92. doi:10.4088/JCP.12m08083.

3. Cohn, Jeffrey, Jon R. Katzenbach, and Guy Vlak. 2008. "Finding and Grooming Breakthrough Innovators." *Harvard Business Review* 86 (12): 62–9. https://hbr.org/2008/12/finding-and-grooming-breakthrough-innovators.

4. Condon, Paul, Gaëlle Desbordes, Willa B. Miller, and David DeSteno. 2013. "Meditation Increases Compassionate Responses to Suffering." *Psychological Science* 24 (10): 2125–7. doi:10.1177/0956797613485603.

5. Weng, Helen Y., Andrew S. Fox, Alexander J. Shackman, Diane E. Stodola, Jessica Z. K. Caldwell, Matthew C. Olson, Gregory M. Rogers, and Richard J. Davidson. 2013. "Compassion Training Alters Altruism and Neural Responses to Suffering." *Psychological Science* 24 (7): 1171–80. doi:10.1177/0956797612469537.

6. Lazar, Sara W., Catherine E. Kerr, Rachel H. Wasserman, Jeremy R. Gray, Douglas N. Greve, Michael T. Treadway, Metta McGarvey et al. 2005. "Meditation Experience Is Associated with Increased Cortical Thickness." *Neuroreport* 16 (17): 1893–7. doi:10.1097/01.wnr.0000186598.66243.19.

7. Condon, Paul, Gaëlle Desbordes, Willa B. Miller, and David DeSteno. 2013. "Meditation Increases Compassionate Responses to Suffering." *Psychological Science* 24 (10): 2125–7. doi:10.1177/0956797613485603; Birnie, Kathryn, Michael Speca, and Linda E. Carlson. 2010. "Exploring Self-compassion and Empathy in the Context of Mindfulness-Based Stress Reduction (MBSR)." *Stress and Health* 26 (5): 359–71. doi:10.1002/smi.1305.

8. Dr. Gard—Tania Singer and Olga Klimecki (2014) describe empathy as resonating with the emotions of others and compassion as having both empathic concern for another and the motivation to help relieve suffering.

Singer, Tania, and Olga M. Klimecki. 2014. "Empathy and Compassion." *Current Biology* 24 (18): R875–R878. doi:10.1016/j.cub.2014.06.054.

9. Kickstarter is a crowdfunding platform (www.kickstarter.com). Kickstarter. 2013. "GoldieBlox: The Engineering Toy for Girls." July 1. Accessed November 12, 2015. https://www.kickstarter.com/projects/16029337/goldieblox-the-engineering-toy-for-girls.

10. GoldieBlox. n.d. "Our Mission." Accessed November 12, 2015. http://www.goldieblox.com/pages/about; Sterling, Debra. 2013. "Inspiring the Next Generation of Female Engineers: Debbie Sterling at TEDxPSU." YouTube video, 17:08. Posted April 19. https://www.youtube.com/watch?v=FEeTLopLkEo.

Chapter 5

1. Johnson, Douglas C., Nathaniel J. Thom, Elizabeth A. Stanley, Lori Haase, Alan N. Simmons, Pei-an B. Shih, Wesley K. Thompson, Eric G. Potterat, Thomas R. Minor, and Martin P. Paulus. 2014. "Modifying Resilience Mechanisms in At-Risk Individuals: A Controlled Study of Mindfulness Training in Marines Preparing for Deployment." *American Journal of Psychiatry* 171(8): 844–53. doi:10.1176/appi.ajp.2014.13040502.

2. Johnson, Douglas C., Nathaniel J. Thom, Elizabeth A. Stanley, Lori Haase, Alan N. Simmons, Pei-an B. Shih, Wesley K. Thompson, Eric G. Potterat, Thomas R. Minor, and Martin P. Paulus. 2014. "Modifying Resilience Mechanisms in At-Risk Individuals: A Controlled Study of Mindfulness Training in Marines Preparing for Deployment." *American Journal of Psychiatry* 171(8): 844–53. doi:10.1176/appi.ajp.2014.13040502; Seeley, William W., Vinod Menon, Alan F. Schatzberg, Jennifer Keller, Gary H. Glover, Heather Kenna, Allan L. Reiss, and Michael D. Greicius. 2007. "Dissociable Intrinsic Connectivity Networks for Salience Processing and Executive Control." *Journal of Neuroscience* 27 (9): 2349–2356. doi:10.1523/jneurosci.5587–06.2007.

3. Uddin, Lucina Q. 2015. "Salience Processing and Insular Cortical Function and Dysfunction." *Nature Reviews Neuroscience* 16 (1): 55–61. doi:10.1038/nrn3857; Menon, Vinod. 2011. "Large-Scale Brain Networks and Psychopathology: A Unifying Triple Network Model." *Trends in Cognitive Sciences* 15 (10): 483–506; Phelps, Elizabeth A., and Joseph E. LeDoux. 2005. "Contributions of the Amygdala to Emotion Processing: From Animal Models to Human Behavior." *Neuron* 48 (October): 175–87. doi:10.1016/j.neuron.2005.09.025; Armony, Jorge L. 2013. "Current Emotion Research in Behavioral Neuroscience: The Role(s) of the Amygdala." *Emotion Review* 5 (1): 104–15. doi:10.1177/1754073912457208.

4. Etkin, Amit, and Tor D. Wager. 2007. "Functional Neuroimaging of Anxiety: A Meta-Analysis of Emotional Processing in PTSD, Social Anxiety Disorder, and Specific Phobia." *American Journal of Psychiatry* 164 (10): 1476–88. doi:10.1176/appi.ajp.2007.07030504; McEwen, Bruce S., Nicole P. Bowles, Jason D. Gray, Matthew N. Hill, Richard G. Hunter, Ilia N. Karatsoreos, and

Carla Nasca. 2015. "Mechanisms of Stress in the Brain." *Nature Neuroscience* 18 (10): 1353–63. doi:10.1038/nn.4086.

5. Tang, Yi-Yuan, Britta K. Hölzel, and Michael I. Posner. 2015. "The Neuroscience of Mindfulness Meditation." *Nature Reviews Neuroscience* 16 (4): 213–25. doi:10.1038/nrn3916.

6. Taylor, Véronique A., Joshua Grant, Véronique Daneault, Geneviève Scavone, Estelle Breton, Sébastien Roffe-Vidal, Jérôme Courtemanche, Anaïs S. Lavarenne, and Mario Beauregard. 2011. "Impact of Mindfulness on the Neural Responses to Emotional Pictures in Experienced and Beginner Meditators." *Neuroimage* 57 (4): 1524–33. doi:10.1016/j.neuroimage.2011.06.001.

7. Hölzel, Britta K., James Carmody, Karleyton C. Evans, Elizabeth A. Hoge, Jeffery A. Dusek, Lucas Morgan, Roger K. Pitman, and Sara W. Lazar. 2010. "Stress Reduction Correlates with Structural Changes in the Amygdala." *Social Cognitive and Affective Neuroscience* 5 (1): 11–17. doi:10.1093/scan/nsp034.

8. Desbordes, Gaëlle, Lobsang T. Negi, Thaddeus W. W. Pace, B. Alan Wallace, Charles L. Raison, and Eric L. Schwartz. 2012. "Effects of Mindful-Attention and Compassion Meditation Training on Amygdala Response to Emotional Stimuli in an Ordinary, Non-Meditative State." *Frontiers in Human Neuroscience* 6 (November): 1–15. doi:10.3389/fnhum.2012.00292; Hölzel, Britta K., Elizabeth A. Hoge, Douglas N. Greve, Tim Gard, J. David Creswell, Kirk W. Brown, Lisa F. Barrett, Carl Schwartz, Dieter Vaitl, and Sara W. Lazar. 2013. "Neural Mechanisms of Symptom Improvements in Generalized Anxiety Disorder following Mindfulness Training." *NeuroImage: Clinical* 2 (1): 448–58. doi:10.1016/j.nicl.2013.03.011; Taren, Adrienne A., Peter J. Gianaros, Carol M. Greco, Emily K. Lindsay, April Fairgrieve, Kirk W. Brown, Rhonda K. Rosen et al. 2015. "Mindfulness Meditation Training Alters Stress-Related Amygdala Resting State Functional Connectivity: A Randomized Controlled Trial." *Social Cognitive and Affective Neuroscience.* Advance online publication. doi:10.1093/scan/nsv066.

9. Allen, Micah, Martin Dietz, Karina S. Blair, Martijn van Beek, Geraint Rees, Peter Vestergaard-Poulsen, Antoine Lutz, and Andreas Roepstorff. 2012. "Cognitive-Affective Neural Plasticity following Active-Controlled Mindfulness Intervention." *Journal of Neuroscience* 32 (44): 15601–10. doi:10.1523/jneurosci.2957-12.2012.

10. Ortner, Catherine N. M., Sachne J. Kilner, and Philip D. Zelazo. 2007. "Mindfulness Meditation and Reduced Emotional Interference on a Cognitive Task." *Motivation and Emotion* 31 (4): 271–83. doi:10.1007/s11031-007-9076-7.

11. Note on the difference between empathy and compassion: Tania Singer and Olga Klimecki (2014) describe empathy as resonating with the emotions of others whereas compassion, or empathic concern, refers to a feeling of concern for the suffering of the other and the motivation to help. Empathy is feeling *with* whereas compassion is feeling *for* the other person. Empathy with negative

emotions can result in empathic distress and be very draining. In the face of negative emotions, responding with compassion might be more adaptive.

With regard to the brain mechanisms of empathy, Tania Singer and colleagues (2004) found that in empathy for pain, that is, when participants watch another person in pain, brain regions were activated that were also activated when participants received painful stimuli themselves. These regions, the dorsal anterior cingulate cortex and anterior insula, are related to the affective (emotional) aspects of the pain experience. During empathy there was no activation in the brain regions that process the sensory aspects of pain. Other studies found similar results (Lamm, Decety, and Singer 2011).

Olga Klimecki and colleagues (2013) compared empathy and compassion. After empathy training, watching video clips of people in distress resulted in increased negative emotions and brain activation in the anterior insula and anterior midcingulate cortex, as in the empathy of pain study of Tania Singer et al. (2004). After a compassion training, watching the video clips resulted in less negative affect (emotions) and more positive affect and in increased brain activation in a network related to reward and positive emotions, including the orbitofrontal cortex and the ventral striatum.

Klimecki, Olga M., Susanne Leiberg, Matthieu Ricard, and Tania Singer. 2013. "Differential Pattern of Functional Brain Plasticity after Compassion and Empathy Training." *Social Cognitive and Affective Neuroscience* 9 (6): 873–9. doi:10.1093/scan/nst060.

Lamm, C., Decety, J., and Singer, T. (2011). "Meta-Analytic Evidence for Common and Distinct Neural Networks Associated with Directly Experienced Pain and Empathy for Pain." *Neuroimage* 54 (3): 2492–502. doi:10.1016/j.neuroimage.2010.10.014.

Singer, Tania, and Olga M. Klimecki. 2014. "Empathy and Compassion." *Current Biology* 24 (18): R875–R878. doi:10.1016/j.cub.2014.06.054.

Singer, Tania, Ben Seymour, John O'Doherty, Holger Kaube, Raymond J. Dolan, and Chris D. Frith. 2004. "Empathy for Pain Involves the Affective but Not Sensory Components of Pain." *Science* 303 (5661): 1157–62. doi:10.1126/science.1093535.

12. Neff, Kristin D., and Katie A. Dahm. 2015. "Self-Compassion: What It Is, What It Does, and How It Relates to Mindfulness." In *Handbook of Mindfulness and Self-Regulation*, edited by Brian D. Ostafin, Michael D. Robinson, and Brian P. Meier. New York: Springer.

13. Jazaieri, Hooria, Kelly McGonigal, Thupten Jinpa, James R. Doty, James J. Gross, and Philippe R. Goldin. 2014. "A Randomized Controlled Trial of Compassion Cultivation Training: Effects on Mindfulness, Affect, and Emotion

Regulation." *Motivation and Emotion* 38 (1): 23–35. doi:10.1007/s11031–013–9368-z; Neff, Kristin D., and Christopher K. Germer. 2013. "A Pilot Study and Randomized Controlled Trial of the Mindful Self-Compassion Program." *Journal of Clinical Psychology* 69 (1): 28–44. doi:10.1002/jclp.21923.

14. Weng, Helen Y., Andrew S. Fox, Alexander J. Shackman, Diane E. Stodola, Jessica Z. K. Caldwell, Matthew C. Olson, Gregory M. Rogers, and Richard J. Davidson. 2013. "Compassion Training Alters Altruism and Neural Responses to Suffering." *Psychological Science* 24 (7): 1171–80. doi:10.1177/0956797612469537.

15. Morishima, Yosuke, Daniel Schunk, Adrian Bruhin, Christian C. Ruff, and Ernst Fehr. 2012. "Linking Brain Structure and Activation in Temporoparietal Junction to Explain the Neurobiology of Human Altruism." *Neuron* 75 (1): 73–9. doi:10.1016/j.neuron.2012.05.021.

16. Hölzel, Britta K., James Carmody, Mark Vangel, Christina Congleton, Sita M. Yerramsetti, Tim Gard, and Sara W. Lazar. 2011. "Mindfulness Practice Leads to Increases in Regional Brain Gray Matter Density." *Psychiatry Research: Neuroimaging* 191 (September): 36–43. doi:10.1016/j.pscychresns.2010.08.006.

17. However, another study found that long-term mindfulness practitioners had lower cortical thickness than controls (Kang et al. 2013).

Kang, Do-Hyung, Hang J. Jo, Wi H. Jung, Sun H. Kim, Ye-Ha Jung, Chi-Hoon Choi, Ul S. Lee, Seung C. An, Joon H. Jang, and Jun S. Kwon. 2013. "The Effect of Meditation on Brain Structure: Cortical Thickness Mapping and Diffusion Tensor Imaging." *Social Cognitive and Affective Neuroscience* 8 (1): 27–33. doi:10.1093/scan/nss056.

Chapter 6

1. Brickman, Philip, Dan Coates, and Ronnie Janoff-Bulman. 1978. "Lottery Winners and Accident Victims: Is Happiness Relative?" *Journal of Personality and Social Psychology* 36 (8): 917–27. doi:10.1037/0022–3514.36.8.917.

2. Please note that while some studies found an association between left-brain activation and positive emotions, others did not, and the lateralization hypothesis of emotions is still debated (Berridge and Kringelbach 2013; Costanzo et al. 2015).

Berridge, Kent C., and Morten L. Kringelbach. 2013. "Neuroscience of Affect: Brain Mechanisms of Pleasure and Displeasure." *Current Opinion in Neurobiology* 23 (3): 294–303. doi:10.1016/j.conb.2013.01.017.

Costanzo, Elsa Y., Mirta Villarreal, Lucas J. Drucaroff, Manuel Ortiz-Villafañe, Mariana N. Castro, Micaela Goldschmidt, Augustina Wainsztein et al. 2015. "Hemispheric Specialization in Affective Responses, Cerebral

Dominance for Language, and Handedness: Lateralization of Emotion, Language, and Dexterity." *Behavioural Brain Research* 288 (April): 11–9. doi:10.1016/j.bbr.2015.04.006.

3. You might enjoy this article in *Esquire*, which includes some details of the study and some life lessons from Matthieu Ricard—http://www.esquire.co.uk/culture/article/4915/matthieu-ricard-what-ive-learned.

4. Davidson, Richard J., Jon Kabat-Zinn, Jessica Schumacher, Melissa Rosenkranz, Daniel Muller, Saki F. Santorelli, Ferris Urbanowski, Anne Harrington, Katherine Bonus, and John F. Sheridan. 2003. "Alterations in Brain and Immune Function Produced by Mindfulness Meditation." *Psychosomatic Medicine* 65 (4): 564–70. doi:10.1097/01.psy.0000077505.67574.e3.

5. Hölzel, Britta K., James Carmody, Mark Vangel, Christina Congleton, Sita M. Yerramsetti, Tim Gard, and Sara W. Lazar. 2011. "Mindfulness Practice Leads to Increases in Regional Brain Gray Matter Density." *Psychiatry Research: Neuroimaging* 191 (September): 36–43. doi:10.1016/j.pscychresns.2010.08.006.

6. Aristotle. 1985. *Nicomachean Ethics*, translated by Terence Irwin. Indianapolis: Hackett; Ryan, Richard M., and Edward L. Deci. 2001. "On Happiness and Human Potentials: A Review of Research on Hedonic and Eudaimonic Well-Being." *Annual Review of Psychology* 52 (February): 141–66. doi:10.1146/annurev.psych.52.1.141; Deci, Edward L., and Richard M. Ryan. 2008. "Hedonia, Eudaimonia, and Well-Being: An Introduction." *Journal of Happiness Studies* 9 (1): 1–11. doi:10.1007/s10902–006–9018–1.

7. Ryan, Richard M., and Edward L. Deci. 2001. "On Happiness and Human Potentials: A Review of Research on Hedonic and Eudaimonic Well-Being." *Annual Review of Psychology* 52 (February): 141–66. doi:10.1146/annurev. psych.52.1.141.

8. Singleton, Omar, Britta K. Hölzel, Mark Vangel, Narayan Brach, James Carmody, and Sara W. Lazar. 2014. "Change in Brainstem Gray Matter Concentration following a Mindfulness-Based Intervention Is Correlated with Improvement in Psychological Well-Being." *Frontiers in Human Neuroscience* 8 (February), 1–7. doi:10.3389/fnhum.2014.00033.

9. Klimecki, Olga M., Susanne Leiberg, Matthieu Ricard, and Tania Singer. 2013. "Differential Pattern of Functional Brain Plasticity after Compassion and Empathy Training." *Social Cognitive and Affective Neuroscience* 9 (6): 873–9. doi:10.1093/scan/nst060.

10. Kong, Feng, Xie Wang, Yiying Song, and Jia Liu. 2015. "Brain Regions Involved in Dispositional Mindfulness during Resting State and Their Relation with Well-Being. *Social Neuroscience*, advance online publication: 1–13. doi:10.1080/17470919.2015.1092469.

CHAPTER 7

1. Cornish, David, and Dianne Dukette. 2009. *The Essential 20: Twenty Components of an Excellent Health Care Team.* Pittsburgh: RoseDog Books; Statistic Brain Research Institute. 2015. "Attention Span Statistics." Accessed November 6, 2015. http://www.statisticbrain.com/attention-span-statistics/.

2. Chiesa, Alberto, Raffaella Calati, and Alessandro Serretti. 2011. "Does Mindfulness Training Improve Cognitive Abilities? A Systematic Review of Neuropsychological Findings." *Clinical Psychology Review* 31 (3): 449–64.

3. Teper, Rimma, and Michael Inzlicht. 2013. "Meditation, Mindfulness and Executive Control: The Importance of Emotional Acceptance and Brain-Based Performance Monitoring." *Social Cognitive and Affective Neuroscience* 8 (1): 85–92. doi:10.1093/scan/nss045; Moore, Adam, and Peter Malinowski. 2009. "Meditation, Mindfulness and Cognitive Flexibility." *Consciousness and Cognition* 18 (1): 176–86. doi:10.1016/j.concog.2008.12.008; Chan, Davina, and Marjorie Woollacott. 2007. "Effects of Level of Meditation Experience on Attentional Focus: Is the Efficiency of Executive or Orientation Networks Improved?" *Journal of Alternative and Complementary Medicine* 13 (November): 651–7. doi:10.1089/acm.2007.7022.

4. Kozasa, Elisa H., João R. Sato, Shirley S. Lacerda, Maria A. M. Barreiros, João Radvany, Tamara A. Russell, Liana G. Sanches, Luiz E.A.M. Mello, and Edson Amaro Jr. 2012. "Meditation Training Increases Brain Efficiency in an Attention Task." *Neuroimage* 59 (July): 745–9. doi:10.1016/j.neuroimage.2011.06.088.

5. Allen, Micah, Martin Dietz, Karina S. Blair, Martijn van Beek, Geraint Rees, Peter Vestergaard-Poulsen, Antoine Lutz, and Andreas Roepstorff. 2012. "Cognitive-Affective Neural Plasticity following Active-Controlled Mindfulness Intervention." *Journal of Neuroscience* 32 (44): 15601–10. doi:10.1523/jneurosci.2957-12.2012.

6. Gard, Tim, Britta K. Hölzel, and Sara W. Lazar. 2014. "The Potential Effects of Meditation on Age-Related Cognitive Decline: A Systematic Review." *Annals of the New York Academy of Sciences* 1307 (1): 89–103. doi:10.1111/nyas.12348.

7. Gard, Tim, Maxime Taquet, Rohan Dixit, Britta K. Hölzel, Yves-Alexandre de Montjoye, Narayan Brach, David H. Salat, Bradford C. Dickerson, Jeremy R. Gray, and Sara W. Lazar. 2014. "Fluid Intelligence and Brain Functional Organization in Aging Yoga and Meditation Practitioners." *Frontiers in Aging Neuroscience* 6 (April): 1–12. doi:10.3389/fnagi.2014.00076.

8. Of the 47 participants in this study, 16 were trained in mindfulness or insight meditation (Goldstein and Kornfield 2001), 16 were trained in Kripalu Yoga (Faulds and senior teachers of Kripalu Center 2005), and 15 had no experience with meditation or yoga. In Kripalu Yoga, *witness consciousness,* which is conceptually very similar to mindfulness, plays an important role, and practicing Kripalu Yoga has been shown to increase mindfulness (Gard et al. 2012). In this study, practitioners of insight meditation and Kripalu were pooled for some of the analyses.

Faulds, Richard, and senior teachers of Kripalu Center. 2005. *Kripalu Yoga: A Guide to Practice On and Off the Mat.* New York: Bantam.

Gard, Tim, Narayan Brach, Britta K. Hölzel, Jessica J. Noggle, Lisa A. Conboy, and Sara W. Lazar. 2012. "Effects of a Yoga-Based Intervention for Young Adults on Quality of Life and Perceived Stress: The Potential Mediating Roles of Mindfulness and Self-Compassion." *The Journal of Positive Psychology* 7 (3): 165–75. doi:10.1080/17439760.2012.667144.

Goldstein, Joseph, and Jack Kornfield. 2001. *Seeking the Heart of Wisdom: The Path of Insight Meditation.* Boston: Shambhala Publications.

9. James, William. 1890. *The Principles of Psychology.* Vol. 1. New York: Holt.
10. Please see Neuro Note 1.2 for an explanation of how habits form.
11. Before developing object permanence, it is thought that when an object disappears from the view of an infant, the object no longer exists (Meyers and Dewall 2015).

Meyers, David G., and C. Nathan Dewall. 2015. *Psychology.* 11th ed. New York: Worth.

Chapter 8

1. Ariga, Atsunori, and Alejandro Lleras. 2011. "Brief and Rare Mental 'Breaks' Keep You Focused: Deactivation and Reactivation of Task Goals Preempt Vigilance Decrements." *Cognition* 118 (3): 439–43. doi:10.1016/j.cognition.2010.12.007; Kong, Feng, Xie Wang, Yiying Song, and Jia Liu. 2015. "Brain Regions Involved in Dispositional Mindfulness during Resting State and Their Relation with Well-Being. *Social Neuroscience*, advance online publication: 1–13. doi:10.1080/17470919.2015.1092469.
2. Ross, Hayden A., Paul N. Russell, and William S. Helton. 2014. "Effects of Breaks and Goal Switches on the Vigilance Decrement." *Experimental Brain Research* 232 (6): 1729–37. doi:10.1007/s00221–014–3865–5.
3. Langner, Robert, and Simon B. Eickhoff. 2013. "Sustaining Attention to Simple Tasks: A Meta-Analytic Review of the Neural Mechanisms of Vigilant Attention." *Psychological Bulletin* 139 (4): 870–900. doi:10.1037/a0030694.
4. Feltman, Rachel. 2014. "Most Men Would Rather Shock Themselves than Be Alone with Their Thoughts." *Washington Post*, July 3. https://www.washingtonpost.com/news/to-your-health/wp/2014/07/03/most-men-would-rather-shock-themselves-than-be-alone-with-their-thoughts/; Wilson, Timothy D., David A. Reinhard, Erin C. Westgate, Daniel T. Gilbert, Nicole Ellerbeck, Cheryl Hahn, Casey L. Brown, and Adi Shaked. 2014. Just think: The challenges of the disengaged mind. *Science* 345(6192), 75–77. doi:10.1126/science.1250830.

5. Fox, Kieran C. R., Savannah Nijeboer, Matthew L. Dixon, James L. Floman, Melissa Ellamil, Samuel P. Rumak, Peter Sedlmeier, and Kalina Christoff. 2014. "Is Meditation Associated with Altered Brain Structure? A Systematic Review and Meta-Analysis of Morphometric Neuroimaging in Meditation Practitioners." *Neuroscience and Biobehavioral Reviews* 43 (June): 48–73. doi:10.1016/j.neubiorev.2014.03.016; Tang, Yi-Yuan, Britta K. Hölzel, and Michael I. Posner. 2015. "The Neuroscience of Mindfulness Meditation." *Nature Reviews Neuroscience* 16 (4): 213–25. doi:10.1038/nrn3916.

6. Craig, A. D. 2002. "How Do You Feel? Interoception: The Sense of the Physiological Condition of the Body." *Nature Reviews Neuroscience* 3 (8): 655–66. doi:10.1038/nrn894; Craig, A. D. "Interoception: The Sense of the Physiological Condition of the Body." *Current Opinion in Neurobiology* 13 (4): 500–5. doi:10.1016/S0959–4388(03)00090–4; Craig, A. D. 2009. "How Do You Feel—Now? The Anterior Insula and Human Awareness." *Nature Reviews Neuroscience* 10 (1): 59–70. doi:10.1038/nrn2555; Critchley, Hugo D., Stefan Wiens, Pia Rotshtein, Arne Öhman, and Raymond J. Dolan. 2004. "Neural Systems Supporting Interoceptive Awareness." *Nature Neuroscience* 7 (2): 189–95. doi:10.1038/nn1176.

7. Singer, Tania, and Olga M. Klimecki. 2014. "Empathy and Compassion." *Current Biology* 24 (18): R875–R878. doi:10.1016/j.cub.2014.06.054.

8. Alkozei, Anna, and William D. S. Killgore. 2015. "Emotional Intelligence Is Associated with Reduced Insula Responses to Masked Angry Faces." *Neuroreport* 26 (10): 567–71. doi:10.1097/WNR.0000000000000389; Takeuchi, Hikaru, Yasuyuki Taki, Rui Nouchi, Atsushi Sekiguchi, Hiroshi Hashizume, Yuko Sassa, Yuka Kotozaki et al. 2013. "Resting State Functional Connectivity Associated with Trait Emotional Intelligence." *Neuroimage* 83 (June): 318–28. doi:10.1016/j.neuroimage.2013.06.044; Takeuchi, Hikaru, Yasuyuki Taki, Yuko Sassa, Hiroshi Hashizume, Atsushi Sekiguchi, Ai Fukushima, and Ryuta Kawashima. 2011. "Regional Gray Matter Density Associated with Emotional Intelligence: Evidence from Voxel-Based Morphometry." *Human Brain Mapping* 32 (9): 1497–510. doi:10.1002/hbm.21122.

CHAPTER 9

1. Taylor, Véronique A., Joshua Grant, Véronique Daneault, Geneviève Scavone, Estelle Breton, Sébastien Roffe-Vidal, Jérôme Courtemanche, Anaïs S. Lavarenne, and Mario Beauregard. 2011. "Impact of Mindfulness on the Neural Responses to Emotional Pictures in Experienced and Beginner Meditators." *Neuroimage* 57 (4): 1524–33. doi:10.1016/j.neuroimage.2011.06.001.

2. Lieberman, Matthew D., Naomi I. Eisenberger, Molly J. Crockett, Sabrina M. Tom, Jennifer H. Pfeifer, and Baldwin M. Way. 2007. "Putting Feelings into Words:

Affect Labeling Disrupts Amygdala Activity in Response to Affective Stimuli." *Psychological Science* 18 (5): 421–28. doi:10.1111/j.1467–9280.2007.01916.x.

CHAPTER 10

1. Bohm, David J., and Basil J. Hiley. 1975. "On the Intuitive Understanding of Non-Locality as Implied by Quantum Theory." *Foundations of Physics* 5 (1): 93–109. doi:10.1007/BF01100319.

2. Modinos, Gemma, Renco Renken, Johan Ormel, and André Aleman. 2011. "Self-Reflection and the Psychosis-Prone Brain: An fMRI Study." *Neuropsychology* 25 (3): 295–305. doi:10.1037/a0021747; Pezzulo, Giovanni, Lawrence W. Barsalou, Angelo Cangelosi, Martin H. Fischer, Ken McRae, and Michael J. Spivey. 2011. "The Mechanics of Embodiment: A Dialog on Embodiment and Computational Modeling." *Frontiers in Psychology* 2 (January): 1–21. doi:10.3389/fpsyg.2011.00005; Chiao, Joan Y., Tokiko Harada, Hidetsugu Komeda, Zhang Li, Yoko Mano, Daisuke Saito, Todd B. Parrish, Norihiro Sadato, and Tetsuya Iidaka. 2009. "Neural Basis of Individualistic and Collectivistic Views of Self." *Human Brain Mapping* 30 (9): 2813–20. doi:10.1002/hbm.20707; Botzung, Anne, Ekaterina Denkova, Philippe Ciuciu, Christian Scheiber, and Lilianne Manning. 2008. "The Neural Bases of the Constructive Nature of Autobiographical Memories Studied with a Self-Paced fMRI Design." *Memory* 16 (4): 351–63. doi:10.1080/09658210801931222; Moll, Jorge, Ricardo de Oliveira-Souza, Griselda J. Garrido, Ivanei E. Bramati, Egas M. Caparelli-Daquer, Mirella L. Paiva, Roland Zahn, and Jordan Grafman. 2007. "The Self as a Moral Agent: Linking the Neural Bases of Social Agency and Moral Sensitivity." *Social Neuroscience* 2 (3–4): 336–52. doi:10.1080/17470910701392024.

3. At least not in the same cell it was in before. Some matter has likely left, been someplace else for a while, and returned to the body, now in a different cell.

4. Robinson, Ken. 2006. Do Schools Kill Creativity? TED video, 19:24. Posted February. http://www.ted.com/talks/ken_robinson_says_schools_kill_creativity?language=en.

5. This statement actually has a serious shortcoming. The awareness that observes the mind, and can even observe where attention is placed, is actually nonlocal. To say that it is "over here" or located in any specific place is not entirely accurate. Although most people have a strong sense that awareness is something that comes from inside our heads (in some Asian countries it is actually experienced as coming from the heart region), eventually, with continued practice, we realize that awareness is, in fact, nonlocal. We cannot find, or point to, a specific place where awareness is. We can only know that it is happening.

6. You might be wondering whether this aspect of ourselves that is more ultimate than the body and mind is the part of ourselves that continues on after the physical body dies. I don't know the answer to that question. Also, a discussion on the topic would be a very lengthy one and isn't relevant for this book. Because this is a business book, I've elected to focus our discussion on what's essential for leadership and personal excellence, which is the fact that we are clearly not our thinking.

7. Killingsworth, Matthew A., and Daniel T. Gilbert. 2010. "A Wandering Mind Is an Unhappy Mind." *Science* 330 (6006): 932. doi:10.1126/science.1192439.

8. Smallwood, Jonathan, and Jonathan W. Schooler. 2015. "The Science of Mind Wandering: Empirically Navigating the Stream of Consciousness." *Annual Review of Psychology* 66 (January): 487–518. doi:10.1146/annurev-psych-010814-015331.

9. Hafenbrack, Andrew C., Zoe Kinias, and Sigal G. Barsade. 2014. "Debiasing the Mind through Meditation: Mindfulness and the Sunk-Cost Bias." *Psychological Science* 25 (2): 369–376. doi:10.1177/0956797613503853.

10. Mason, Malia F., Michael I. Norton, John D. Van Horn, Daniel M. Wegner, Scott T. Grafton, and C. Neil Macrae. 2007. "Wandering Minds: The Default Network and Stimulus-Independent Thought." *Science* 315 (5810): 393–5. doi:10.1126/science.1131295; Christoff, Kalina, Alan M. Gordon, Jonathan Smallwood, Rachelle Smith, and Jonathan W. Schooler. 2009. "Experience Sampling during fMRI Reveals Default Network and Executive System Contributions to Mind Wandering." *Proceedings of the National Academy of Sciences of the United States of America* 106 (21): 8719–8724. doi:10.1073/pnas.0900234106; Greicius, Michael D., Ben Krasnow, Allan L. Reiss, and Vinod Menon. 2003. "Functional Connectivity in the Resting Brain: A Network Analysis of the Default Mode Hypothesis." *Proceedings of the National Academy of Sciences of the United States of America* 100 (1): 253–8. doi:10.1073/pnas.0135058100; Buckner, Randy L., Jessica R. Andrews-Hanna, and Daniel L. Schacter. 2008. "The Brain's Default Network: Anatomy, Function, and Relevance to Disease." *Annals of the New York Academy of Sciences* 1124 (March): 1–38. doi:10.1196/annals.1440.011; Raichle, Marcus E. 2015. "The Brain's Default Mode Network." *Annual Review of Neuroscience* 38 (July): 433–47. doi:10.1146/annurev-neuro-071013-014030; Raichle, Marcus E., Ann Mary MacLeod, Abraham Z. Snyder, William J. Powers, Debra A. Gusnard, and Gordon L. Shulman. 2001. "A Default Mode of Brain Function." *Proceedings of the National Academy of Sciences of the United States of America* 98 (2): 676–82. doi:10.1073/pnas.98.2.676.

11. Mrazek, Michael D., Michael S. Franklin, Dawa T. Phillips, Benjamin Baird, and Jonathan W. Schooler. 2013. "Mindfulness Training Improves Working

Memory Capacity and GRE Performance While Reducing Mind Wandering." *Psychological Science* 24 (5): 776–81. doi:10.1177/0956797612459659.

12. Hafenbrack, Andrew C., Zoe Kinias, and Sigal G. Barsade. 2014. "Debiasing the Mind through Meditation: Mindfulness and the Sunk-Cost Bias." *Psychological Science* 25 (2): 369–376. doi:10.1177/0956797613503853.

13. Brewer, Judson A., Patrick D. Worhunsky, Jeremy Gray, Yi-Yuan Tang, Jochen Weber, and Hedy Kober. 2011. "Meditation Experience Is Associated with Differences in Default Mode Network Activity and Connectivity." *Proceedings of the National Academy of Sciences of the United States of America* 108 (50): 20254–9. doi:10.1073/pnas.1112029108.

14. Bornemann, Boris, Beate M. Herbert, Wolf E. Mehling, and Tania Singer. 2015. "Differential Changes in Self-Reported Aspects of Interoceptive Awareness through 3 Months of Contemplative Training." *Frontiers in Psychology* 5 (January), 1–13. doi:10.3389/fpsyg.2014.01504; Bornemann, Boris, and Tania Singer. 2015. "Taking Time to Get in Touch with Our Body: Heart Beat Perception Accuracy Increases Linearly over Nine Months of Contemplative Training." Paper presented at the International Convention of Psychological Science, Amsterdam, Netherlands, March; Sze, Jocelyn A., Anett Gyurak, Joyce W. Yuan, and Robert W. Levenson. 2010. "Coherence between Emotional Experience and Physiology: Does Body Awareness Training Have an Impact? *Emotion* 10 (6): 803–14. doi:10.1037/a0020146; Fox, Kieran C., Pierre Zakarauskas, Matt Dixon, Melissa Ellamil, Evan Thompson, and Kalina Christoff. 2012. "Meditation Experience Predicts Introspective Accuracy." *PLoS ONE* 7 (9): e45370. doi:10.1371/journal.pone.0045370.

15. Farb, Norman A. S., Adam K. Anderson, Helen Mayberg, Jim Bean, Deborah McKeon, and Zindel V. Segal. 2010. "Minding One's Emotions: Mindfulness Training Alters the Neural Expression of Sadness." *Emotion* 10 (1): 25–33. doi:10.1037/a0017151; Farb, Norman A. S., Zindel V. Segal, and Adam K. Anderson. 2013. "Mindfulness Meditation Training Alters Cortical Representations of Interoceptive Attention." *Social Cognitive and Affective Neuroscience* 8 (1): 15–26. doi:10.1093/scan/nss066; Farb, Norman A. S., Zindel V. Segal, Helen Mayberg, Jim Bean, Deborah McKeon, Zainab Fatima, and Adam K. Anderson. 2007. "Attending to the Present: Mindfulness Meditation Reveals Distinct Neural Modes of Self-Reference." *Social Cognitive and Affective Neuroscience* 2 (4): 313–22. doi:10.1093/scan/nsm030; Gard, Tim, Britta K. Hölzel, Alexander T. Sack, Hannes Hempel, Sara W. Lazar, Dieter Vaitl, and Ulrich Ott. 2012. "Pain Attenuation through Mindfulness Is Associated with Decreased Cognitive Control and Increased Sensory Processing in the Brain." *Cerebral Cortex* 22 (11): 2692–702. doi:10.1093/cercor/bhr352; Hölzel, Britta K., Ulrich Ott, Tim Gard, Hannes Hempel, Martin Weygandt, Katrin Morgen, and Dieter Vaitl. 2008. "Investigation of Mindfulness Meditation Practitioners with Voxel-Based

Morphometry." *Social Cognitive and Affective Neuroscience* 3 (1): 55–61. doi:10.1093/scan/nsm038; Lazar, Sara W., Catherine E. Kerr, Rachel H. Wasserman, Jeremy R. Gray, Douglas N. Greve, Michael T. Treadway, Metta McGarvey et al. 2005. "Meditation Experience Is Associated with Increased Cortical Thickness." *Neuroreport* 16 (17): 1893–7. doi:10.1097/01.wnr.0000186598.66243.19.

16. Craig, A. D. 2002. "How Do You Feel? Interoception: The Sense of the Physiological Condition of the Body." *Nature Reviews Neuroscience* 3 (8): 655–66. doi:10.1038/nrn894; Craig, A. D. 2003. "Interoception: The Sense of the Physiological Condition of the Body." *Current Opinion in Neurobiology* 13 (4): 500–5. doi:10.1016/S0959–4388(03)00090–4; Craig, A. D. 2009. "How Do You Feel—Now? The Anterior Insula and Human Awareness." *Nature Reviews Neuroscience* 10 (1): 59–70. doi:10.1038/nrn2555; Critchley, Hugo D., Stefan Wiens, Pia Rotshtein, Arne Öhman, and Raymond J. Dolan. 2004. "Neural Systems Supporting Interoceptive Awareness." *Nature Neuroscience* 7 (2): 189–95. doi:10.1038/nn1176.

CHAPTER 11

1. Berna, Chantal, Siri Leknes, Emily A. Holmes, Robert R. Edwards, Guy M. Goodwin, and Irene Tracey. 2010. "Induction of Depressed Mood Disrupts Emotion Regulation Neurocircuitry and Enhances Pain Unpleasantness." *Biological Psychiatry* 67 (11): 1083–90. doi:10.1016/j.biopsych.2010.01.014.

2. Lutz, Antoine, Daniel R. McFarlin, David M. Perlman, Tim V. Salomons, and Richard J. Davidson. 2013. "Altered Anterior Insula Activation during Anticipation and Experience of Painful Stimuli in Expert Meditators." *Neuroimage* 64 (January): 538–46. doi:10.1016/j.neuroimage.2012.09.030; Grant, Joshua A., and Pierre Rainville. 2009. "Pain Sensitivity and Analgesic Effects of Mindful States in Zen Meditators: A Cross-Sectional Study." *Psychosomatic Medicine* 71 (1): 106–14. doi:10.1097/PSY.0b013e31818f52ee; Gard, Tim, Britta K. Hölzel, Alexander T. Sack, Hannes Hempel, Sara W. Lazar, Dieter Vaitl, and Ulrich Ott. 2012. "Pain Attenuation through Mindfulness Is Associated with Decreased Cognitive Control and Increased Sensory Processing in the Brain." *Cerebral Cortex* 22 (11): 2692–702. doi:10.1093/cercor/bhr352; Perlman, David M., Tim V. Salomons, Richard J. Davidson, and Antoine Lutz. 2010. "Differential Effects on Pain Intensity and Unpleasantness of Two Meditation Practices." *Emotion* 10 (1): 65–71. doi:10.1037/a0018440.

3. Gard, Tim, Britta K. Hölzel, Alexander T. Sack, Hannes Hempel, Sara W. Lazar, Dieter Vaitl, and Ulrich Ott. 2012. "Pain Attenuation through Mindfulness Is Associated with Decreased Cognitive Control and Increased Sensory Processing in the Brain." *Cerebral Cortex* 22 (11): 2692–702. doi:10.1093/cercor/bhr352; Grant, Joshua A., Jérôme Courtemanche, and Pierre Rainville. 2011. "A Non-

Elaborative Mental Stance and Decoupling of Executive and Pain-Related Cortices Predicts Low Pain Sensitivity in Zen Meditators." *Pain* 152 (1): 150–6. doi:10.1016/j.pain.2010.10.006.

4. Grant, Joshua A., Jérôme Courtemanche, and Pierre Rainville. 2011. "A Non-Elaborative Mental Stance and Decoupling of Executive and Pain-Related Cortices Predicts Low Pain Sensitivity in Zen Meditators." *Pain* 152 (1): 150–6. doi:10.1016/j.pain.2010.10.006.

5. Zeidan, Fadel, Nakia S. Gordon, Junaid Merchant, and Paula Goolkasian. 2010. "The Effects of Brief Mindfulness Meditation Training on Experimentally Induced Pain." *Journal of Pain* 11 (3) 199–209. doi:10.1016/j. jpain.2009.07.015; Zeidan, Fadel, Katherine T. Martucci, Robert A. Kraft, Nakia S. Gordon, John G. McHaffie, and Robert C. Coghill. 2011. "Brain Mechanisms Supporting the Modulation of Pain by Mindfulness Meditation." *Journal of Neuroscience* 31 (14): 5540. doi:10.1523/JNEURO-SCI.5791–10.2011; Kingston, Jessica, Paul Chadwick, Daniel Meron, and T. Chas Skinner. 2007. "A Pilot Randomized Control Trial Investigating the Effect of Mindfulness Practice on Pain Tolerance, Psychological Well-Being, and Physiological Activity." *Journal of Psychosomatic Research* 62 (3): 297–300. doi:10.1016/j.jpsychores.2006.10.007.

6. Brown, Christopher A., and Anthony K. P. Jones. 2013. "Psychobiological Correlates of Improved Mental Health in Patients with Musculoskeletal Pain after a Mindfulness-Based Pain Management Program." *Clinical Journal of Pain* 29 (3): 233–44. doi:10.1097/AJP.0b013e31824c5d9f; Jensen, Karin B., Eva Kosek, Rikard Wicksell, Mike Kemani, Gunnar Olsson, Julia V. Merle, Diana Kadetoff, and Martin Ingvar. 2012. "Cognitive Behavioral Therapy Increases Pain-Evoked Activation of the Prefrontal Cortex in Patients with Fibromyalgia." *Pain* 153 (7): 1495–503. doi:10.1016/j.pain.2012.07.004; Zeidan, Fadel, Katherine T. Martucci, Robert A. Kraft, Nakia S. Gordon, John G. McHaffie, and Robert C. Coghill. 2011. "Brain Mechanisms Supporting the Modulation of Pain by Mindfulness Meditation." *Journal of Neuroscience* 31 (14): 5540. doi:10.1523/jneurosci.5791–10.2011.

7. Taylor, Véronique A., Joshua Grant, Véronique Daneault, Geneviève Scavone, Estelle Breton, Sébastien Roffe-Vidal, Jérôme Courtemanche, Anaïs S. Lavarenne, and Mario Beauregard. 2011. "Impact of Mindfulness on the Neural Responses to Emotional Pictures in Experienced and Beginner Meditators." *Neuroimage* 57 (4): 1524–33. doi:10.1016/j.neuroimage.2011.06.001.

8. Ireland, T. (2014). *What Does Mindfulness Meditation Do to Your Brain?* Article retrieved from http://blogs.scientificamerican.com/guest-blog/what-does-mindfulness-meditation-do-to-your-brain/.

9. To be most precise here, when we are perfectly mindfully self-aware, there is no sense of *me* that exists apart from experience. A feeling of like or dislike actually

can't arise because there's no ego there determining whether it likes something. I felt this concept is a little too deep for the main text. However, if you'd like to explore this further, you could pay close attention to experiences of *selflessness* that you likely have every day. It happens when we first wake up from sleep, before the brain reconstructs our sense of self, it happens when we're in what's known as *flow state*, and it happens whenever we are truly being mindfully self-aware. There's nothing too mysterious about it. It's just experiencing sensations, and the awareness of those sensations, without a false sense of *me* that seems to be in our heads running the show. It's a nonlocal, nonpersonal knowing that "experience is happening."

CHAPTER 12

1. Although I thought this was a little too deep for the main text, this exercise can actually start to break down the firmly held notions we have about what is *inside* and what is *outside*. When we really look closely at reality, it can be quite challenging to find anything other than a very arbitrary boundary—a line in the sand, if you will—between *inside* and *outside*. Does a sound happen *outside* of the mind or *inside* of it? Are the inner voice and the sounds in the office happening in the same place?

CHAPTER 13

1. Wisdom 2.0. n.d. "Wisdom 2.0 | February 20th-22nd, 2016 | San Francisco." Accessed November 12, 2015. http://www.wisdom2summit.com.
2. Cornish, David, and Dianne Dukette. 2009. *The Essential 20: Twenty Components of an Excellent Health Care Team.* Pittsburgh: RoseDog Books.
3. Weinschenk, Susan. 2012. "Why We're All Addicted to Texts, Twitter and Google." *Brain Wise* (blog). *Psychology Today*, September 11. https://www.psychologytoday.com/blog/brain-wise/201209/why-were-all-addicted-texts-twitter-and-google.
4. Rosenberg, Marshall B. 2003. *Nonviolent Communication: A Language of Life.* 2nd ed. Encinitas, CA: PuddleDancer Press.

AFTERWORD

1. Hölzel, Britta K., Sara W. Lazar, Tim Gard, Zev Schuman-Olivier, David R. Vago, and Ulrich Ott. 2011. "How Does Mindfulness Meditation Work? Proposing Mechanisms of Action from a Conceptual and Neural Perspective." *Perspectives on Psychological Science* 6 (6): 537–59. doi:10.1177/1745691611419671; Tang, Yi-Yuan, Britta K. Hölzel, and Michael I. Posner.

2015. "The Neuroscience of Mindfulness Meditation." *Nature Reviews Neuroscience* 16 (4): 213–25. doi:10.1038/nrn3916.

2. Vago, David R., and David A. Silbersweig. 2012. "Self-Awareness, Self-Regulation, and Self-Transcendence (S-ART): A Framework for Understanding the Neurobiological Mechanisms of Mindfulness." *Frontiers in Human Neuroscience* 6 (October): 1–30. doi:10.3389/fnhum.2012.00296; Lutz, Antoine, Amishi P. Jha, John D. Dunne, and Clifford D. Saron. 2015. "Investigating the Phenomenological Matrix of Mindfulness-Related Practices from a Neurocognitive Perspective." *American Psychologist* 70 (7): 632–58. doi:10.1037/a0039585.

APPENDIX

1. Berger, Abi. 2002. "Magnetic Resonance Imaging." *British Medical Journal* 324 (7328): 35. doi:10.1136/bmj.324.7328.35.

2. Kalat, James W. 2015. *Biological Psychology*. 12th ed. Boston: Cengage Learning.

3. Bullmore, Ed, and Olaf Sporns. 2009. "Complex Brain Networks: Graph Theoretical Analysis of Structural and Functional Systems." *Nature Reviews Neuroscience* 10 (3): 186–98.

ACKNOWLEDGMENTS

MATT TENNEY

There are countless people I would like to thank for their help throughout my life, without whom I would not be who I am or doing what I do. For the sake of brevity here, I would like to acknowledge and thank those who have had the greatest impact on the success of this book.

First, I thank those of you who have been in the audiences of my keynotes and training programs over the past few years, and to the clients who have invited me to serve those audiences. You have shown such an inspiring thirst for mindfulness and other tools that can help you not only realize greater professional success and better business outcomes but also become kinder, more compassionate human beings. You inspired me to write this book much sooner than I had originally intended to.

Thank you, Mom and Dad. Without your unconditional support, this book never would have come to be.

Thank you, Leah, my wonderful wife and best friend. You inspire me every day with your incredible thoughtfulness, your care for the people around you, and your devotion to being as Christ-like as possible.

Thank you, Tim Gard. Despite your grueling academic schedule and the quick deadlines we faced, you took this project on with enthusiasm and precision and made the book significantly better than what it would have been had I written it alone. Also, I thank your wife and son for supporting you on this project.

Thank you, Jon Gordon and Simon Sinek. Your help was instrumental in launching my writing career.

Thanks to the other mentors in my life who played a significant role in helping this book come to be: Michael Carroll, Chade-Meng Tan, John Spence, and Ted Prince.

Special thanks to Chade-Meng Tan for being so innovative and creating the Search Inside Yourself program at Google. You paved the way for books like this one to have a chance of succeeding.

Thanks to Shannon Vargo, Liz Gildea, and Peter Knox at John Wiley & Sons for being so gentle with my naïveté and so patient with my endless questions.

Thank you, Arianna Huffington, for inviting me to write for the *Huffington Post*, which has helped me share mindfulness and servant leadership with a large number of people I might have never reached.

Thank you, Tim Ferriss, for being so generous with what you learn from your countless experiments. Nearly my entire marketing plan for this book was inspired by your efforts.

Thanks to all those who took the time out of their very busy schedules to read an advance copy of this book and write endorsements: John Spence, Michael Carroll, Skip Prichard, Bob Hottman, Greg Serrao, Chis Thoen, Tara Swart, Rick Staab, Scott Halford, Martin Sirk, Colin Melvin, Chad Paris, Britta Hölzel, and Wibo Koole.

Tim Gard

A variable that is related to mindfulness and predicts happiness is gratitude. Writing an acknowledgment is a beautiful practice of gratitude, and I am delighted to have the opportunity of doing so here.

I am deeply grateful for the beauty of life in general. With regard to this book I am very grateful to my wife, Marasha, and my parents, Karin and Wolfgang, who supported me in many ways and made it possible for me to make time available to work on this exciting project. I am also grateful to my sons, Max and Lex, who are a continuous source of love and inspiration. The photograph of me was made by a very talented 83-year-old, semiprofessional photographer, my grandmother Susanne. Thanks, Grandma! I also would like to thank Sara Lazar for the MRI image, David Vago for the brain template and my brother Fritz for his help with editing the photograph and brain illustration.

Of course I am very grateful to Matt for inviting me to join him in this inspiring and fun project. Matt, you are a very motivating and inspiring person, and it has been a true pleasure to work with you. Thanks for your patience and the wonderful collaboration! I also would like to thank the entire John Wiley & Sons team, including Peter Knox, Lauren Freestone, Judy Howarth, Liz Gildea, and Shannon Vargo, for all their great work, for guiding us through the process, and for turning plain text into an actual book. John Spence, Michael Carroll, Skip Prichard, Bob Hottman, Greg Serrao, Chis Thoen, Tara Swart, Rick Staab, Scott Halford, Martin Sirk, Colin Melvin, Britta Hölzel, Chad Paris, and Wibo Koole, thanks for your endorsements!

I could not have done the job without my training in neuroscience and mindfulness, and I am very grateful to my teachers, colleagues, and friends in the field. In particular I would like to thank Britta Hölzel, Ulrich Ott, Sara Lazar, Dieter Vaitl, Rainer Goebel, Alexander Sack, Carolyn West, and Laurie Rhoades. I am also grateful to the wider contemplative neuroscience community with the Mind and Life Institute at its core. The scientists of this community are the ones who conducted much of the research that I cited in this book. Of course a scientist is nowhere without participants and funding, and I would like to thank all who contribute to this field in their own way. Last but not least, I would like to thank you, the reader, for your interest, time, and trust to work with this book.

ABOUT THE AUTHORS

MATT TENNEY

Matt Tenney works to develop highly effective leaders who achieve extraordinary long-term business outcomes—and live more fulfilling lives—as a result of realizing high levels of self-mastery and more effectively serving and inspiring greatness in the people around them.

Matt is a social entrepreneur and the author of *Serve to Be Great: Leadership Lessons from a Prison, a Monastery, and a Boardroom.* He has been teaching mindfulness in various capacities since 2002. He is also an international keynote speaker, a corporate trainer, and a consultant with the prestigious Perth Leadership Institute. Matt's clients include Wells Fargo, Marriott, Keller Williams, Four Seasons, and many other companies, associations, and universities.

To connect with Matt, please visit www.MattTenney.com, or connect via one of the social media platforms below:

Twitter: @MattTenney1
LinkedIn: www.linkedin.com/in/matttenney
Facebook: www.facebook.com/MattTenneyServes

TIM GARD

Tim Gard, PhD, is a neuroscientist, keynote speaker, and mindfulness trainer. His research focuses on the neural and psychological mechanisms of mindfulness in a variety of contexts. Tim is affiliated with the Lazar lab for neuroscience of mindfulness research at Massachusetts General Hospital, Harvard Medical School, Boston, MA. Other leading institutes where he conducted his research include the Ott group at the Bender Institute of Neuroimaging, Giessen, Germany; Maastricht University, the Netherlands; and the Tata Institute of Fundamental Research, Mumbai, India. Furthermore, Tim was trained in mindfulness-based stress reduction and mindfulness-based cognitive therapy at the Center for Mindfulness at the University of Massachusetts Medical School, Worcester, MA. In his talks and workshops, Tim integrates the practice of mindfulness with the latest insights from neuroscience.

To connect with Tim, see www.timgard.eu or find him on LinkedIn: www.linkedin.com/in/timgardeu.

INDEX

Note: Page references in *italics* refer to figures.